the Undaunted garden

the Undaunted

garden

Planting for Weather-Resilient Beauty

TEXT AND PHOTOGRAPHS BY

Lauren Springer

FULCRUM PUBLISHING
GOLDEN, COLORADO

Springer, Lauren.
    The undaunted garden : planting for weather-resilient beauty /
text and photographs by Lauren Springer.
        p.   cm.
    Includes index.
    ISBN 1-55591-115-3
    1. Natural landscaping—United States. 2. Landscape plants—United States.
3. Natural landscaping. 4. Landscape plants.
    I. Title.
SB473S68 1994
635.9'52—dc20   93-42137
                                                                              CIP

Printed in Korea

0 9 8 7 6 5 4 3

Fulcrum Publishing
350 Indiana Street, Suite 350
Golden, Colorado 80401-5093
800/992-2908

For Dad, Jessy and Henry.
I miss you.

COVER AND FRONTISPIECE: *Old favorites dianthus, iris, poppy and peony are joined by less common white* Tanacetum niveum *and, in back, the giant foamy sea kale,* Crambe cordifolia.

TABLE OF CONTENTS:
Left top: Dwarf bearded iris 'Lemon Blossom' and moss phlox in spring.
Left center: Crambe cordifolia, *pinks, 'Husker Red' penstemon, yellow* Onosma echioides, *lady's mantle and Oriental poppy 'Helen Elizabeth' in late spring. Left bottom:* Delosperma nubigenum *(hardy iceplant) and fallen blue flax petals. Center: The pastel east-facing border in June: roses 'Félicité Parmentier' and 'William Lobb', cranesbills,* Digitalis grandiflora, *campanulas, penstemons, columbines, lady's mantle, golden feverfew, Oriental poppies,* Crambe cordifolia.
Right top: The hot-colored west-facing border in midsummer: orange Papaver rupifragum, *mullein, blue alkanet, red penstemons, yarrow, grasses, red hot poker, goldenrod, yellow dyer's broom, tawny Grecian foxglove. Right center: California poppies and* Zauschneria californica *'Solidarity Pink'. Right bottom: Autumn in the garden: red-leaved* Euphorbia epithymoides, *California poppies, 'Mary Stoker' mum, 'Goldsturm' rudbeckia seedheads,* Crocus speciosus, *sand cherry, grassy blue* Poa baldensis.

ENTS

 I don't understand the concept of the low-maintenance garden. Landscape yes, but not garden. Gardening may be many things to many people, but it is always an active relationship between a person and a group of plants. Don't get me wrong—there are times when even the most devoted gardener wishes for the help of an energetic group of weeding elves. But to desire a garden that requires no time spent except the occasional stroll through in well-laundered clothes is like having the most beautiful and appetizing food laid out on a table before you and not wanting to take a bite.

Real gardeners are a mixed lot. Some love the sun, the rain, the soil—the whole sense of being part of something greater than themselves. Some are guided by the aesthetic spirit within: The garden is an artistic expression, a creative exercise and release, like that well-worn but true cliché, painting with plants. Some respond to a nurturing instinct and derive their pleasure from the sowing and growing. Some are fascinated by the scientific intricacies of the natural world and observe the garden as a marvelous microcosm thereof. Most gardeners see a little of themselves in all these inadequate explanations of the urge to garden.

Whatever it is that calls the gardener to the garden, it is strong, primeval and infinitely rewarding. A friend, in her late seventies and wracked with crippling arthritis and back problems, still spends most of her days in the garden. She crawls on her belly, drawing herself forward on her elbows since bending and kneeling are too painful. She says she sees things in ways she never saw before. The garden is transformed now that she experiences it at eye and nose level. At the end of the day, she is the filthiest, happiest old woman I know. Low maintenance? Why on earth would gardeners want to stay away from the very thing that calls them out?

The undaunted garden is an outgrowth of my dissatisfaction with the low-maintenance concept. I certainly have my least favorite gardening chores—washing pots and turning compost topping the list. Almost all miserable garden work becomes tolerable if the garden seems to thrive because of it. One would like to believe that time in the garden correlates directly with the health and beauty of the plants. Some success is due to experience. Mostly I think the gardener's influence is more illusory

than real. The gardener's main role is to entertain him- or herself. Plants grow in spite of the gardener. The supreme example of this self-satisfying illusion that gardeners perpetuate is what they go through when growing from seed. Find me the gardener who doesn't hover over a batch of newly germinated seed with a combination of surprise and wonder and a large modicum of smug pride. Gardening is a fine balance between human intervention and the natural course of things. It is the natural forces beyond our control that shape the garden as much as the trowel and the hand.

The undaunted garden is lovingly composed and cared for by the gardener, yet thrives not so much because of him or her, but because it is in tune with the natural forces around it. Plant choices reflect these forces. The undaunted garden looks beautiful and satisfies the gardener because the plants are ideally suited to its conditions. The gardener lavishes attention on the garden and feels directly responsible for its success, yet it succeeds quite well with less intervention. It is like being part of a happy game where the ultimate outcome has already been determined, yet the game is a great joy to play.

In North America, vast regions of great climactic diversity all share one attribute: They discourage many a gardener with their extremes. While the milder maritime regions offer environments where gardens and gardeners flourish in carefree abundance, the interior continental regions suffer from excessive heat, cold, wind and drought, and outrageous weather phenomena, namely torrential rainstorms, tornadoes and hail. These all take their toll—both physical and emotional—on the gardens and gardeners of these regions. This needn't be the case.

North American gardeners have their roots for the most part in a European, primarily English, gardening tradition, especially in the case of ornamental gardening. Certain plants such as peonies, hollyhocks and lilacs have become tried and true favorites over much of this continent because they have adapted so well to the vagaries and extremes of the continental climate, but the majority of plants known and coveted via tradition and gardening literature are those suited to the mild, moist maritime climate of the British Isles. Billowing perennial borders brimming with delphiniums bloom for months in the gentle temperatures and soft light there, never facing the stifling heat and fierce sun of one-hundred-degree days, the pelting wall of water of summer showers or the wicked wrath of hail stones. Tender roses are not subjected to the disruptive and onerous mummification and burial routines necessary where winters regularly send the thermometer careening to thirty below.

What continental North American gardeners need are new models for their gardens. While the classics of English and coastal garden writing serve as wonderful bedtime reading and artistic inspiration, what we need out here are some new plants, combinations and ideas that help gardens face the severity of our climates with beauty and diversity. We need to create undaunted gardens.

The most beautiful gardens, be they a subtle, evocative combination of shapes and textures in Japan, a formal and beckoningly green oasis in Italy, a friendly, casual profusion in front of a cottage in England or a Wisconsin prairie garden bustling with birds and butterflies, all share a basic quality. No matter how exotic the plants may be or how elaborate and artificial the plan, the overall effect is one of harmony between nature and the gardener's hand. Even the most tortured topiary can be breathtaking when the pruned plant appears healthy and adapted to the rigors of regular shearing. A garden becomes beautiful when the plants in it adapt to their surroundings and thrive. Artistic combination of plants and overall design go a long way in determining the aesthetic fate of a garden, but the bottom line is how well the plants like growing within the individual constraints of the design and the greater constraints of climate, exposure and soil.

(facing page) Native and adapted plants mingle in undaunted profusion along the path, with luminescent yellow Aquilegia chrysantha lighting the way.

◄ *Chartreuse donkey-tail spurge, dwarf bearded iris, purple rock cress, blue woolly veronica and a pale yellow cultivar of basket-of-gold, 'Citrina', burst into unabashed spring bloom.*

Out in the wild, unrestrained landscapes of continental North America, the gardener needs to approach both design and plants in new ways. Light, color, space—all are experienced differently here. Many of the plants that grow so well on the coasts and in England don't thrive, let alone survive. Some will, but a great many require a lot of cajoling in the form of back-ruining soil amendments, expensive additional watering and protective winter mulches. Some of these plants are so dear to us that we don't mind the extra money and effort. I think many would be quickly forgotten and relegated to their place in glossy gardening books were there a good selection of tough yet beautiful plants with which to replace them. In this book, I hope to champion a rich and diverse group of such plants. They are the new pioneers of North American gardening. Just as the people who came to this land brought with them cherished traditions, objects and ideas from their roots, the gardens in this land will continue to draw inspiration from other countries for design and choice of plants. But the settlers turned their backs on many parts of their past they found distasteful or useless in their new homeland. Continental gardeners need to do the same.

warmer soil. The plants get busy putting out roots rather than attempting to grow tops and roots at the same time. Never in my wildest dreams would I have imagined such success with fall planting in the harsh climate of northern Colorado. One of the world's finest plantsmen, a Colorado native, warned me that as long as no snow lies on the ground, there is no excuse not to garden. He has successfully planted a rock garden in January. That is a bit extreme for me—cold soil and days that turn frigid and dark by midafternoon aren't my idea of fun, let alone the psychological trauma of worrying over the new garden. But in my garden, the vast majority of tiny November-planted seedlings have come through a winter that boasted minus thirty-two degrees Fahrenheit in December.

Native Versus Exotic

▲ Three foreigners—sea lavender, pink Lycoris squamigera *and blue-leaved sea kale—thrive as an ensemble.*

Native plants aren't the only ones to look to when planning an undaunted garden, although some purists would have one believe that to plant any exotic is heresy. That's absurd. The act of creating a garden is a disturbance and partial, if not total, destruction of the natural ecosystem that, either recently or many, many years ago, thrived on that spot of land. To plant with a palette of only natives, even regional natives, on the site as it now stands isn't always easy or desirable, well-intentioned as it may seem. Disturbed soil, a house or other man-made structure on the site, usually a population of previously planted exotics in various stages of health or decay, plus lusty, well-adapted weeds to round out the picture all can mean trouble for the reintroduced natives. A purist, to avoid hypocrisy, should remove the house along with the existing plants and let the natural cycle begin again. Few of us would live long enough to see the ecosystem return, and even fewer of us are willing to sacrifice the house, the paths, the garage and so on.

Certainly native plants can beautify a garden, especially by helping it look regionally appropriate. To think that natives can go it alone, planted out into the

▶ On the plans of southeastern Wyoming, abandoned bearded iris 'Flavescens' shimmers, a ghost of a homestead long gone.

(facing page) Iris 'Flavescens' is welcome at a newer homestead, the author's garden in northern Colorado.

"wilderness" that is an uncontrolled garden just as they do in the natural environment, is wrong. Many exotics, not to mention weeds, will out-compete the natives unless removed first. Overly aggressive plants, be they native or exotic, are a hazard in the careful balance of control and havoc that is a garden. But many exotics deserve their place. They have earned it by being tough and beautiful. It is a crime to remove a well-established, thriving lilac hedge, to dig up a large clump of peonies, to saw down a beautifully grown crabapple to make way for only native plants. If an attractive plant has adjusted to the climate of a garden and is not so self-important and antisocial as to preclude its being joined by other plants, why remove it, just because it wasn't a part of the natural landscape at one time?

One need only travel to a few ghost towns, abandoned farmsteads and the like to see what plants, over and over, have made themselves at home in the harsh North American climate—Harison's yellow rose, mock orange and hollyhocks are a few that have become as much a part of the landscape near these buildings as the native plants that have reclaimed the territory that was once theirs. For some reason, either due to an adaptive ability buried deep inside their heredity, or because these plants come from regions with similar climates and growing conditions, these exotics are happy here without much help on the part of the gardener.

Many, many more plants like these exist, but they haven't reached the horticultural spotlight yet. Countless are yet to be discovered. Perhaps they don't thrive in the maritime climates where most of this country's gardening trends originate. Perhaps they lack exposure because only a few people have grown them. When a plant is obscure, new or not particularly popular with the mainstream of horticulture, it is all the more reason to give it a try. The most important thing is to find out a little about its origins.

There is an ongoing battle among gardeners regarding the merit of botanical names versus common ones. It seems that any information about a plant that goes a step beyond height, bloom time and flower color becomes a burden to many gardeners. I heartily endorse finding out as much as possible about the conditions that prevail where a particular plant grows in the wild. Rock gardeners do this as second nature; only with this information are they able to coax plants from the high mountains to grow and thrive in their gardens. For some reason, other gardeners haven't taken to this approach. An undaunted garden comes about by taking the rock gardener's approach in reverse— finding out what a plant needs and, instead of artificially trying to simulate those needs, the gardener chooses plants that have needs that match what the garden and climate offers. This is Darwinian gardening—only the fit survive and thrive.

This book is the result of a lot of experimentation, translating into a merry-go-round of plants coming and going in my garden. I hate to admit the nasty truth that the newcomers I have killed may outnumber the successes. The lovely winners of the survival game in my garden and in the gardens of others who have created beauty in this land of extremes are the reason for this book.

▲   *In autumn, colchicum blooms through sweet woodruff leaves.*

◀   *Winter has not yet given in to spring when* Crocus biflorus *pushes past dormant penstemon, stonecress and cactus.*

▼   *The spikes of native penstemons harmonize with the opulent blossoms of Oriental poppies.*

The Adapted Plant Palette

Several regions in the world are homeoclimactic with one another, meaning they share similar climates. The western half of continental North America, for instance, with its grasslands, deserts and montane forests, has parallels in both hemispheres. My northern Colorado garden mirrors the extreme climate of the steppes and dry mountains of Central Asia and the eastern Mediterranean. As expected, plants from those regions do exceptionally well in my garden. Luckily, these regions are amazingly rich in plants. Unluckily, they are difficult to explore botanically for they are rugged and often ruled by politically hostile regimes. No one knows what horticultural wonders grow there, waiting to be discovered. Fortunately, a number of beauties are being brought into cultivation every year by a handful of plant collectors and growers.

For plants not accustomed to intense heat, huge differences in day and night temperatures, drought, mineral soils poor in organic matter or lack of humidity, the unaltered parts of my garden are a death trap.

Microclimates—a sheltered, east-facing area, a shady, cool spot on the north side of the house, the addition of manure and compost and water-conserving mulch—help me accommodate plants that need a little protection from the unadulterated high plains climate. By knowing where a plant originates, I have a much better idea where it should go in the garden. Just as a child blossoms when his or her talents are discovered and encouraged, a garden flourishes when the right plants are chosen for it.

The wonderful thing about selecting well-adapted plants is that they not only look better because they are healthy, but also because they often look as if they belong to the region. Homeoclimactic plants resemble each other. Many of the plants growing in the hot, dry, exposed parts of my garden have silver, gray or bluish leaves, often with hairs. They look like brethren, though they may come from Central Asia, the mountains of Greece, Turkey, the Great Basin or from just down the road. A harmony results that could not be accomplished by the gardener's hand alone.

A Sense of Place

Yet gardening is more than just choosing good plants. The best gardens, I'm convinced, not only add beauty to their immediate surroundings, they belong. They belong to their maker, the yard they have transformed, the home they enhance; they belong to the local landscape as well. Let the colors, forms and textures of the natural environment nearby make their impression. The natural landscape, with its predominant colors, shapes and vistas, should inspire an echo of some sort in the garden microcosm. Nothing is sadder in the gardening world than the homogeneity of North American landscapes. Each region has its own history, style, flavor and natural landscape. Why these haven't inspired more gardens is a mystery. It must be lack of horticultural confidence. A nation of bold pioneers and innovators withers when it comes to adventurous gardening and plants the same few dozen plants in the same few dozen ways, from sea to shining sea. Aside from being unsound from a practical and ecological perspective, this sameness is as stultifying as the ubiquitous American commercial strip, replete with fast-food joints and gas stations.

INTRODUCTION

I was taught a lesson in regional adaptation quite graphically when I moved from the East Coast to Colorado. On the very first flight, something seemed odd. Taking off and flying over Pennsylvania, I saw a soft green patchwork of fields and woods, undulating and flowing around dotted towns. Approaching Denver, I looked down on a totally different landscape. A wall of behemoths, the Rockies, stood guard over the city. And how the colors had changed. In place of lush greens, brown, russet and sage predominated. Suburban settlements stood out like psychedelic checkerboards—little squares of screaming green lawns. I knew right then and there that lawns looked much more out of place than they did back in the moist, green East. I decided to do something that would compliment this stark, dry, open landscape better, both in terms of looks and in terms of environmental needs.

Once I settled in, I noticed immediately that here in the shadow of the Rockies, rock gardens look great, better than many other garden forms, while back East they often appear stilted and artificial. Not only do the western rock gardens mirror the surrounding landscape, the plants growing in them look especially healthy and robust, since they are adapted to harsh, high-altitude extremes the world over. This is what is meant by a sense of place.

Regional landscapes help inspire good gardens, but the more immediate environment—the neighborhood and the house—plays just as important a role. For me, this meant a slight adjustment to my original dream. Here I was, full of fresh images of mountainsides strewn with boulders and wildflowers, the prairie alive with waving grasses. Well, I bought a prim, seventy-year-old clapboard house, picket fence and all. I wasn't about to give in to my fond memories of home and put in the bluegrass lawn and climbing roses I wistfully associated with this style of house. I wanted to make a garden for Colorado, yet I realized for a happy result, I would have to marry the planting style with the quaintness of the house. I think I found the best of both worlds by using native and homeoclimactic plants, all with a natural, unpolished look about them, but growing them in the jumbled, full, old-fashioned cottage garden style, not spread out and sparse as they grow in the wild.

The casual cottage style isn't for everyone. A fine landscape architect has chastised me for lack of elegance and structure. I admit, the backbone of my garden (which does include a few evergreen trees and shrubs and a patchwork of evergreen perennial foliage) tends to become a bit tenuous and droopy by midwinter, while a garden with more emphasis on overall shape and year-round interest would beat mine in January and February, hands down. The style of garden that inspires the gardener and enhances its surroundings is a highly personal thing. And style is relatively unimportant in determining the success of the garden. Whatever the style, let it be a personal expression, not some carbon copy of the neighbors'. My only plea is for individuality. I believe that by growing a diversity of adaptive plants and by combining their varied colors, forms and textures, any gardener can create a beautiful undaunted garden.

I

Through the Seasons in the Lush Dry Garden

The past few years, a new consciousness has emerged among gardeners, both professional and amateur. People are beginning to overcome the centuries-old need to dominate and harness nature in their gardens; instead, a sensitivity to regional conditions is developing, coupled with a desire to adapt to them rather than enslave a garden to a particular style or group of plants. Burgeoning interest in native plants and naturalistic styles such as rock, prairie, desert and meadow gardens reflect this change.

This book is based on these premises. One needs to feel a sense of place before plowing ahead blindly with a fixed idea in mind when one goes about creating a garden. As much as Americans move, they drag along the same horticultural prejudices with them just as they do the tired old sofa, bringing the same look and the same dozen plants to places as varied as Savannah, San Antonio and Seattle.

With the recent surge of interest in environmentally conscious gardening, a parallel trend has surfaced, that of using native plants to the exclusion of exotics. This is far too radical and confining to benefit most gardens—native plants, contrary to popular claims, are not necessarily more pest resistant or more adaptable. Many have evolved in very specific niches: One penstemon may grow perfectly in a sand pocket on the plains a mile from the more clay-like soil of the foothills, yet because it is a "native," it may be deemed more appropriate for the foothills garden than, say, a Central Asian plant which actually may do better on the clay than that penstemon. Just because a plant comes from a particular state doesn't make it ideally suited to gardens throughout that state.

Native plants have been sorely underused, and the untapped wealth of floristic beauty with garden potential on this continent boggles the mind. To see them begin to take their deserved place in gardens is a delight, but to become rigid and adamant about using native plants to the exclusion of worthy exotics is ridiculous. Certainly one needs to exercise caution with imported plants; witness what havoc invasive, aggressive foreigners the likes of purple loosestrife, kudzu and porcelain berry have wreaked in certain regions of the United States. Yet it is nearsighted to ban them outright—loosestrife is a pest in the water-rich regions of the upper Midwest where it is choking out native lake and pondside plants, but it can hardly be expected

(preceding pages) The late-summer garden—blue sea kale, purple coneflower, yellow Verbesina encelioides, *sea lavender, Ozark sundrop and tall pink* Agastache barberi—*spills over the sidewalk.*

to jump ship from an irrigated garden patch in Wyoming to the adjacent arid landscape. One needs to consider the conditions that favor their escape and avoid planting them in areas that offer these. As is so typical of human nature, the pendulum swings from one extreme—careless introduction of plants that have become impossible to eradicate and the bigoted opinion that all native plants are weeds, to the other—fascist bans on exotic, nonnative plants in the landscape of certain new "progressive" developments. Just as in the political arena, in horticulture the extreme right meets the extreme left and they become indistinguishable.

 One trend taking a strong hold in the drier half of this continent is water- *Wise About Water* conscious gardening. Whether by force during extended drought and the accompanying water restrictions, or by financial incentives as good, clean water becomes more and more of an expensive luxury, or purely motivated by a desire to garden in harmony with one's conditions rather than taking on nature in a power struggle, waterwise gardens are popping up all over. There is even a trendy term coined for this kind of sensible gardening: *xeriscape*—from the Greek word for dry—a dry landscape. Unfortunately, many people still associate this concept with the parched, sterile cliché of a sea of stone mulch and a few yuccas and cacti strewn about, perhaps with a cow skull or wagon wheel thrown in to give that western feel. I avoid the term for this reason, and also because it is so often mispronounced "zeroscape." Somehow its nonmellifluous sound reminds me not of a beautiful drought-tolerant garden but of a dry skin condition. I hear "xeriscape" and I want to scratch the back of my neck. Whether the term works or not is a matter of debate; whether the concept does is not. Drought-tolerant, waterwise landscapes are a wonderful new development in North American horticulture.

Many California gardeners have looked to the Mediterranean horticultural tradition for plants to create such environmentally friendly gardens. South Africa and Australia offer an almost unlimited palette for the West Coast garden as well. Sadly, the majority of South African and Australian plants are too tender to be grown as perennials in the rigorous climates of the interior West. While many Old World plants, including most of the aromatic herbs and a large number of well-known rock garden plants, grow well in this severe climate, some aren't winter hardy either.

One needs to look into the flora of regions with similar extreme conditions, especially the Irano-Turanian region, sparsely populated and politically hostile to the United States, for hardy plants. And indeed, this is one of the richest floristic regions of the world, barely tapped, brimming with untold treasures that may soon be destroyed by warfare or more pastoral yet equally damaging overgrazing.

And so, with a choice of thousands of beautiful plants from the North American plains, Great Basin deserts, dry foothills and mountains, from the rocky, sunbaked cliffs,

fragrant maquis and garigue of the Mediterranean regions and the parched steppes and stark mountains of the near East and Central Asia, the most varied and beautiful waterwise gardens can be created. They are environmentally sound and easy to care for, and they somehow look right, echoing the surrounding natural landscape.

My garden is made up mostly of drought-tolerant plantings. The only two areas that receive regular irrigation are my Irish garden, on the east side of the house, where pampered traditional border perennials—lilies, delphiniums, foxgloves—join old garden roses with fanciful French names, and the kitchen garden, a German four-square garden where all the vegetables and flowers for cutting and drying are grown each year. The rest of the garden is remarkably stingy with water and yet decadently overflowing with plants. The waterwise part of the garden can be divided into three distinct areas, reflecting distinct moods, fulfilling varied roles, requiring slightly different culture and making use of different groups of plants.

I should admit right off that I have no lawn in these parts of the garden. My property is just shy of half an acre. Half of this is not a garden; it is a yard. Here there

▲   A froth of honey-scented sea kale flowers borders old-fashioned miniature tall bearded irises.

▶   Sandy Snyder's dormant buffalo grass lawn comes alive each spring with hundreds of jewel-like snow iris and crocus.

is lawn. I have nothing against lawn; it sets off a garden beautifully with its restful green monotony, it is soft underfoot on paths—the perfect outdoor carpet. But it can never be a garden, only in service to a garden. I use it for my three large dogs to romp on and lie in on hot days, to cool their furry undersides. My daughter crawls around in it; I relax on it; we set up meals and gatherings on it. It controls erosion and water runoff, cools the area and keeps everyone's feet clean, whether human or animal, when they come in from outside. I have nothing but praise for it, along with the easy-care trees and shrubs growing here in the backyard, but a garden it is not.

My garden, on the other hand, is not utilitarian. It serves no purpose other than to feed my soul. It is a place for never-ending experimentation, for feeling renewed, in awe, a child again—a place to consort with the natural world, to express the artistic side of oneself. When I moved out West, I dreamed of a garden setting with a dramatic backdrop of foothills, mountains or mesas, with hills and rock outcrops and a good stand of native vegetation. No such luck. We bought a small clapboard home in a tidy plains town in northern Colorado, where large Siberian elms, sugar maples and ash trees line the wide streets, and the only glimpse one has of the snowcapped Front Range peaks is from the middle of Main Street. At first glance, one might think this is Anytown, Iowa, or Indiana—small, green, well kept. Porch-sitting, car-washing, evening strolls and neighborly chats are as much a part of life here as the ubiquitous churches and American flags. Everyone grows peonies, lilacs, bearded iris, hollyhocks and vast expanses of Kentucky bluegrass, which get watered at any and all times of the day. Mowing and sprinkling are regular summer activities along with softball and barbeques.

I have a long rectangular corner lot encircled by concrete sidewalks, beyond which stretch 250 feet of narrow "hell strips," areas owned by the municipality but to be maintained by the homeowner. The plot is so flat that not even a marble will roll. Once I removed the car parts, swing sets, doghouses and other various and sundry junk that had accumulated from years of being a rental property, I surveyed the vegetation: a ragtag collection of half-dead Siberian elms, lilacs, *Campanula rapunculoides* (also known as cancer-of-the-garden), parched Kentucky bluegrass, a sea of dandelions and, on the hottest edges of the property near the street, a tangle of bindweed and that sadistic paw-piercing, tire-puncturing pest, *Tribulus terrestris* (which means "demon of the earth" in Latin).

I was determined to have a waterwise garden. After removing most of the ratty plants except for eighty feet of a wonderful, overgrown lilac hedge that I pruned drastically to rejuvenate, I set about removing weeds. Spreading perennial weeds like bindweed and cancer-of-the-garden were sprayed monthly for the entire first spring and summer with glyphosate, one of the least environmentally toxic herbicides. I pulled out the dandelions with an asparagus knife and turned under the weakened, dried-out turf with a spade. We spread several pickup truck loads of rotted cow and horse manure on the turned-over lawn, six to eight inches deep, and left this over the first winter. The following spring, we tilled it under. The grass had been smothered and was now decomposing and adding organic matter to the dusty soil. Noxious annual weeds such as spotted spurge and puncture vine were pulled out by hand, but over the years they had left such a legacy of seed that I am still pulling out seedlings four years later.

The "hell strips" were thick with weeds. I decided these were to be the toughest plantings, to receive no supplemental water at all once established. After a spring and summer of weed killing, I planted them in the cooler days of September, my favorite month for planting perennials. The town ordinance requires all plants be twelve inches or less on these strips; I stretch this a little, maybe to fifteen or eighteen inches, but when choosing plants for this area, short, compact stature and heat and drought tolerance are traits of highest priority.

 The longest strips, running north-south, follow a heavily traveled route to the elementary school at the end of the road. Dozens of children, some very rambunctious, pass by daily. Here I decided I had best stick with grasses. One half is planted with short native buffalo grass (*Buchloe dactyloides*), which I planted as tiny plugs a foot apart in mid-June. I spent the following two months watering and weeding regularly, but since then, it has pretty much taken care of itself. Buffalo grass is a warm-season grass, so seeding or plugging is best left for late May or June, unlike cool-season grasses like Kentucky bluegrass or tall fescue. This preference for warm weather keeps buffalo grass from greening up early; it stays tawny and dormant-looking until around Memorial Day. A fellow gardener pioneered a wonderful way of dealing with its boring spring appearance: She planted small drought-tolerant bulbs—species crocus and tulips and little snow iris—in the grass in naturalistic sweeps. I copied this idea in a big way, planting five thousand of these bulbs into the grass the fall after the grass went in. This was no mean feat; the grass had proven so vigorous and filled in so well in just three months that it was a real pain grubbing down into the mats to get to the soil to poke in the bulbs. Fortunately, I have a sandy soil, so I moistened it before planting, and with the help of a good friend and several beers, we spent a weekend sitting in the soft grass, dibbling holes into the ground and stuffing in hundreds of bulbs. It was well worth the effort. From late February until mid-April, large sweeps of colorful bulbs take their turn blooming. First comes golden *Crocus ancyrensis*, followed by lavender *C. sieberi*. Then yellow *I. danfordiae* opens, followed by a host of purple, indigo and sky blue *Iris reticulata*. Then come the rest of the crocus, mainly various yellow, white, lavender, purple and striped forms of *Crocus chrysanthus*. Last, the species tulips bloom—rich magenta and warm pink *Tulipa humilis* selections followed by scarlet *T. linifolia* and *T. maximowiczii* and gold-flushed-red

A Bulb Lawn

▲ *Daughter Daphne nestles in the buffalo grass among* Tulipa humilis.

▶ *Another selection of* Tulipa humilis *glows in the early spring sunlight amid the buffalo grass.*

(facing page) Leadplant, Amorpha canescens, *is a wonderful large summer-flowering plains native that deserves more garden use.*

T. kolpakowskiana. Finally, the large-headed orange-red *T. vvedenskyi,* deep red *T. wilsoniana* and the more petite, softer colored yellow and copper forms of *T. batalinii* bloom.

The thin bulb foliage ripens quickly in the heat and drought of late spring, and by early June I can rake down the whole area, removing the remains of the bulb foliage along with dead grass from last year. The bulbs have started to seed themselves and produce bulblets; each passing year, the clumps grow bigger. Luckily, these self-sufficient little plants don't require dividing like their larger, more pampered cousins, for this would be quite an unthinkable chore. Raking and spot weeding is the only work this area requires. The dense turf of the buffalo grass and the lack of irrigation both see to it that weeds have a hard time gaining any foothold. One could mow the grass, but I like the tawny little seedheads, and I am also establishing clumps of various prickly pear cactus (*Opuntia* spp.) throughout, to echo the grasslands just east of town where irrigated agriculture comes to an abrupt halt and the overgrazed dry ranchland has become endless stretches of buffalo grass studded with cacti. In early summer, the effect is spectacular—yellow, gold and pink cactus flowers dot the landscape. I'm hoping my little strip will soon look that good. So I pass on the mowing. The grass never gets more than four to six inches tall and is a soft-textured gray-green, perfect for setting off the wild, colorful chaos of my cottage garden on the other side of the sidewalk. The daily parade of children with skateboards and bikes do the grass little harm. All in all that strip, the garden's showcase in early spring and good companion for the rest of the year, has been a real success.

A Prairie Planting

 The lower half of this same north-south strip, also planted in grass, has a totally different look. Here, juxtaposed across the sidewalk, is not a frothy cottage garden but a six-foot-high lilac hedge and graying cedar picket fence that enclose our backyard. I decided I could go a little more colorful and wild here without risking the effect becoming overbearing. I wanted to have color here in the summer and fall; the bulbs in the buffalo grass have spring covered. On a trip to the Nebraska sandhills, I fell in love with the way wildflowers spangled the soft, undulating sea of grass. I'm drawn to wide-open vistas; as a child I'd spend hours on a bench on the boardwalk at the New Jersey shore, looking out on the ocean and the horizon beyond. The parallel between ocean and prairie has been drawn before, and it works for me—I feel at home with both.

Prairie gardening is becoming quite popular in the Midwest, as people begin to treasure the vanishing landscape of that region. I wanted grass to dominate, with just a few patches of color threaded throughout, to give an evocative, restful feel rather than the rock-'em sock-'em color of annual meadows. It also needed to be a drought-tolerant, weed-choking planting that would stay less than a foot and a half in height.

Buffalo grass did not have the right look—it is too short to sway in the breeze. It also is a spreading rather than clump-forming grass, aggressive enough that perennial wild-flowers have a hard time competing. Research has been done at the North Platte Agricultural Experiment Station in Nebraska, and the results suggest that one needs to establish the perennials and then plant the buffalo grass if such a mix is to be successful. I chose blue grama grass (*Bouteloua gracilis*) instead; it is a lovely native perennial bunchgrass, fine textured and soft green in color, with charming little seedheads that suggest its other common name, eyelash grass. My rather unpoetic husband calls it toothbrush grass; I guess the seedheads do resemble a tiny toothbrush. Blue grama's clump-forming ways make it easy to grow perennials throughout the planting.

Unlike the buffalo grass area, where I did nothing to the soil but rid it of weeds and till before planting, over the prairie strip I added about two to three inches of aged horse manure. The sandy, rather sterile soil needed some organic matter: Many of the plants I wanted to grow there originate from regions where the topsoil is deeper and richer from eons of grass breaking down into humus. Prairie grasses, after all, begat the enormously fertile soil that has made the Midwest the rich farming region it is.

I planted tiny plugs of blue grama in June (it too is a warm-season grass, like buffalo grass) and interplanted a host of seed-grown wildflowers that September. Again, irrigation and weeding took up much of my time that summer, but since then, the planting has been off and running with very little help from me. In the winter, the softly textured buff clumps of grass and remaining seedheads are appealing.

If one doesn't have a height restriction, there are several larger shrubby plants that would look good in such a planting: silver sagebrush (*Artemisia tridentata* and *A. cana*) and two butterfly favorites, rabbitbrush (*Chrysothamnus nauseosus*), with its late-season golden flowers, and leadplant (*Amorpha canescens*). Leadplant grows in the Nebraska sandhills in great colonies, its sage green pinnate foliage punctuated with deep purple flower spikes with prominent orange anthers in late summer. Larger, western native perennials that give a shrubby effect yet die down to the ground each winter are bush morning glory (*Ipomoea leptophylla*), its graceful, willowlike foliage on arching stems that bear large pink funnel-shaped flowers in midsummer, and showy four o'clock (*Mirabilis multiflora*), with gray-green leaves and rose-pink flowers that open in late afternoon and evening. These plants could not be expected to heed the town height ordinance, so I had to find a place for them in other parts of the garden. Their absence, however, makes it possible to give the grass an annual mow and raking in early spring, bringing air and sunlight to the plants hiding under a mat of last year's dead grass, as well as allowing the grass more room for new growth. It simulates the grazing the buffalo used to do for the prairie. By mowing time, all the seedheads of the grass and the wildflowers have shattered, their jobs of reseeding and giving interest during the winter finished.

◄ *A blossom of plains native bush morning glory,* Ipomoea leptophylla, *is framed by blue grama grass.*

▼ *Showy western native four o'clock,* Mirabilis multiflora, *opens its tubular flowers every afternoon for two months in the summer.*

In late spring, when the blue grama is just beginning to turn green and push out of its tawny dormant tufts, two penstemons bring color to the slowly greening strip. The smaller, more dainty one, *Penstemon secundiflorus*, has orchid lavender flowers thickly crowded along one side of a twelve- to eighteen-inch narrow stem. The other, known commonly as shell-leaf penstemon or wild snapdragon, is *P. grandiflorus*, which grows wild in the sandhills and elsewhere on the Great Plains, as well as parts of the more eastern tallgrass prairie. This showstopper reaches anywhere from two to four feet in height, depending on moisture and soil. Its evergreen foliage rosette, the leaves beefy, slightly wavy-edged and a lovely waxy blue-gray, sets off the pastel flowers perfectly. The spikes in bloom are as dramatic as the most overbred hybrid snapdragon. Huge one and one-half inch puffy blossoms bloom in tight whorls all up and down the stem. The most common color is a washy lavender, but white, rosy-lilac and reddish purple forms exist as well. *P. grandiflorus* grows easily from seed, and although it has the reputation of being short-lived, as is the case with many of the penstemon clan, I've known individuals to live well over five years if grown dry and given lots of sunshine. Several self-sown seedlings appear every year, so the colony replenishes and increases itself.

As these two penstemons finish, the grass has filled in and turned the strip into an inviting soft billow of green. My cats now get lost in it, and spend hours napping or crouching low and stalking young grasshoppers here in their own private Serengeti plain. Late spring brings on the start of blue flax's (*Linum perenne* ssp. *lewisii*) two-month-long flowering season. In the morning, the pale blue and occasionally white blossoms are at their best; by early afternoon, the heat and relentless sunshine have wilted that day's crop of flowers. Deep purple and indigo spires of Rocky Mountain penstemon (*Penstemon strictus*) begin to bloom. This most adaptable of penstemons can grow both in very dry and regularly irrigated gardens, an unusual feat that has led to its popularity. As with most penstemons, it blooms only two to three weeks. But while many of this group of plants are unsuitable for the typical perennial border, even a dry one, because they bloom for so short a period and their leaves have so little substance that a hole remains for the rest of the season once they finish blooming, Rocky Mountain penstemon has great evergreen foliage in lush six-inch-tall evergreen mats that bely its ability to withstand drought. Beautiful fiery scarlet bugler penstemon, *P. barbatus*, blooms for over a month, starting just as *P. strictus* finishes. Its scanty foliage is well hidden when planted in the blue grama; only the tall, airy flower spikes rise above. Many sparsely clothed penstemons mix ideally in this manner with grasses, since the grass conceals their weak points, and one doesn't notice any holes once they have gone out of bloom. A really fine variant of *P. barbatus*, 'Schooley's Yellow', looks best when its creamy yellow flowers are paired with blue flax, and both these delicate plants, almost without substance, are surrounded and visually supported by the green of the grass.

▲ *NeeNee the cat stalks grasshoppers in a sea of blue grama, paper flower (Psilostrophe tagetina) and Indian blanket.*

◄ *Western natives skyrocket gilia and Indian blanket glow like embers on an August evening.*

► *Prairie coneflower, Ratibida columnifera, sends a parade of shuttlecock-like daisies toward the summer sky for weeks on end.*

I grew seed of several species of the lovely western bulbous genus *Calochortus*, known romantically as mariposa lilies or fairy lanterns, and planted well over one hundred seedlings throughout the grass. Their foliage is so fine at this young age that I couldn't find the plants now if I tried. I'm eagerly awaiting the first cream, yellow, purple or orange three-petaled flower to arise from the grass. I've been told it may be five to seven years, so I try not to think about them much since patience is not my strong suit.

As early summer begins to heat up, scarlet bugler penstemon is still going strong, joined now by its lookalike, skyrocket gilia (*Ipomopsis aggregata* aka *Gilia aggregata*). From a distance, the two are indistinguishable. Skyrocket's flowers are starry trumpets rather than the snoutlike blossoms of the penstemon. The bright reds of these two tall spiky flowers and the gold and red daisy mounds of dwarf Indian blanket (*Gaillardia* x *grandiflora* 'Goblin') marry well. I've grown plain Indian blanket and the cultivar 'Burgundy' several times, first in a perennial border where they flopped miserably, and then much drier, where they still flopped miserably, so I've finally banished them both from the garden. Little 'Goblin' stays a compact eight to fifteen inches tall, the brilliant daisies just barely peeking up over the grass. With a monthly deadheading, this plant blooms from June until October.

Late June and July, the grassy strip is aflame with oranges, reds and golds. The penstemon and skyrocket are still at their peak, as is Indian blanket. Now one of my all-time favorite plants, butterfly weed (*Asclepias tuberosa*), adds orange to the scene. Unlike many members of its genus, butterfly weed is highly drought tolerant. I picked it along abandoned railroad beds in the parched, sandy soil near the coast of southern New Jersey; a long-lived cut flower, it found its way into my wedding bouquet.

Touches of gold come from three members of the daisy family: the small but profuse blossoms of paper flower (*Psilostrophe tagetina* and shorter *P. bakeri*); prairie coneflower (*Ratibida columnifera*); and coreopsis-like greenthread (*Thelesperma ambiguum*). Vast golden ribbons of the latter run through fields along Interstate 80 in central Nebraska. All three of these plants are short-lived but reseed themselves. I collect seed annually just in case nature leaves me high and dry. I would hate to be without their cheerful summer-long bloom.

I've attempted to integrate two of the smaller native sages—*Artemisia frigida*, the fringed sage, and *A. filifolia*, sand sage. I was hoping that they would help host some of the beautiful orange-red dryland species of Indian paintbrush (*Castilleja integra* and *C. chromosa*), semiparasitic wildflowers that have frustrated many gardeners by refusing to be tamed. A few people, including a phlegmatic gardener who barely notices them sprouting in huge clumps from a container originally slated for petunias, have the magic touch. I do not. Every year I have tried sowing seed—in with the sage, in with the grass, in pots, directly into the planting. I have yet to succeed with this beautiful trickster of a plant.

At the north end of the blue grama strip, where it comes closer to the pastel east-facing garden, softer colors dominate. Wiry stems of *Gaura lindheimeri*, appropriately dubbed apple blossom grass by a friend for its ethereal white flowers, rise above the grass in a three-month long succession of bloom. Magenta prairie wine-cup, also known as buffalo rose (*Callirhoe involucrata*) and its more upright relative *C. triangulata* sprawl at the edges of the planting, also blooming for months on end. Large white prickly poppy flowers (*Argemone platyceras*) shimmer in the sunlight; this short-lived prairie native self-sows dependably. Purple prairie clover (*Dalea purpurea*) attracts bumblebees; night-flowering *Mentzelia decapetala* draws moths.

I first found this mentzelia while driving back from an evening visit to the Pawnee Buttes in northeastern Colorado. These mysterious stone formations that rise so abruptly from the plains are a favorite place for local botanizers and solitude seekers. The ruddy sandstone and eroding soil host an abundance of unusual cushion plants and night-blooming flowers. Down in a canyon created by periodic flooding from the strong thundershowers of late spring and summer, dark, gnarled silhouettes of juniper and limber pine dot the landscape. In this out-of-the-way place coyotes sing and antelope still roam; osprey and bald eagle ride the hot afternoon wind currents in lazy circles against a horizon of purple thunderclouds, orange lightning and misty gray rain shadows. It is no wonder the Pawnee Indians considered this haunting landscape sacred. As night falls slowly on the buttes, the warm tones of the soil and stone slip into lavender and gray, and the drive back down the dirt roads is lit by the reflections of a thousand eyes. The hot sun is gone and the land comes alive with busy animals. Birds swoop out of the darkness into the car's headlights to gather roadkill or bathe in rain puddles in the road's ruts. The moon sneaks in and out of the clouds; on the northern horizon, the clearing sky offers an August shower of falling stars. All of a sudden, around a sharp turn, a cluster of four-inch, creamy white stars glows from the roadside: *Mentzelia decapetala* has opened its blossoms for the night. After several unsuccessful attempts at photography, I made a mental note of the spot for a return visit later in the season to collect seed. Now this wild beauty graces the grass along the roadside by my house.

As summer slips into autumn, the grassy strip takes on a more tawny color. The dainty seedheads have dried, but several flowers still add bright notes of color. Indian blanket is still blooming, as is paper flower. The fine-textured sprays of golden broomweed, *Gutierrezia sarothrae*, have opened. Lavender hues join the reds and golds: *Machaeranthera bigelovii*, with large aster-like flowers, and the more purple spikes of *Liatris punctata*, the most drought tolerant of this genus of showy North American plants. Purple and gold thread through the softly browning grass, just like on the prairie. I recall the same colors from memories of meadows aflame with asters and goldenrod back in Pennsylvania. For me, this is more romantic than the most velvety crimson rose, the most delicate violet. These are the colors of autumn in America.

▲ Iris reticulata 'Clairette' unfurls between still-dormant evergreen sempervivum and veronica.

◄ Crocus chrysanthus 'Aubade' pokes through ruddy sempervivums and 'Dragon's Blood' sedum.

▶ *Snow iris bulbs multiply dependably, growing into sizeable clumps in a couple of years.*

▼ *Hardy cacti plump up in the warm spring soil:* Pediocactus simpsonii *blooms alongside* Corynopuntia sp.

From Hell to Heaven

 On the hell strips running east-west along the property, the plants are much more diverse. Few children walk along here, so I was less worried about trampling and picking. Here, with completely unamended soil—an alkaline, sandy loam with a pH above 8—I'm experimenting with the toughest, most heat-, cold- and drought tolerant plants from around the world. I want high drama on these strips; Mediterranean herbs, native wildflowers, mountain plants all combine in an unabashed, brilliant color jamboree.

Not only must the plants be attractive and tough, they also should stay under a foot and a half in height and have good-looking, perhaps even evergreen foliage. A mulch of three-eighths-inch local pea gravel, a nice mauve-gray color, moderates the soil temperature and slows runoff from heavy summer showers. It also has proven itself the perfect seed bed for many of these plants; each spring I'm greeted with a whole new group of offspring, some highly desirable, some less so.

Spring starts early on these strips, for the sandy soil and stone mulch warm up quickly. *Iris reticulata* often blooms in February, followed by sand lilies (*Leucocrinum montanum*) with their starry white flowers. Soon after, dark blue grape hyacinths (*Muscari armeniacum*) open, releasing their delicious musky fragrance. I'm sure to remove their spent flower heads, for their self-sowing is legendary. Silver mats of low-growing *Centaurea stricta* foliage are backdrop to glowing magenta *Tulipa humilis*; ruddy maroon hens and chicks host clumps of lavender and white crocus. The bluish, whorled foliage of donkey-tail spurge (*Euphorbia myrsinites*) lolls on the ground, the tips festooned with brilliant chartreuse-bracted flower clusters. Orange-red *Tulipa vvedenskyi* blooms alongside. Mat thyme, *Penstemon caespitosus* 'Claude Barr', *Achillea serbica* and Turkish veronica (*Veronica liwanensis*) will bloom a little later, but their ground-hugging, lush evergreen foliage sets the stage for several other small bulbs.

The earliest bees venture out to the pink flowers of snowball cactus (*Pediocactus simpsonii*). Little Easter daisy (*Townsendia hookeri*) opens its disproportionately large white flowers. Gold and lemon flowers form rings around the silvery evergreen rosettes of various bladderpod species (*Physaria* and *Lesquerella* spp.). Later these will ripen into curious inflated pale green and mauve seedpods.

My favorite color combination on these strips in the spring is brilliant magenta locoweed (*Oxytropis lambertii*) with robin's egg blue *Penstemon angustifolius*. *P. nitidus*, also a short, early flowering species, has coarser flowers in shades of vivid blue mixed with rosy lavender. A friend combines this penstemon with bright pink moss phlox (*Phlox subulata* 'McDaniel's Cushion') in his dry garden; I would love to copy this vibrant mix but that phlox fries on my strips. I can only grow the more heat-tolerant white plains phloxes *P. andicola*, *P. hoodii* and *P. bryoides* in this area of the garden.

Several diminutive bearded iris bloom in April; my favorite is the six-inch white and purple plicata called 'Scribe'. Three good companions to the upright, jaunty foliage and flowers of the irises are candytuft-like, white-flowered *Schivereckia podolica*, with pretty evergreen foliage rosettes; pink-flowered *Dracocephalum botryoides*, with lovely sage-green woolly foliage mats, also evergreen; and the furry, finely dissected gray-green leaves of *Erigeron compositus*, bearing lavender and white daisies that harmonize well with pale yellow iris flowers.

Two early blooming, shrubby members of the pea family stay low enough to be allowed on the strips. *Cytisus austriacus*, with pale, creamy yellow flowers, is the larger of the two, growing about a foot in height and three feet in spread. Vibrant yellow *Genista sagittalis* 'Nana', with curiously winged stems, stays at about six to eight inches in height and probably would prefer it a little cooler.

Bright yellow dominates when *Alyssum montanum* and *Lithospermum incisum* burst into flower. The alyssum continues on for a good six weeks, overlapping with the intense late May flower flush. Silver foliage helps cool the fiery yellows: partridge feather (*Tanacetum densum* var. *amani*), buckwheat (*Eriogonum ovalifolium*, *E. niveum* and *E. jamesii*), lavender cotton (*Santolina chamaecyparissus* 'Nana') and shrubby, short *Verbascum dumulosum*, the latter two blooming yellow later on. Blue flowers also soften and complement the strident yellows: mats of purple-blue 'Claude Barr' penstemon and several low-growing, spring-flowering veronicas can take the heat and drought of these strips, making a good foil for the strong colors. Two evergreen spreading veronicas, Turkish and woolly veronica (*Veronica pectinata*), lap out onto the pavement like green surf, softening the straight lines of the property, while *V. cinerea* and *V. armena* form discrete mounds.

The month of May on the strips is outrageous. Depending on my mood, I either revel in the colors or feel somewhat embarrassed and reach for the sunglasses. The two areas are separated by a short piece of sidewalk that goes to the street, and I have used this as a stop in the action to divide color—bright red, orange and the fiercer yellows are held captive on the western strip, while pink, lavender, white, magenta and pale yellows stay obediently on the east side. Blue and purple are allowed to jump the path and mingle with all, adding richness and depth to the paler planting while cooling and unifying the more jarring colors.

On the pale side, two-foot lavender and white spires of shell-leaf penstemon mock the height ordinance for a couple of weeks. The strong indigo blues of Wasatch beard-tongue (*Penstemon cyananthus*), *P. virgatus asa-grayi* and Rocky Mountain penstemon join in. Shocking pink blossoms of the hardy cactus *Coryphantha vivipara* punctuate the pebbles. Large white tufted evening primrose flowers (*Oenothera caespitosa*) open in early evening, sending out a sweet perfume until mid-morning the next day, when they close once again, the oldest blossoms fading to pink. Several dianthus species and hybrids smother themselves in pink, rose, white, maroon and bicolor clove-scented flowers. *Salvia jurisicii* offers many compact lavender blue spikes over hairy, finely dissected foliage.

▲ Cytisus austriacus.

▲ Echinocereus triglochidiatus, *claret-cup cactus.*

▲ Schivereckia podolica.

◀ *The cool chartreuse flower heads of donkey-tail spurge,*
Euphorbia myrsinites, *temper bright tulips and* Alyssum montanum.

To accentuate these more dramatic plants, I make use of fillers with profuse, small flowers and a mounded rather than upright habit. Stone cress (*Aethionema grandiflorum* and *A.* x *warleyense*) creates a sugar pink foam throughout the planting, while white and pink sunroses (*Helianthemum nummularium*) sprawl in between. White flower clusters of *Achillea serbica* carpet its evergreen foliage mat, and the white daisies with ruby-red reverses of ground-hugging *Anacyclus depressus*, Mt. Atlas daisy, add charm without taking away from the showier plants. When evening approaches and the oenotheras have opened, the whites and pale yellows begin to glow. Most luminescent are creamy yellow *Scutellaria supina*, with flowers like a miniature snapdragon, pale yellow *Sideritis hyssopifolia*, white-flowered, fragrant-leaved *Dracocephalum multicaule* and *D. renatii*, and the tufted chartreuse flower heads of *Thymus mastichinus*, which remain pretty for weeks after the flowers themselves have passed.

In late May on the hot-colored western strip, yellow *Alyssum montanum* is just finishing. The golden daisies of *Eriophyllum lanatum* open above silver filigree foliage. More of the same flower color comes with *Hypericum cerastioides*, lying flat to the ground. The richest of the yellows, *Linum bulgaricum*, has contrasting leaves of the darkest green. Blue foliage plants cool the sunny tones: rue, the doily-like rosettes of biennial apricot-flowered poppy *Papaver triniifolium*, and ubiquitous California poppies, here in their more common orange flowered form. Prairie-fire penstemon (*Penstemon pinifolius*) and claret-cup cactus (*Echinocereus triglochidiatus*), with contrasting lime green stigmas, add red to the brilliant color display. The indigo spires of biennial *Dracocephalum nutans*, navy blue annual desert bluebells (*Phacelia campanularia*), perennial blue Rocky Mountain penstemon and sky blue flax pull together the cacophony of bright color, interwoven with orange cowboy's delight (*Sphaeralcea coccinea*). Two excellent native evening primroses included in the planting are *Oenothera brachycarpa*, a dwarf with huge lemon yellow flowers that open from dusk until mid-morning, and the smaller-flowered, day-blooming *O. serrulata*.

Once summer begins in earnest, the rest of the garden takes center stage and the strips, having had their day, complement it. On the west strip, annuals California poppy and golden Texas blazing star (*Mentzelia lindleyi*) continue on bravely in the heat, joined by yellow moss rose (*Portulaca grandiflora*). Various prickly pear cacti (flat-segmented *Opuntia polyacantha*, *O. phaeacantha*, *O. humifusa* and oval-segmented *O. fragilis*) bloom, their lemon, cream, bright yellow and apricot flowers shining like silk in the sun. Floppy little Rocky Mountain zinnia, *Zinnia grandiflora*, begins a long succession of amber flowers. Old faithful dwarf Indian blanket 'Goblin', orange butterfly weed and yellow paper flower are welcome not only in the prairie strip amid the blue grama grass, but also here in the hot-colored strip for summer color. Blue-leaved *Sedum reflexum* and the tiny silver mats of Spanish dandelion, *Andryala agardhii*, slip in and out of the brighter flowers. The ratty yellow daisies of *Berlandiera lyrata* are not much to look at, but in the morning they smell just like milk chocolate, which more than redeems them. The seed heads are quite pretty, too—scalloped green affairs reminiscent of the *Bupleurum* tribe.

On the other side, lipstick pink and magenta still add pizzazz to the pastels: Hardy purple iceplant (*Delosperma cooperi*), weavers such as prairie wine-cup and *Verbena bipinnatifida* and annuals *Talinum mengesii* and catchfly (*Silene armeria*) bloom well into autumn. Frothy white *Eriogonum niveum* and *Goniolimon tataricum*, known as German statice in flower arranging circles, add airiness to the planting, as do lavender *Limonium binervosum* and tiny *L. bellidifolium*, both close relatives of the statice. Pink *Petrorhagia saxifraga* (aka *Tunica saxifraga*) has the appeal of a low-growing pink baby's breath, as does late-blooming *Dianthus nardiformis*. The tissue-paper flowers of *Oenothera speciosa*, pink Mexican evening primrose, bloom nonstop until October. The plant spreads by underground runners, as does rose-pink *Teucrium webbianum*, but the stems are so fine and the leaves of so little substance, that they never crowd out other plants, only poke out a pretty flower here and there. A creamy, pale form of California poppy reseeds every year, adding a touch of soft yellow, while plains native blackfoot daisy (*Melampodium leucanthum*) tirelessly sends up white zinnia-like flowers. Foliage interest comes from spiny biennial thistle *Cirsium spinosissimum* and, as a soft counterpoint, furry *Sideritis scardica*, looking like a refined lamb's ear. This plant sends up pale yellow flower spikes earlier in the season, but like lamb's ear, the blossoms are secondary to the foliage.

Favorites at this time are the showy oreganos. A deep pink form of cooking marjoram with purple stems, *Origanum vulgare*, is the tallest at eighteen inches, growing next to its herbal partner, dark-blue-flowered hyssop (*Hyssopus officinalis*). Large chartreuse bracts, giving the plants a shrimplike appearance, make *Origanum libanoticum* and *O. acutidens* so appealing and useful with all other colors. The bracts remain showy for almost two months, well into late summer, before turning brown and shattering.

The queen of this pale strip in mid- and late summer, however, is the long-flowering desert penstemon, *Penstemon ambiguus*. It is well named, for when I first saw it, I was sure it was a phlox, not a penstemon. We were driving through the Painted Desert in northern Arizona, where miles of great billowing pink, lavender and white mounds of this plant shimmer against red stone and sand in the evening light. The beautiful blossoms seem to hover above a tangle of wiry, almost leafless stems.

The dutiful self-sowing annuals continue on into fall, when they are joined by the low-growing golden aster-like *Haplopappus spinulosus*, the yellow haze of broomweed and dwarf rabbitbrush and an autumnal showstopper, the fiery orange-red trumpets of *Zauschneria garrettii*, hardiest member of this gorgeous genus.

Winter is not a lost, desolate time on the strips. Snow melts off quickly, exposing the geometry of petite *Yucca harrimaniae*, larger *Y. glauca* and *Y. angustissima*, both narrow-leaved soapweeds, and the thick, wider-leaved rosette of *Y. baccata*. The cacti are particularly pretty until late winter, when they have shriveled and sunken into the ground. Bright red berries of *Coryphantha* (aka *Neobesseya*) *missouriensis* help lessen my

▲   Veronica armena *and sunrose intertwine along the warm flagstone path.*

◄   *George the cat lolls in his own private opium den, a planting of fragrant catmint.*

(facing page, far right) The hell strips in full glory: penstemons, cacti, blue flax, stone cress, pinks, lavender Salvia jurisicii *and pale green* Sideritis scardica.

▲ *Tufted evening primrose and pinks make a fragrant pair.*

▲ *Mounds and spikes fill the unwatered June hell strip.*

▲ *Coryphantha vivipara, a hardy cactus.*

▼ *Penstemon caespitosus 'Claude Barr'.*

nostalgia for the holiday hollyberries of the east. Tiny *Ephedra minima* raises its blue-green stems a few inches from the ground; sedums and sempervivums take on their deeper, more reddish and purple cold-weather hues. Hardy iceplant (*Delosperma nubigenum*), a cheerful spreading ground cover with lime green, succulent foliage during the growing season, turns a scrumptious raspberry rose in the winter. Many of the perennials—dianthus, donkey-tail spurge, thymes, penstemons, bladderpods, buckwheats—retain their foliage all winter, adding texture and color to the pebbled strips. Most fun of all are the *Acantholimon* species with their spiky, mounded humps, like a gathering of snow-dusted porcupines huddling against the wind. Soon enough the earliest seedlings will form a soft green haze over the stones, and the first snow iris will bravely unfurl a blue flower in the warming sunlight.

The Dry Cottage Garden

 The largest part of the garden is what I like to call the dry cottage garden. This area was given over to a weedy, poorly maintained bluegrass lawn when we moved in. I turned that one foot under with a spade and spread six inches of rotted horse manure on top for the winter, which we then tilled in the following spring. The first year, both new plants and weeds grew enthusiastically out of bounds thanks to this oversupply of nitrogen until a late-season hailstorm struck, turning the lush, floppy tangle into lime sherbet in a few foul minutes. Each year since that ignominious beginning, the garden looks better and better. The soft, floriferous cottage gardens of the British Isles that I loved so much when I worked there inspired the style of this garden; our quaint old clapboard house begged for it.

With the help of amended soil, a wide range of tough, water-stingy plants give a big, blowsy, romantic effect with about two inches of water a month during the hottest season and one inch each month thereafter. By choosing plants from homeoclimactic regions—areas of the world with similar growing conditions—I've been able to create a garden with year-round interest that looks very English, without the rain. As with the strip plantings, the cottage garden consists of a mélange of herbs and Mediterranean plants, native western wildflowers and a large group from the Near East and Central Asia. Here, however, bigger plants are allowed; I have more space—almost a quarter acre—and I'm not restrained by any height ordinance. Plants with attractive foliage and a host of self-sowing annuals and biennials that pop up in places and mingle in ways my hand could never hope to imitate give the garden staying power through the summer months. Several shrubs and dwarf conifers add structure and winter interest, as do the flagstone paths snaking through, dividing the garden into discrete asymmetrical, curved patterns. These areas are not beds or borders per se, for the entire ground from house to sidewalk is planted.

To describe the whole dry cottage garden in detail, I could go on ad infinitum. The choice of plants for this kind of garden is virtually limitless. Each year, I move and rearrange so much, adding over a hundred new species and removing nearly as many that I've either killed, that don't seem to like me and are languishing or whose looks

▲ Penstemon pinifolius, *prairie fire penstemon.*

▲ Mt. Atlas daisy, Anacyclus depressus, *closes its flowers when clouds roll over, revealing red undersides.*

▲ *Several* Opuntia *species bloom alongside blue flax in early summer.*

I've decided I don't like. Throughout the seasons, however, a number of combinations have worked especially well. Color, form and texture of foliage and flower, as often by accident as by plan, somehow harmonize. In all honesty, only a handful of these combinations were planned out on paper or ahead of planting time. Often they occurred by my walking around the garden, plant and trowel in hand, holding the newcomer up against others, imagining the effect at its peak. Most commonly I notice certain plants in the garden that are not growing together and suddenly realize how well they would look side by side, so I dig one or the other up and compose this way, called the "trowel and error" method. Formal perennial borders with repetition and a finite palette of plants can be created on paper. This kind of wild jumble, with constant change and a large number of plants—over a thousand species—makes that sort of design process impossible here.

Edges In early spring, the smaller plants tucked along the edge of the sidewalk and stone paths are at their showiest. As elsewhere in the garden, small bulbs are framed by companion plants with evergreen foliage: gray felted rosettes of dwarf pussytoes (*Antennaria parvifolia*) set off rose-purple *Tulipa humilis*, pale yellow *T. batalinii*, especially endearing for its plump, rounded rather than pointy flowers, rises from a mat of sage green rock-cress leaves (*Aubrieta macedonica*), whose purple blossoms are just beginning to open.

Blue and yellow dwarf bearded iris bloom with chartreuse-yellow spring spurge (*Euphorbia epithymoides* aka *E. polychroma*) and blue woolly veronica. Lavender iris joins pale yellow basket-of-gold (*Aurinia saxatilis* 'Citrina'); deep purple iris glows with biennial orange Siberian wallflower (*Cheiranthus allionii*). Other iris cultivars mix with moss phloxes. *Phlox douglasii* 'Boothman's Variety' is lavender with a dark purple eye; *P. subulata* 'Blue Emerald', hardly blue but a pleasing dusky lilac, grows like a weed and has the hardiest, lush, glossy evergreen foliage of the bunch. *P. subulata* ssp. *brittonii* is tiny, with starry baby pink flowers, and the sand phloxes, white *P. bifida* 'Alba' and lavender 'Betty Blake', are tough and dependable. Purple Corsican violet (*Viola corsica*), in bloom every month of the year, self-sows between the iris spikes and the phlox mats, improving many a combination.

The pasqueflowers begin, their furry stems and buds glistening in the bald spring sunlight. Pale blue *Anemone pulsatilla* 'Budapest' is the loveliest, with a skirt of frosty, freshly emerged silver lamb's ear (*Stachys byzantina*). The paths come alive as the pinks start to bloom. The bright pink double buttons of *Dianthus gratianopolitanus* 'Tiny Rubies', the large blush pink flowers of the cultivar 'Pike's Pink', and the maroon-and-white-patterned petals of 'Waithman's Beauty', like Spanish mosaic, are among the best. Tufts of blue fescue (*Festuca ovina* var. *glauca*) soften the brilliant magenta of the small, mounded *Geranium cinereum* var. *subcaulescens* and *G. sanguineum*. Mauvy, pink-veined *Geranium cinereum* 'Ballerina' and pink-veined white *G. sanguineum* var. *striatum* are paired with the silver foliage and electric indigo blue of *Veronica incana* 'Saraband', longer-flowering than the straight species. A refined little knapweed, *Centaurea bella*, with eight-inch rosy bachelor's button flowers and deeply cut leaves with silver undersides, is framed by sprawling, woolly silver *Nepeta phyllochlamys*, with modest lavender-blue flowers. Silver and pink is echoed by *Onosma alboroseum*, its creamy, blush-pink flower drops dangling over the path above pewter foliage. *O. echioides* hangs yellow drops over dark green, hairy leaves. Both are joined by the long-blooming, deep rose flower clusters of storksbill, *Erodium daucifolium*, and dwarf rock soapwort, *Saponaria ocymoides* 'Nana'.

Farther into the planting, the larger spring flowers demand their share of attention. The smoky arilbred irises, mauve, lavender, chocolate brown and amber, often finely veined and spotted, precede the flashy tall bearded iris, in shades of lavender, plum and almost black-purple. Similarly toned four-foot drumstick alliums (*Allium aflatunense*) and white Oriental poppies take center stage with a backdrop of six-foot, frothy white *Crambe cordifolia*, once well described by a friend as baby's breath with a glandular problem. This giant sea kale has a smaller, finer textured, four-foot cousin, *Crambe orientalis*, with grayer, deeply incised leaves rather than the great green, rhubarb-like foliage of *C. cordifolia*. Its foamy white inflorescence frames the large single white blossoms of early flowering *Rosa rugosa* 'Alba', backed by the unfurling purple foliage of smokebush, *Cotinus coggygria* 'Royal Purple'. White, lavender and purple together is a color combination I seem to repeat over and over without being fully aware. I've always loved the color purple, ever since my psychedelic days as a wannabe hippie, too young to march on Washington but not too young to plaster Jimi Hendrix posters on my walls. "Purple Haze" was not just a song, it was a state of mind. While my juvenile fascination with incense, bell-bottoms and Woodstock faded, my predilection for purple has not.

Warm salmon-pink 'Helen Elizabeth' Oriental poppies join similarly toned *Penstemon barbatus* 'Elfin Pink'. The more common orange-red poppies find a home next to the blue lupinelike spikes of wild indigo (*Baptisia australis*). Tall, long-flowering alkanet, *Anchusa azurea*, has a more vivid, true blue tone than false indigo and pairs well with the butter yellow, almost single flowers of hardy, early flowering shrub rose 'Frühlingsgold'. Few roses can tolerate dry conditions, but this, as well as the rugosas, the red-leaf rose (*Rosa glauca* aka *R. rubrifolia*) and *R. x alba* do well. *R. x alba* 'Semiplena', a substantial, lush gray-green shrub rose that also blooms earlier than the majority of roses, joins another giant sea kale towards the back of the garden. A huge silver biennial thistle, *Onopordum acanthium*, fattens up nearby. The silver and white forms and textures shimmer in the still benevolently soft spring sunshine. I grow this thistle only for its

▶ *Violas and moss phlox dress the base of dwarf bearded iris.*

▼ *Pasqueflowers don fuzzy halos in the early spring light.*

(facing page) Mounds of lamb's ear, pinks, Geranium cinereum 'Ballerina', pale yellow Scutellaria supina and the dusky foliage of Sedum x 'Vera Jameson' soften the path's edges.

dramatic silver silhouette; once it begins to bloom, the foliage goes to pot and the unremarkable purple flowers quickly produce an army of unwanted seed. My retired farmer neighbors view this plant with wary distrust, and each year when I pull it out, armed with thick leather gloves and an axe, I wonder whether I have gone as mad as they think. Then I was told by a friend fluent in Greek that the botanical name for the plant means donkey fart. One would think that would be the coup de grace for the plant, but each year I save one or two of the self-sown seedlings, and for the few weeks when they stand so statuesquely with the rose and the crambe, I forget all the thistle's shortcomings.

As the poppies begin to fade, the peonies take over. A perfect companion to the romantic, double pink flowers of 'Sarah Bernhardt' are the icy white and gray vertical stripes of spiky *Iris pallida* 'Argentea Variegata' leaves. The flowers of this iris are puny, gnarled, almost deformed, so I remove them and grow it only as a foliage plant. *I. orientalis*, an old-fashioned garden plant rarely seen in nurseries today, blooms later than the bearded irises. I find it the most elegant of the irises. Its long, narrow green

foliage stays healthy and erect all summer, adding clean vertical lines to the multitude of mounded, busy textures and shapes. Stylish white and yellow flowers, while not large and frilly like the bearded iris, nevertheless are quietly beautiful and more classical in form. They pair well with the lemon yellow spikes of pea flowers of *Thermopsis fabacea*, which takes more drought than its brassier yellow American cousins.

As in most gardens, late spring and early summer brings on a flush of color unmatched by any other time of year. While I try to include as many early and late-flowering plants as I can, June is still the most spectacular month in this part of the garden. Misty lavender-blue spikes of *Nepeta* x 'Six Hills Giant', a taller version of common catmint, set off the shimmering flat flowerheads of *Achillea* x 'Moonshine', a particularly fine sulphur yellow yarrow with feathery gray foliage. That same yellow, a preferred color in my garden, is found in two smaller western natives, both evergreen: *Eriogonum umbellatum*, appropriately named sulphur flower, with fluffy rounded flower clusters, and *Penstemon pinifolius* 'Mersea Yellow', a pale yellow variant of the orange-red prairie-fire penstemon. Deep blue Rocky Mountain penstemon, at two to three feet, stands behind.

I also like pale yellow with purple. A fine cultivar of basket-of-gold, *Aurinia saxatilis* 'Dudley Neville', with creamy, variegated foliage and pale yellow flowers, is a gem of a plant. It blooms at the same time as two dainty lilacs that are ideal for integrating with perennials: cut-leaf lilac, *Syringa laciniata*, and the small-leaved Korean lilac, *S. meyeri*, both much prettier than the earlier-flowering common lilac. These are quite drought tolerant, not inclined to mildew, but unfortunately not nearly as fragrant as old *S. vulgaris*. The non-flowering form of furry lamb's ear, 'Silver Carpet', and the waxy, opalescent lavender-gray leaves of little *Orostachys furusei* front the combination. Seedlings of annual *Atriplex hortensis* 'Rubra' abound, and one has fortuitously popped up next to the pale yellow basket-of-gold. Known as red orach or summer spinach by cooks but grown by me only for its lovely reddish purple foliage, atriplex joins bronze fennel (*Foeniculum vulgare* 'Purpureum'), lavender, white and purple opium poppies (*Papaver somniferum*), blue love-in-a-mist (*Nigella damascena*), purple *Verbena bonariensis* (aka *V. patagonica*) and ruby flax (*Linum grandiflorum* 'Rubrum') in a melee of self-sown seedlings throughout the garden. I have these carefree "perennial" annuals to thank for brightening many a combination and filling many a gap. Red orach looks especially good with *Phlomis russeliana*, a perennial with unusual, tiered whorls of creamy flowers over large, hairy, light green leaves. A most unexpected brushstroke of red orach's vibrant foliage united an otherwise undistinguished planting when it joined tawny cream and brown-freckled Grecian foxglove (*Digitalis lanata*) and the profuse white froth of daisies that is *Tanacetum niveum*. I am crazy about both these plants, but their colors are so similar that they are lost on each other. Enter red orach to the rescue; a rich purple seedling planted itself squarely between them.

Penstemon digitalis 'Husker Red', with a more muted maroon leaf color than red orach and small white flowers, pairs with white Greek valerian (*Centranthus ruber* 'Albus'), the three-foot pewter filigree of *Artemisia* x 'Powis Castle', a short-lived perennial for me but easily grown from cuttings, and the dusky purple, felted leaves of the low-growing shrublet *Salvia officinalis* 'Purpurea'. Thin, almost without substance, the airy spikes of promiscuous toadflax, *Linaria purpurea* and its pink form 'Canon Went' are allowed here, but its seedlings are pulled out by the bushel-full in other parts of the garden. This pretty plant, reminiscent of a snapdragon but much more delicate, blooms and sets seed all summer, and it seems every seed is viable.

Foliage plays a role equally important to that of flowers in my combinations. *Foliage* Just as I suffer icy stares and nasty prickles for the silver silhouettes of my donkey farts, I pull out thousands of biennial mullein seedlings each spring for the few that I save and let grow into large, animal-like felted rosettes. *Verbascum bombyciferum* has the whitest foliage of all. Its thin, tall flower stems are equally white, with lemon yellow flowers dotted up and down. *V. densiflorum* has lime green, hairy leaves and the best flowers of the lot—two-inch golden saucers that go on for most of the summer. *V. undulatum* shouldn't even bother blooming, and I'm always tempted to remove its ratty flower stalk, except that I need the thing to set seed. So I indulge it, for the wavy, undulate foliage is out of this world. The hairs are yellow, as if the plant had been dusted with sulphur. The last of the biennial, drought-tolerant mulleins that have found a happy home in my garden is white-leaved, purple-flowered *V. wiedemannianum*, a plant whose aristocratic looks bely its weedy ways. Now, after three years, all the mulleins have decided they are quite fond of each other and have started to breed. The seedlings are becoming more muddled and difficult to classify each year. I'm hoping some will be even more beautiful than their parents, but I am growing the true species from seed acquired elsewhere just in case my troop of mongrels turns out to be all dogs.

One particular grouping of plants, blue, green and yellow, gets a lot of attention from passersby, and yet there isn't a single flower to be seen. Foliage adds all the color, form and texture to make this a good marriage. The wavy, lolling waxy leaves of blue sea kale (*Crambe maritima*) are interrupted by yellow-and-green-striped *Iris pallida* 'Variegata' foliage, with a fountain of blue avena grass (*Helictotrichon sempervirens*) at the rear.

Such drama with the exclusion of flowers is the exception rather than the rule in my garden, however. I think too many unusual foliages grouped together start to look artificial, restless and contrived. Rather, simple coupling of a good foliage plant with a contrasting flower can be counted on for success. The hairy-leaved horehounds, *Marrubium* spp., are perfect partners to more showy flowering perennials. Take for example the long-blooming pink spikes of *Veronica spicata* 'Red Fox' with the velvety, pale

▲ *Dwarf 'R.H. Montgomery' spruce frames the mysterious blossoms of arilbred iris 'Oyez'.*

green, rounded leaves of *Marrubium rotundifolium*. Or the raspberry-red, dense drumstick blossoms of summer-flowering bulb *Allium sphaerocephalum* rising on naked stems through a thick gray pelt of silver horehound, *Marrubium incanum*. Or perhaps the clear pink mallow flowers of *Malva alcea* 'Fastigiata' fronted by chartreuse, furry *Marrubium cylleneum*, with a cloud of white baby's breath behind.

Midsummer in the garden relies heavily on herbs for color and fragrance. Lavender, blue-flowered hyssop, culinary oregano and its pale-green bracted relatives, and the pungent foliage of lacy blue rue and sage green southernwood, *Artemisia abrotanum*, all complementary plants rather than dominant, join the daylilies that now stand out. Fragrant pale yellow 'Hyperion' and soft pink 'Catherine Woodbery', with a green throat, are two of my favorites. 'Irish Limerick', a shorter daylily with cool lemon yellow flowers, supports the scrambling stems of blue *Clematis integrifolia*. Steely blue globe thistle (*Echinops ruthenicus*) holds court over an unnamed tall peach cultivar. Behind these, even taller perennial hollyhock, *Alcea rugosa*, opens clear yellow flowers. This underused, tough plant never suffers from the rust and insect damage that trouble the more common, shorter-lived hollyhocks. Powder blue spires of white-stemmed Russian sage accompany various other daylilies a bit later, in August.

▲ *Red orach enlivens creamy* Digitalis lanata *spikes, framed by airy white* Tanacetum niveum *daisies and giant sea kale.*

▼ Iris orientalis.

▲ *Old-fashioned tall bearded iris 'Wine and Roses'.*

▼ Onosma echioides.

The most colorful late summer composition, right near the front of the house, echoes the flower colors of late summer in the wild—lavender, purple, yellow and gold. A cloud of sea lavender (*Limonium latifolium*) frames yellow Ozark sundrop (*Oenothera macrocarpa*), flanked by the large, orange-centered rose daisies of purple coneflower (*Echinacea purpurea*) and spiky magenta prairie gayfeather, *Liatris spicata* 'Kobold'. Taller goldenrod (*S. puberula*) stands guard behind. Most solidagos are invasive, water-greedy sorts best left to grace the wild places to which they are native, but this species, as well as *S. sempervirens, S. rugosa, S. spathulata* and some of the named selections are more drought tolerant and well behaved in the garden.

As summer gives way to autumn, blue mist spirea (*Caryopteris* x *clandonensis*), a shrubby semiwoody perennial that should be cut to the ground early each spring, shares a place with golden aster, *Chrysopsis villosa*. Navy blue *Salvia arizonica* is still flowering close by, and the whole group has dark green bristlecone pine (*Pinus aristata*) as a backdrop. Lavender, white and purple combine once again, this time with white garlic chives (*Allium tuberosum*), dusky plum *Sedum* x 'Vera Jameson' foliage and self-sown purple annual *Verbena bonariensis* hovering above. Close to the path, the wavy blue leaves of *Allium senescens* 'Glaucum' now give rise to many short pink umbels, paired with the smoky gray-tinted foliage and bright carmine flowers of *Sedum* x 'Ruby Glow'. The odd brick red of 'Autumn Joy' sedum and the more crimson *S.* x 'Brilliant', mixed in with all these colors, would burn my eyes at any other time of the year, but come autumn, I couldn't care less about so-called color clashes. With the onset of cool nights and shorter days, the glossy leaves of sand cherry (*Prunus besseyi*) and three-leaf sumac (*Rhus trilobata*) take on glorious scarlet and orange tints. Purple, lavender and magenta fall-blooming crocus and colchicum open. Orange-red *Zauschneria arizonica*, at three feet the tallest of its genus, glows like a beacon beside sprawling 'Blue Chip' juniper. This is my idea of a seasonal grand finale in the garden.

In winter, the dry cottage garden is quietly serene. The mauve flagstone paths become more apparent, now that all the vegetative chaos has once again retreated. Evergreen thyme softens the cracks between the stones. Junipers and several dwarf spruces and pines dominate the landscape now, with evergreen perennial foliage forming a swirling carpet of muted silver, green, plum and gray. Here and there, a bright rose hip adds an exclamation point. I am thankful for this soporific, peaceful time. It lets me recharge for the coming spring, plan new combinations, order new seed and plants. If we get no snow for a month or so, I venture out and water the conifers, hauling ice-cold watering cans, dreaming of spring.

PLANTS FOR SUNNY, DRY GARDENS

When only the genus is listed, this means that all species in this genus are drought tolerant.

KEY

D: insists on very dry conditions.
GC: provides good ground cover.
PP: featured in plant portrait section.
B: biennial.

PERENNIALS

Achillea yarrow **some GC**
Aethionema stone cress
Agastache giant hyssop
Agave parryi century plant **D**
Agave utahensis century plant **D**
Alcea hollyhock **PP**
Alyssoides utriculata bladder pod
Alyssum **PP**
Amsonia jonesii desert blue stars **D**
Anacyclus depressus Mt. Atlas daisy
Anchusa azurea alkanet
Andryala agardhii **D**
Antennaria pussytoes **GC, PP**
Anthemis marguerite
Aquilegia bertolonii, *A. laramiensis*, *A. saximontana* columbine
Arabis rock cress **GC**
Argemone prickly poppy
Armeria sea thrift
Asclepias tuberosa butterfly weed
Aster ericoides heath aster **PP**
Aster kumleinii pink prairie aster
Aster linearifolius
Aster porteri
Aster sericeus silky aster
Astragalus pea vetch **D**
Aubrieta rock cress
Aurinia saxatilis basket-of-gold
Ballota
Baptisia australis wild blue indigo
Baptisia leucantha white prairie indigo
Berlandiera lyrata chocolate flower **D**
Bouteloua gracilis blue grama **GC**
Buchloe dactyloides buffalo grass **GC**
Calamagrostis x acutiflora 'Stricta' feather reed grass
Calamintha
Callirhoe buffalo rose **GC, PP**
Campanula aucheri, *C. bellidifolia*, *C. sarmatica*, *C. thessela*, *C. tridentata*
Carlina thistle

Castilleja Indian paintbrush **D**
Catananche Cupid's dart
Centaurea knapweed
Centranthus ruber Greek valerian
Cephalaria alpina giant pincushion flower
Cerastium snow-in-summer **GC**
Ceratostigma plumbaginoides false plumbago, leadwort **GC**
Chrysopsis golden aster
Cirsium thistle
Convolvulus several noninvasive species **D**
Coreopsis grandiflora garden coreopsis
Coreopsis verticillata threadleaf coreopsis
Coryphantha vivipara **D**
Crambe sea kale **PP**
Dalea purpurea prairie clover
Delosperma iceplant some **GC**
Dianthus pinks **GC**
Dictamnus gas plant
Digitalis lanata Grecian foxglove
Digitalis obscura Spanish foxglove
Dracocephalum dragonshead
Echinacea coneflower
Echinocereus hedgehog cactus **D**
Echinops globe thistle
Enceliopsis sunray **D**
Erianthus ravennae hardy pampas grass
Erigeron fleabane
Eriogonum buckwheat **D, PP**
Eriophyllum lanatum woolly sunflower **D, GC**
Erodium storksbill
Eryngium sea holly
Erysimum wallflower
Euphorbia epithymoides (aka *E. polychroma*) spring spurge
Euphorbia myrsinites donkey-tail spurge, snakeweed **D**
Euphorbia nicaensis
Euphorbia rigida
Ferula
Festuca fescue
Gaillardia Indian blanket **D**
Galega goat's rue
Gaura
Geranium cinereum, *G. sanguineum*, *G. sessiliforum* 'Nigricans', *G. subcaulescens* cranesbill
Goniolimon tataricum German statice
Gutierrezia sarothrae broomweed **D**

Gypsophila baby's breath
Haplopappus **D**
Hedysarum alpinum
Helianthus maximiliani Maximilian's sunflower
Helichrysum everlasting
Helictotrichon sempervirens blue avena grass
Heliopsis summer sun
Hemerocallis daylily
Hieracium lanatum, *H. waldsteinii* silver hawkweed
Hymenoxys perky Sue **D**
Hypericum St. John's wort
Iberis candytuft
Incarvillea olgae
Ipomoea leptophylla bush morning glory **D**
Iris arilbred hybrids
Iris germanica bearded iris
Iris orientalis
Iris pallida
Iris pumila dwarf bearded iris
Iris spuria
Jurinea
Jurinella
Knautia macedonica, **PP**
Kniphofia red hot poker
Koeleria cristata June grass
Lamium eriocephalum
Lathyrus polymorphos plain's pea **GC**
Lavatera shrub mallow **PP**
Lesquerella bladderpod **D**
Leuzea conifera
Limonium sea lavender
Linaria toadflax
Linum flax **PP**
Lithospermum canescens, *L. carolinianum*, *L. incisum* puccoon
Lupinus argenteus
Malva mallow **PP**
Manfreda virginica (aka *Agave virginica*)
Marrubium horehound **PP**
Melampodium leucanthum blackfoot daisy **D**
Mertensia lanceolata chiming bells
Mirabilis multiflora desert four o'clock **D, GC**
Miscanthus maiden grass
Nepeta catmint **GC, PP**
Neobesseya missouriensis cactus **D**
Nolina microcarpa bear grass **D**
Oenothera evening primrose (all but *O. biennis*, *O. tetragona*) **some GC, PP**

▲ Centaurea stricta.　　　　▼ Erigeron compositus.

▲ Limonium binervosum, Goniolimon tataricum, Cirsium spinosissimum.

▼ Fragrant dwarf bearded iris 'Lemon Blossom', moss phlox 'Blue Emerald'.

▲ Dracocephalum botryoides.　　　▼ Onosma alboroseum.

▼ Eryngium bourgatii.

▼ Veronica incana foliage; Phlox bifida 'Betty Blake'.

▲ Petrorhagia saxifraga *'Rosea Plena'*.

▲ Nemastylis acuta, *prairie iris*.

▲ Origanum acutidens; Mirabilis multiflora.
▼ Origanum libanoticum, Dianthus chinensis *var.* amurensis.

▲ Linaria purpurea *'Canon Went'*.

▼ Melampodium leucanthum, *blackfoot daisy*.

▲ Aster kumleinii *'Dream of Beauty'*.   ▼ Hedysarum alpinum.

PERENNIALS, CONT.

Ononis
Onosma
Opuntia prickly pear, beaver tail, cholla cactus **D**
Origanum oregano some **GC, PP**
Oryzopsis hymenoides Indian rice grass
Oxytropis locoweed **D**
Paeonia peony **PP**
Papaver poppy
Pardanthopsis dichotoma vesper iris
Pediocactus simpsonii snowball cactus
Penstemon beardtongue many **D, PP**
Petalostemon purpureum prairie clover
Petrorhagia saxifraga (aka *Tunica saxifraga*)
Phlomis **PP**
Phlox andicola **D**
Phlox bifida sand phlox **GC**
Phlox bryoides **D**
Phlox douglasii
Phlox hoodii **D**
Phlox missoulensis **D**
Phlox multiflora **D**
Phlox nana **GC D**
Phlox subulata moss phlox **GC**
Phlox tumulosa **D, GC**
Phlox woodhousei
Physaria bladderpod **D**
Potentilla nevadensis creeping cinquefoil **GC**
Psilostrophe paper flower **D**
Pterocephalus **GC**
Ptilotrichum spinosum
Pulsatilla pasqueflower
Ratibida prairie coneflower
Rudbeckia black-eyed Susan
Ruellia wild petunia
Rumex venosus wild begonia **GC**
Ruta graveolens rue
Salvia sage (the less hardy species from Mexico, Central and South America tend to need more water) **PP**
Saponaria soapwort **GC**
Scabiosa graminifolia
Scabiosa ochroleuca yellow pincushion flower **PP**
Schivereckia podolica
Schizachyrium scoparium little bluestem
Schlerocactus whipplei **D**
Schrankia sensitive briar
Scutellaria skullcap **GC, PP**
Sedum **GC**
Sempervivum hens and chicks
Sidalcea checkerbloom
Sideritis **PP**

Silene laciniata Indian pink **D**
Solidago puberula, S. rugosa, S. sempervirens, S. spathulata goldenrod
Sorghastrum avenaceum Indian grass
Sphaeralcea cowboy's delight **D, GC**
Sphaeromeria capitata **D**
Spraguea umbellata **D**
Stachys betony **some GC**
Stanleya prince's plume **D**
Stipa comata needle and thread grass
Tanacetum densum var. *amani* partridge feather **GC**
Tanacetum niveum snow daisy **PP**
Teucrium germander **some GC**
Thermopsis fabacea **PP**
Thermopsis rhombifolia golden banner **D, GC**
Thymus thyme **GC**
Townsendia Easter daisy **D**
Tradescantia occidentalis western spiderwort
Vella spinosa
Verbascum mullein
Verbena some **GC**
Veronica the shorter and mat-forming species some **GC, PP**
Viguiera multiflora golden eye
Zauschneria California fuchsia **GC, PP**
Zinnia grandiflora Rocky Mountain zinnia **D**

BULBS

Allium ornamental onion **PP**
Anemone blanda Grecian windflower
Asphodeline Jacob's rod
Calochortus mariposa, sego lily **D**
Colchicum autumn crocus
Crocus crocus **PP**
Eremurus foxtail lily
Fritillaria persica
Gladiolus byzantinus hardy gladiolus
Iris aucheri **PP**
Iris bucharica
Iris danfordiae
Iris graeberana
Iris histrioides
Iris oncocyclus group **D**
Iris reticulata snow iris
Leucocrinum montanum sand lily **D**
Lewisia rediviva bitterroot **D**
Liatris aspera, L. punctata **D**, *L. spicata* prairie gayfeather
Lycoris squamigera naked ladies
Muscari grape hyacinth
Nectaroscordum
Nemastylis acuta prairie iris
Ornithogalum umbellatum star of Bethlehem
Scilla squill

Sternbergia autumn daffodil
Tulipa tulip **PP**

TREES

Acanthopanax sieboldianus
Ailanthus altissima tree of heaven
Amelanchier alnifolia western serviceberry
Catalpa speciosa western catalpa **PP**
Celtis occidentalis hackberry
Corylus colurna Turkish filbert
Crataegus ambigua Russian hawthorn
Elaeagnus angustifolia Russian olive
Euonymus europaeas spindle tree
Gleditsia triacanthos honey locust
Gymnocladus dioicus Kentucky coffee tree
Juniperus monosperma one-seeded juniper **D**
Juniperus scopulorum Rocky Mountain juniper
Juniperus virginiana Eastern red cedar
Koelreuteria paniculata golden rain tree
Maackia amurensis
Morus alba, M. rubra mulberry
Phellodendron amurense cork tree
Picea omorika Serbian spruce
Pinus aristata bristlecone pine
Pinus edulis pinyon pine **D**
Pinus flexilis limber pine
Pinus leucodermis
Pinus mugo mugo pine
Pinus nigra Austrian pine
Pinus parviflora Japanese white pine
Pinus ponderosa Ponderosa pine
Pinus sylvestris Scots pine
Prunus americana wild plum
Ptelea trifoliata hop tree
Pyrus ussuriensis Ussurian pear
Quercus gambelii Gambel oak
Quercus macrocarpa bur oak
Robinia neomexicana New Mexico locust
Robinia pseudoacacia, R. x 'Idaho' black locust
Tamarix ramosissima tamarisk

SHRUBS

Acantholimon spike thrift **D**
Amorpha leadplant
Arctostaphylos bearberry, manzanita **GC**
Artemisia sagebrush **some D, some GC**
Atriplex saltbush **D, some GC**
Berberis koreana Korean barberry
Berberis thunbergii, 'Atropurpurea', 'Aurea' barberry
Buddleia butterfly bush
Caragana Siberian pea shrub
Caryopteris x clandonensis blue mist spirea
Ceratoides lanata winter fat **D**
Cercocarpus mountain mahogany

Chamaebatiaria millefolium fern bush **D**
Chamaecytisus broom
Chrysothamnus rabbit brush, chamisa **D**
Cotinus coggygria, *C. obovatus* smokebush
Cowania neomexicana cliff rose **D**
Cytisus broom
Ephedra joint fir **D**
Fallugia paradoxa Apache plume **D, PP**
Fendlera rupicola fendler bush **D**
Forestiera neomexicana New Mexico privet
Genista broom some **GC**
Helianthemum sunrose **GC**
Hibiscus syriacus rose of Sharon
Hippophae rhamnoides sea buckthorn
Holodiscus dumosus rock spirea
Hypericum kalmianum, *H. kouytchense*
    St.John's wort
Hyssopus hyssop
Juniperus some **GC**
Kolkwitzia amabilis beauty bush
Lavandula lavender
Lespedeza thunbergii bush clover
Lonicera honeysuckle
Mahonia fremontii **D**
Mahonia haematocarpa **D**
Onobrychis
Peraphyllum ramosissimum squaw apple
Perovskia Russian sage
Philadelphus mock orange
Prunus besseyi sand cherry
Purshia tridentata antelope bitterbrush **D**
Rhamnus smithii
Rhus aromatica **GC**, *R. glabra*, *R. trilobata*,
    R.typhina sumac
Rosa eglanteria sweet briar rose
Rosa foetida **PP**
Rosa glauca red-leaf rose **PP**
Rosa hugonis Father Hugo rose
Rosa rugosa
Rosa spinosissima burnet rose
Rosa woodsii Wood's rose
Rosa x alba **PP**
Rosa x harisonii Harison's yellow rose
Rubus deliciosus boulder raspberry **PP**
Salvia dorrii gray ball sage **D**
Salvia lavandulifolia lavender-leaf sage
Salvia officinalis culinary sage
Santolina lavender cotton
Senecio longilobus silver groundsel **D**
Shepherdia argentea, *S. canadensis* buffalo berry
Syringa lilac
Thymus thyme **GC**
Yucca

VINES
Campsis radicans trumpet creeper

Clematis ligusticifolia, *C. orientalis*,
    C. tangutica
Humulus lupulus hops vine **PP**
Lathyrus latifolius perennial pea **PP**
Lonicera honeysuckle
Parthenocissus quinquefolia Virginia creeper,
    Englemann ivy
Polygonum aubertii silver lace vine
Wisteria floribunda, *W. sinensis* wisteria

ANNUALS AND BIENNIALS
Abronia sand verbena **B, D**
Aeoniopsis cabulica **B, D**
Antirrhinum majus snapdragon
Arctotis African daisy
Baileya multiradiata desert marigold **D**
Borago officinalis borage
Brachycome iberidifolia Swan River daisy
Calandrinia umbellata rock purslane
Calendula officinalis pot marigold
Catharanthus roseus Madagascar
    periwinkle
Centaurea cyanus bachelor's button
Cheiranthus allionii Siberian wallflower **B**
Clarkia amoena satin flower
Cleome spider flower
Consolida ambigua larkspur
Coreopsis tinctoria calliopsis
Cosmos
Crepis rubra pink hawksbeard
Datura meteloides angel's trumpet
Daucus carota Queen Anne's lace
Dianthus chinensis annual pinks
Diascia twinspur
Dimorphotheca Cape marigold
Dracocephalum nutans **B, PP**
Dyssodia tenuiloba Dahlberg daisy
Echium viper's bugloss
Emilia javanica tassel flower
Erigeron karvinskianus Santa Barbara daisy
Eriogonum annuum buckwheat
Eryngium giganteum silver sea holly **B, PP**
Eschscholzia California poppy
Euphorbia marginata snow on the mountain
Foeniculum vulgare 'Purpureum' bronze
    fennel **PP**
Gaillardia pulchella annual Indian blanket
Gazania rigens treasure flower
Gilia/Ipomopsis **B, D** except *I. rubra*
    skyrocket
Glaucium horned poppy **B**
Godetia satin flower
Gomphrena globosa globe amaranth
Gypsophila elegans annual baby's breath
Helipterum strawflower

Hunnemannia fumariifolia Mexican poppy
Iberis umbellata annual candytuft
Ipomoea purpurea morning glory
Kallstroemia grandiflora desert poppy **D**
Kochia scoparia burning bush
Lavatera trimestris rose mallow
Layia tidy tips
Limonium sinuatum statice
Linaria maroccana toadflax
Linum grandiflorum annual flax
Linum usitatissimum annual blue flax
Lobularia maritima sweet alyssum
Machaeranthera Tahoka daisy **B, D**
Matricaria recutita German chamomile
Matthiola bicornis evening scented stock
Mentzelia blazing star some **B, D**
Michauxia **B**
Mirabilis jalapa four o'clock
Nemophila baby blue-eyes, five-spot
Nigella love-in-a-mist
Nolana paradoxa Chilean bellflower
Oenothera annual evening primrose
Onopordum Scots thistle **B**
Orthocarpus purpurascens owl clover
Papaver poppy **PP**
Pelargonium graveolens scented geranium
Pennisetum fountain grass
Perilla frutescens beefsteak plant
Phacelia campanularia desert bluebells
Phlox drummondii annual phlox
Portulaca grandiflora moss rose
Rudbeckia hirta Black-eyed Susan
Rudbeckia triloba **B, PP**
Salvia many tender ones can be grown
    as annuals
Salvia aethiopis **B**
Salvia coccinea Texas scarlet sage
Salvia columbariae chia
Salvia farinacea mealy-cup sage
Salvia sclarea clary sage **B**
Sanvitalia procumbens creeping zinnia
Senecio cineraria dusty miller
Silene armeria annual catchfly,
    none-so-pretty
Silybum marianum milk thistle **B**
Talinum fame flower
Thelesperma greenthread
Tropaeolum majus nasturtium
Venidium fastuosum Cape daisy
Verbascum mullein **B, PP**
Verbena **PP**
Verbesina encelioides butter daisy
Viola corsica Corsican pansy **PP**
Xeranthemum annuum immortelle
Zinnia angustifolia narrow-leaf zinnia

II

Through the Seasons in the Shaded Garden

It's easy to fall in love with the wide-open, larger-than-life landscapes of the West. What can be better than the big skies, red and amber mesas, stark snowy peaks and endless grasslands where one may actually catch a glimpse of the curvature of the earth, or at least feel wrapped in the great black cloak of the universe at night as the stars touch the horizon?

What I do miss is the gentle green of deciduous woodlands, softly dappled by light and shade, that I grew up with in the East. From the earliest spring walks through rustling tawny beech leaves among white bloodroot and yellow erythronium, on to the crescendo of spring bloom under the chartreuse haze of freshly unfurling oak, hickory and tulip poplar, the understory dotted with flowering dogwood and redbud, the woods feel like home. Blue phlox, trilliums, wild azaleas and mountain laurel will always strike a deeper note in my heart than the showiest wildflower from the high mountains. Summer under the trees is a tangle of green, a temperate jungle of sorts, heavy with sap and life. Then, as the nights grow cooler and longer, the trees begin to take on those outlandish hues, as if nature had decided to turn the landscape into an infrared photograph. And then, after the leaves have fallen and the underbrush has slunk back into the ground, it is once again easy to walk among the graceful giant trunks of the trees, the sweet smell of fallen leaves turning to humus kicked up at every step. I have to be content to recreate a microcosm of this in my garden out here in the West.

And to think that most gardeners find shade a curse rather than a blessing. What I would do for a mature stand of trees. There is something primeval about a shady garden; everything is more subtle and mysterious. The play of light and shadow changes hour by hour, minute by minute. The plants, less inclined to dramatic displays of boisterous color, nevertheless have a grace and charm, a refinement of form and texture augmented by the subdued light that one never sees in sunny gardens. The tranquility of a shade garden soothes the soul. After a day of working in the sunnier parts of the garden, shoulders burned and eyes fixed in a permanent squint, I long for the cool soil and soft light of the shadier areas. How much more romantic it is to imagine the beginnings of mankind as sultry Eve's seduction of Adam in a lush Garden of Eden than as our harsh first years on the sunbaked grasslands of the Dark Continent.

Shade is more complex than the little five-letter word lets on. It can range from the gently luminescent green light of a woodland understory, so supportive of life, to the dank recesses beneath evergreens or on the north side of large structures where nothing but mulch and a few

(preceding pages) In the benevolent light of the east side of the house, pale roses 'Bredon' and 'Sparrieshoop', 'Annabelle' hydrangea, white pea vine, musk mallow, columbine, 'Husker Red' penstemon and the spikes of white fireweed and Digitalis lutea flourish.

ghostly fungi will grow. Shade can be intermittent, as the wind and the movement of the sun change the patterns cast by the foliage canopy of tall trees, or it can occur in large, predictable stretches of time, such as on the eastern or western sides of a house.

The east-facing garden is my favorite site; many sun-loving plants receive enough light the first half of the day to flourish, and the cooling shade that falls over the more shade-demanding plants in the early afternoon protects them from frying. Thus I can grow plants from both sides of the fence, so to speak—roses and hostas can mingle on the east side. An exposed west side, however, is useless for shade lovers. Encased in darkness until noon or so, suddenly the plants are awakened by the jolt of a fiercely hot afternoon sun. West-facing gardens need to be populated with hardy, heat- and sun-loving plants.

The quality of shade is not the only determinant of what plants will grow there and how well—the soil and its moisture content make as much difference as the amount and type of shade. Dry, sterile soil under the eaves of a house, devoid of seedling or worm, is inhospitable to plant and animal life, while the crumbly, humusy soil of a mature woodland floor is literally crawling with it. If shade is cast by a structure or a tree impenetrable to rain, the only answer is to find some artificial way of introducing moisture to the area—by drip irrigation, soaker hose or some other device—or leave the area to bare soil, stones or mulch. Perhaps building a patio might be a good solution.

If the shade that is cast lets in ample moisture, but the tree that casts it is of the gluttonous, self-important sort that sends out a battalion of thick surface roots in every direction, plants won't have a chance either. Typical offenders of this type are poplar, cottonwood, elm, silver and Norway maple, beech and horse chestnut. Deep-rooted trees like oak, hackberry, honey locust and yellow-wood (*Cladrastis lutea*) make much more benevolent partners for a shade garden. The very worst offenders are the all-and-all-out chemical warfarers, tree of heaven (*Ailanthus altissima*) and black walnut. These trees are so territorial that they actually secrete substances from their roots into the soil that stunt the growth of plants other than themselves, the ultimate in antisocial behavior.

No matter what type of tree casts the shade, be it friend or foe, it drinks and dines from the surrounding soil and keeps out some rain and the warmth of the sun, lessening beneficial microbial activity in the soil. If the well-meaning but misguided seasonal cleanup of fallen leaves also has taken place, the natural replenishment of organic matter stops. What's usually left is a dry, sterile, dusty soil. Vital to a successful shade garden is the liberal addition of compost and leaf mold on a regular basis. The majority of shade plants thrive in this kind of soil; in nature they have adapted to a woodland situation where leaves are not raked but instead are allowed to break down into nutritious, water-retentive humus.

▲ *Double-flowered*
Trillium grandiflorum *and*
Phlox stolonifera *enjoy the*
indirect light of a north-facing
wall in the Rock Alpine
Garden at Denver Botanic
Gardens.

Most shade gardens still benefit from a light raking since many gardeners find the appearance and amount of leaves that fall onto a shade garden not aesthetically pleasing, and in the case of some of the larger-leaved trees and those whose leaves form soggy mats when moistened, the plants underneath may actually be smothered and rot. Several gardeners I know rake off the leaves, shred them and then put them back, which not only looks good but speeds the conversion to leaf mold and smothers no plants or seedlings in the process. These shredded leaves are the finest mulch I can think of, and I have started to do this in my shady areas, using the lawn mower as my shredder since I can't bring myself to buy any more machines. Usually this happens around Thanksgiving, when the lawn mower is already dull and tired from a summer of duty, so I don't feel bad about dulling it a bit more and dirtying it with leaf dust. It will get a spring overhaul shortly anyway. A topdressing of compost goes on in early spring,

◀ *'Annabelle' hydrangea and a trumpet lily make an elegant picture in late summer.*

▼ *Variegated bulbous oat grass, 'Janet Fisk' pulmonaria, Geranium* x cantabrigiense *'Biokovo', 'Herman's Pride' lamiastrum, red-leaf plantain and violas crowd under the arching branches of boulder raspberry, Rubus deliciosus.*

when the plants are still small enough to make spreading easy. These two procedures have gone a long way in making the shaded garden more lush and vigorous.

I have three very different areas of shade in my garden. The first is the easiest and most hospitable—the east side of the house where ample amounts of horse manure, compost and a soaker-hose system have turned this into the place for all my more traditional, temperamental plants—roses, foxgloves, lilies, delphiniums and the like. I call it my Irish garden, for it reminds me of the softly billowing pastel borders of the British Isles and is filled with many plants grown from seed collected while I worked in gardens on the Emerald Isle. Plants that tend to be sun-lovers in the more muted light

of Ireland and the northern coasts of North America appreciate protection from the harsh afternoon sunlight here in the dry air and high altitude of the northern Colorado plains. Roses of delicate pale shades bleach less and their blossoms last several days longer than if they were subjected to sun all day. Closer to the house, where shade falls earlier than at the edge of the bed, true shade plants thrive, pampered by rich soil and extra water.

The second shade area is smaller, yet changes in size from season to season. It is on the north side of the house, open to the sky, yet gets no direct sunlight from October until April or so, due to the lower arc the sun travels in the sky during that time. In midsummer, only a small sliver of plants huddled right up against the wall remains shaded; the rest is in full sun. This is a difficult area due to these extremes and discouragingly slow to wake up in the spring. Snow remains here weeks after it has melted elsewhere, which protects the plants yet also keeps spring at bay a lot longer than I would like. Snowdrops bloom here in April, whereas they are finished by late February in other parts of the garden. The lateness wouldn't bother me so much, in fact it could be seen as an asset having plants blooming at such different times throughout the garden, except that my front door is on this side so several times a day I have to go by this dormant little area that is still all drab while the rest of the garden has exploded into riotous growth and bloom. I have since put in a number of evergreen plants to offset the brown of the excessively long winter this spot must endure. The rounded, leathery, dark green leaves of *Synthyris missurica*, *Bergenia cordifolia* 'Silberlicht' and tiny *Bergenia stracheyi*, combined with silver-mottled *Heuchera sanguinea* 'Green Ivory' and *Asarum hartwegii* foliage and the bronze-purple of semievergreen *Tiarella wherryi* and *Viola labradorica* all help to make this area pretty even when it is asleep. In the cracks between the path and the steps to the door, the lime-encrusted foliage rosettes of various saxifrages make themselves a cool, shady home. Variegated *Daphne* x *burkwoodii* 'Carol Mackie' and the plum-blue winter foliage of *Juniperus squamata* 'Blue Star' give shrubby winter effect, while *Cornus alba* 'Elegantissima', leafless, shows off its burgundy stems.

The most challenging shaded area is on the west side of the house, where when we arrived, the skirt of an enormous hulk of a spruce from my neighbor's property all but obliterated most of the ground. Seeing how eager I was to get the garden going, my neighbor generously decided to limb up the old behemoth, leaving it looking sorry and embarrassed but giving me a good two hundred square feet of additional garden space. But what I faced was no ordinary gardening experience. The spruce had turned the soil to dust, and greedy roots ran everywhere. Over the past three years I have dumped more horse droppings and compost there than in any other place, even the vegetable garden. It has slowly turned into a garden, but the plant choices are still limited since I decided not to irrigate any part of my garden heavily except the so called

Irish border. Here under the spruce, receiving only the most obtuse angles of the late afternoon sun, a host of plants that can take dry shade have proven themselves. Dry shade is a term that will send a gardener running almost as surely as the term dry shave will send a man. But I have found that with a group of tough plants even this can become an attractive oasis, although I'm not as inclined to spend time under the spruce as I am in other shaded gardens, due to needles prickling my sandaled feet and kamikaze bird droppings courtesy of this well-populated tree.

The one kind of shade I do not have and for which I long is that dappled woodland shade, under the canopies of deciduous trees, that I rhapsodized about earlier. I have planted several small trees and in a decade or so, some of the sunnier parts of the garden slowly will be transformed into those woodland areas I crave. I envy gardeners with good mature trees already gracing their gardens, but I will have to bide my time for now. These woodland situations offer the unique combination that so many spring-blooming bulbs and perennials prefer—sun in winter and spring when they bloom, and cool, moisture-conserving shade and its accompanying humidity during the hot, dry part of the year.

The closest thing I have to a cool, moist woodland shade garden is that small area on the north side of the house where spring comes so slowly. When it does come, however, it lasts a long time. Being so close to the house, the delicate flowers aren't subjected to drying winds. It is in this area that I can play with variegated foliage best, for direct sunlight never touches the leaves of these plants that are so prone to scorching. My relationship with these striped and spotted plants is a somewhat ambivalent one. Once, as an ignorant garden intern, I had a disastrous encounter with a variegated plant. I was given the nebulous orders to "clean up the herb garden." This I did, or so I thought: I proceeded to pull out all the variegated mint because I was sure it was diseased. The moral of the story (aside from not letting novices loose in a garden) is that some variegated plants cross that fine line between sublime and sickly looking. The best, however, can transform a shaded garden into a subtle masterpiece. In soft light, the pale leaf markings contrast with the predominant greens, appearing fresh and cool.

I'm partial to subtle, evenly distributed variegation, as in the case of the cream-edged, heart-shaped leaves of Siberian forget-me-not *Brunnera macrophylla* 'Hadspen Cream' as opposed to another, much blotchier and less attractive form, 'Variegata'. 'Carol Mackie' daphne, *Cornus alba* 'Elegantissima' and *Acanthopanax sieboldianus* 'Variegatus', a large, tough shrub with pretty, palmate leaves, form the variegated shrub backbone for the small planting. *Hydrangea arborescens* 'Annabelle', with large green foliage that dies down to the ground each year, acts as a foil between all the variegation to

The Never-Summer Garden

▲ Brunnera macrophylla *'Hadspen Cream', variegated Siberian forget-me-not.*

▲ *'Roy Davidson' pulmonaria and white bleeding heart join shrubs variegated dogwood and dwarf Colorado spruce 'Globosa' on the north side of the house.*

▶ *Early daffodils and a deep purple Lenten rose,* Helleborus orientalis, *give color to spring's emerging foliage.*

anchor it. Its large white billows of summer flowers further brighten this dark spot. Among the deep green foliages of various perennials, the almost entirely white, wavy-edged leaves of *Hosta undulata* 'Variegata'; sprawling silvery *Lamium maculatum* 'White Nancy'; plum and pewter Japanese painted fern (*Athyrium nipponicum* 'Pictum'); and two favorite pulmonarias, 'Janet Fisk', almost completely pale in leaf, and strongly spotted 'Roy Davidson' with sky blue flowers, round out the variegated palette. Spilling onto the path and creeping into the cracks between the flagstones, where it is joined by emerald green Irish moss (*Sagina subulata*), is petite *Arabis sturii* 'Variegata'.

Spring is the showiest season for this garden nook. Soft colors and delicate flower shapes predominate. Only the smallest bulbs are allowed: In such a restricted space and one that gets extremely close scrutiny—right by the house entrance—I don't want quantities of flaccid bulb foliage for weeks on end. Daffodils 'Jenny', 'Jack Snipe' and 'Thalia', all small and soft-colored, take over once the snowdrops, snowflakes, deep periwinkle blue *Chionodoxa sardensis* (which I like better than the coarser, white-eyed *C. luciliae*) and pale aquamarine-striped puschkinias have finished. I'm partial to the smaller daffodils altogether, especially the cyclamineus types, named for mimicking the reflexed petals of that plant. I once heard them described as a hound dog with its muzzle out the window of a moving car, ears blown back by the wind.

The cream and primrose yellow daffodils are joined by a deep plum-flowered lenten rose (*Helleborus orientalis*) and the exotic, ephemeral white blossoms of double bloodroot, *Sanguinaria canadensis* 'Multiplex', looking just like a land-locked water lily. Then various white, yellow and rose-pink epimediums start to bloom, along with the

forget-me-not-like flowers of *Omphalodes verna*, an underused charmer of a ground cover. More blue flowers follow with the pulmonarias and then the long-lasting sprays of Siberian forget-me-not, which is seeding itself around. These bulkier plants are joined by pink and white old-fashioned bleeding heart (*Dicentra spectabilis*), with ferny foliage that offsets the substantial, rounded leaves of the brunnera.

I have never been a great fan of primroses, probably because I find them very hard to grow in my garden, and also because they seem almost a bit too cute. I am, however, a sucker for pale yellow, and three obliging primroses for those of us who struggle with the more persnickety types have found a happy home among the blue, white and pink spring flowers in this small area. *Primula veris*, the cowslip, is the coarsest and easiest to accommodate. Its flowers are born in clusters and are the strongest yellow. The oxlip, *Primula elatior*, has bigger flowers in smaller numbers, in a more pleasing soft yellow. An heirloom form of this plant, passed around from garden to garden in the Northeast for years, made it to my garden by way of a wet paper towel in my mother's purse. It is a "hose-in-hose" form, where two flowers are fused back to back, making for a showier, longer-lasting display. The soft yellow is that of its ancestor, and a sweet scent accompanies this lovely primrose. Finally, I grow the English primrose, *P. vulgaris*, with large single flowers nestled in its fresh green foliage rosette. Again, the color is that wonderful pale yellow, and the fragrance as demure and enchanting as the flower.

Once the primroses have gone over and late spring moves in, blue Jacob's ladder (*Polemonium foliosissimum*), with fernlike foliage, and long-blooming *Corydalis lutea*, a petite, yellow-flowered bleeding heart lookalike, start off. The hosta foliage has finally unfurled. Fernleaf bleeding heart (*Dicentra eximia*) fills in where the larger old-fashioned bleeding heart leaves off; its old-rose flowers are echoed in color by the dainty blossoms of *Semiaquilegia ecalcarata* nodding along the path. This is my favorite columbine. The foliage has hints of dusky purple; the stems are wiry and almost invisible, leaving the flowers hovering as if suspended in air. To add to the pink tones, the plum-colored leaves and washy lavender flowers of low-growing *Penstemon hirsutus* var. *pygmaeus*, one of the few beardtongues native to the East and tolerant of moist shade, grows along the path. Lilac, snapdragon-like flowers of creeping *Mazus reptans* (there is also a pretty white form) and the chubby white bells of cockleshell campanula (*Campanula cochleariifolia* 'Alba') spread merrily in the cracks between the stones of the path.

As summer begins, coralbells send graceful sprays of white, pale green and pink flowers arching along the path and spreading *Geranium* x *clarkei* 'Kashmir White' opens its fresh-faced symmetrical flowers. As summer stretches toward fall, the heady scent of white-flowered *Hosta* 'Royal Standard' wafts toward the front door and blue monkshood (*Aconitum henryi* 'Spark's Variety') blooms with tall, late altissima daylilies in pale yellow. Just as I think that part of the garden is closing up shop for the year, with longer shadows encasing it in early slumber, patches of pink cyclamen rise between burgundy and silver Japanese painted ferns like tiny naked fairies. Their mottled foliage disappears early in the summer, and I forget about them until now, at the very end of the season, when they reemerge bashfully to bloom.

 Over in dry shade under the spruce, more robust plants take their place, many of which have somewhat invasive habits that usually would inspire fear but are welcome in this inhospitable site. Here, in place of the white and cream variegated plants, I rely on golden shades to lighten the area. Generally, leaves of golden tones are a little less likely to suffer from drought and sun scorch than their paler counterparts. Golden barberry (*Berberis thunbergii* 'Aurea') glows from the recesses beneath the tree. Its brilliant foliage is toned down by somber evergreen *Microbiota decussata*, which looks deceptively like a sprawling green juniper but is much more shade tolerant. It has the alarming habit of turning brown in the winter; a catalog called it plum, but it is the brown of death. The first year I was sure I'd killed the plant, until it greened up again in April. Its ability to handle dry shade is its best attribute. Closer to the path, lime green flowers of *Helleborus foetidus* open when spring is little more than wishful thinking. It is the toughest of the hellebores and the only one tolerant of dry shade. Golden feverfew (*Tanacetum parthenium* 'Aureum'), at its most luminescent in early spring, echoes the tones of the barberry. The creamy yellow flowers of ground cover *Symphytum grandiflorum*, nodding above rough dark green leaves, carry on the green-and-yellow color scheme in April.

By mid-spring, self-sowing biennial woad (*Isatis tinctoria*), a dye plant worth its weight in gold as a filmy background plant but used shamefully little as an ornamental, blooms in great chartreuse-yellow billows toward the back, along with pale lavender, fragrant sweet rocket (*Hesperis matronalis*). The lemon yellow, single-flowered peony known as "Mollie the witch" for its unpronounceable Latin name, *P. mlokosewitschii*, follows suit. It, along with red-flowered fernleaf peony (*P. tenuifolia*), handles more shade than the typical garden variety peony. The famed Wayside Gardens catalog cover girl of a few years back, going at sixty dollars a pop, fernleaf peony fails to send me into the expected tailspin. I love its foliage, but the blood-red flowers with garish yellow stamens are not colors I particularly want in the shade.

Spreading their small round leaves like so many bright golden coins across the ground are shallow-rooted golden moneywort (*Lysimachia nummularia* 'Aurea') and golden oregano (*Origanum vulgare* 'Aureum Compactum'). They tangle with shade tolerant little *Penstemon procerus*, a mat-forming, long-blooming blue species with fine-textured but profuse eight-inch flower spikes. Blue mist penstemon (*Penstemon virens*) can also take a good amount of dry shade; it grows well on north-facing cliffs and under ponderosa pines in the foothills of the Rocky Mountains and thrives similarly under the spruce in

55

▲ Sanguinaria canadensis *'Multiplex', double bloodroot.*

▲ *Tiny* Mazus reptans *and woolly thyme creep between flagstones.*

▲ *The misty blues of* Penstemon procerus *and* Phlox divaricata *are brightened by golden moneywort.*

◄ *Emerging* Semiaquilegia ecalcarata *foliage.*

my garden. The lavender-blue of these two penstemons tones down the brassy golds of the many yellow-toned leaves and flowers.

Toward the base of the tree trunk, creeping perilously close to the property line and toward the thin lawn under the spruce on my neighbor's side, two dogged ground covers are duking it out: *Geranium macrorrhizum* 'Album', with its handsome, herb-scented foliage and late-spring flowers, and white-flowered sweet woodruff (*Galium odoratum*). Closer to the path, two more conservatively growing ground covers do battle: mauve-pink *Geranium* x *cantabrigiense*, which has *G. macrorrhizum* as a parent but is more refined in leaf, flower and growth habit, and that rarity in shady areas, a silver-leaved plant, *Rumex scutatus*, with foliage shaped much like an arrowhead. *Arabis caucasica*, which I always thought of as a sun lover, is actually happiest here in dry shade. While it blooms less profusely, it is more drought tolerant and the luxuriant foliage rosettes turn a beautiful pink-tinted sage green in winter. Candytuft (*Iberis sempervirens*) has shown similar tendencies, so now is relegated to dry shade and appreciated as much if not more, as is

▲ *Blue and white peach-leaf bellflowers have golden feverfew as a softly hued foil.*

▼ *Petite* Campanula cochleariifolia 'Alba' *squeezes between flagstones, joined by variegated* Arabis sturii *and* Mazus reptans.

arabis, for its attractive evergreen foliage as for its showy white flowers in early spring. Various shade-tolerant sedums join these plants at the edge of the path. In the cracks of the flagstones, dwarf silver pussytoes (*Antennaria parvifolia*) and the tiniest thyme (*Thymus serpyllum* 'Minus')—both remarkably shade tolerant, fight it out.

Foliage also is a major drawing card with several of the early summer bloomers. *Lamiastrum galeobdolon* 'Herman's Pride' has yellow nettlelike flowers that are passable, but the pewter-variegated leaves are fabulous, reminiscent of the tender houseplant known as aluminum plant. The fleeting, creamy flowers of dropwort (*Filipendula vulgaris*) are quite nice, but the fernlike leaves, thriving in a place where few ferns would dare tread, are the reason I covet this plant. Likewise goat's rue (*Galega officinalis*), with white or washy lavender lupinelike spikes for two weeks in midsummer, blooms less in shade but grows into a lush, large mound of fine, pinnate foliage with little sun or water. *Penstemon richardsonii*, on the other hand, blooms well, in rose-pink, during the dog days of summer, with very little sun. Its site preference, bloom time and serrate foliage are unusual for the genus.

Late spring under the spruce melds pale yellow, rose-pink, blue and lavender. *Verbascum phoeniceum*, also known as purple mullein, veers away from its tall, sun-loving yellow brethren in preferring shade and remaining under two feet in height. I was also thrilled to find it is reliably perennial as well as a prolific self-sower; the sumptuous flower spikes in various shades of pink, rose and purple, are poking up all over. Showy betony (*Stachys grandiflora*), in white and mauve, makes a more substantial foliage clump, but the flower spikes are a bit less dramatic. True blue *Cynoglossum nervosum* joins pale yellow perennial foxgloves *Digitalis grandiflora* and taller, smaller-flowered *D. lutea*, while a woodland salvia, *Salvia forskaohlei*, sends up deep indigo spires behind. Low-growing creeping bellflower (*Campanula poscharskyana*) spills powder blue starry flowers onto the path.

Summer is the domain of various white-flowered perennials. *Lychnis coronaria* 'Alba', with gray felted foliage and usually a brilliant magenta flower, does remarkably well in dry shade. I chose the white form because of all the golden foliage nearby, with which it would otherwise clash terribly. Spreading *Campanula punctata* has a less shining white flower, but the soft nodding bells are quietly charming and I appreciate how happy it is in its surroundings. My favorite, however, is the musk mallow (*Malva moschata*). I have a weakness for the mallow family, for their delicate yet showy flowers and attractive foliage, tendency toward long bloom periods and drought tolerance. Pink or white, musk mallow blooms tirelessly for almost two months, and its rich green, deeply cleft leaves grow in great masses in spite of a lack of water. Just as the mallows finally begin to fade, bulbous *Lycoris squamigera*, named surprise lily or better yet, naked ladies for its sensuous, tropical-looking pink flowers that rise on leafless stems in late summer, begins to bloom. Fragrant white autumn clematis (*Clematis maximowicziana* aka *C. paniculata*) joins in on the fence nearby. I would have never guessed this godforsaken area could become such an asset to the garden, but with compost topdressings, leaf mulching and a group of stalwart plants, it has come a long way from the barren brown wasteland populated only by fallen spruce needles, cones and bird droppings four short years ago.

 The last and most benevolent shaded area in my garden is the so-called Irish garden, which receives morning sun. In cooler, more cloud-enshrouded climates, many of the plants I grow here would thrive in full sun. With the dry air, hot summers and intense sunlight of forty-eight hundred feet above sea level, an average of twelve inches of rainfall and over three hundred sunny days a year here in northern Colorado, as with any other region where harsh extremes dominate the growing season, traditional "sun" plants like roses, lilies and delphiniums need some shade. The east side of the house works wonderfully well for these plants. To frame these show-stealing prima donnas in late spring to midsummer, I chose more delicate-looking, airy, subtle plants as a supporting cast. They thrive in the rich, moist soil the divas require, and bring out the best in their showier companions.

The East-Facing Garden

Various columbines offer an extended period of bloom, as does frothy chartreuse lady's mantle (*Alchemilla mollis*). My favorite columbine is the long-spurred, yellow *Aquilegia chrysantha*. Hybrid 'Yellow Queen' is also pretty, if not quite as graceful. Old-fashioned, dusky purple-blue *A. vulgaris* mingles with spurless pink and white hybrids 'Dailey' and 'Clematiflora Alba'. The very double forms, also known as "congested," of which pink 'Nora Barlow' and deep purple 'Millicent Bowden' are the most famous, look a bit odd, almost deformed to me, but I have one or two. The individual flowers, as so often the case with doubles, have lost much of the grace of the singles but are more able to withstand wind and weather and last longer on the stem.

The white form of fireweed (*Epilobium angustifolium* 'Album'), while still invasive, is much less rambunctious than its magenta-flowered cousin. This beautiful, opportunistic plant is among the first plants to recolonize fire-ravaged areas—in London after the Blitz, it is said to have turned rubble into lush gardens of flowers, like the phoenix rising from the ashes. It must have helped the courageous Londoners take heart that life does go on, even after such devastation. I saw a similar sight on Mount St. Helens three years after the volcanic eruption; hillsides were carpeted in brilliant pink as far as the eye could see. I let fireweed run among the shrub roses and delphiniums toward the back of the border. Unfortunately, the clapboards of the house are also white; I look forward to appreciating the beauty of this plant when we repaint the house next year in a darker color. Its subtle spikes mirror the gaudier delphiniums, but bloom a good month longer and don't require any staking.

▲ Salvia forskaohlei *joins white musk mallow and rose campion in dry shade.*

▲ Galega officinalis, *goat's rue.*

▼ *Crocus, puschkinia and winter aconite spangle a thin lawn under leafless trees in early spring.*

I get more of that spike effect that goes so well with the rounded blossoms of the roses from a tall lavender-blue catmint, *Nepeta sibirica*. It blooms for six weeks in early summer with the roses and is such a fine border plant that I am puzzled by its relative obscurity.

Four quiet plants add subtle charm to the lightly shaded garden in May and June: fragrant, tall white valerian (*Valeriana officinalis*), Eastern native bowman's root (*Gillenia trifoliata/Porteranthus trifoliatus*), with airy maroon stems and white flowers, and two plants I brought over from Ireland that are not very well known in gardens here as of yet, but have proven themselves hardy in this harsh climate. The first is *Silene fimbriata*. This tall perennial is not to everyone's liking—a friend of mine says it ranks right up there with green nicotianas (which I happen to like as well). Its puffy lime calyces are carried airily far above pale green foliage. Fringed white petals emerge from these; the flowers, by no means striking, nod with a quiet charm that invites closer scrutiny. The other, along the same lines, is *Nepeta govaniana*, with small pale yellow flowers in delicate sprays reminiscent of coralbells. It blends beautifully with deep pink and magenta roses and mallows, and equally well with the vibrant blues and purples of delphinium and larkspur.

In the back, almost under the eaves of the house and far away from passing children, biennial poison hemlock (*Conium maculatum*) hovers high above the largest shrub roses. Its finely dissected leaves and white flower umbels add a lacy framework to the picture. In the middle of the border, various meadow rues (*Thalictrum* spp.), with columbine-like foliage and frothy lavender, white and pale yellow flowers, blend well with the clean, elegant lines of Siberian irises.

Come late summer, several shade-loving annuals take over bloom duty: tall powder blue cultivars of ageratum, those much-maligned green nicotianas, the white starbursts of gargantuan *Nicotiana sylvestris*, foxglove lookalikes rose-pink *Rehmannia angulata* and taller mauve and white *Ceratotheca triloba*, and blue Chinese forget-me-not (*Cynoglossum amabile*). They continue on into fall, when they are joined by two large, lushly leaved perennials: Japanese anemones, with round, simple blossoms in white and rose, and *Cimicifuga simplex* 'White Pearl', a great contrast, with white bottlebrush flower spikes. Perennial spreader *Eupatorium coelestinum*, a late bloomer that looks deceptively like the annual ageratum, sneaks in and about the roses and larger perennials. The soft colors and textures of this garden bring the season to a quiet close.

No matter the depth or type of shade that falls on one's garden, it can transform an area into a place of peace. Paths through a shaded garden allow one to experience subtle sensual pleasures—heightened fragrance, as well as form, texture and soft pastel colors. One should walk into a garden rather than remain on the edge—just as one misses the whole essence of a woodland if one doesn't venture in among the trees, the subtleties of a shaded garden go unnoticed if viewed only from a window or the road. A winding path among these most graceful and gentle of plants, the plants that prefer and delight in the cool tranquility of shaded places, is an oasis for the soul.

PLANTS FOR SHADED GARDENS

GROUND COVERS—BEYOND VINCA, IVY AND AJUGA

Most of these are somewhat spreading, but those with pernicious ways that are hard to control or pull out are marked as invasive.

Acaena New Zealand burr **I, L**
Aegopodium podagraria goutweed, bishop's weed **I**
Ajuga reptans carpet bugle **I**
Alchemilla lady's mantle **L**
Anemone canadensis, A. sylvestris wood anemone **I**
Antennaria pussytoes **I, L, PP**
Arabis rock cress **L**
Asarum ginger
Astilbe chinensis false spiraea
Bolax glebaria plastic plant

Brunnera macrophylla Siberian bugloss
Ceratostigma plumbaginoides false plumbago, leadwort
Chrysogonum virginianum green-and-gold
Convallaria majalis lily-of-the-valley **I**
Crucianella stylosa (aka *Phuopsis stylosa*) crosswort
Cynoglossum nervosum hound's tongue **PP**
Duchesnea indica false strawberry **I**
Epimedium barrenwort
Fragaria vesca strawberry
Galax urceolata fairy wand
Galium odoratum sweet woodruff **I**
Geranium macrorrhizum
Glechoma hederacea **I**
Hedera helix English ivy **I**
Hemerocallis daylily **L**
Houttuynia cordata **I**
Lamiastrum galeobdolon yellow archangel **I**
Lamium maculatum dead nettle
Lysimachia nummularia creeping Jenny, moneywort **I**
Mahonia repens grapeholly **I**
Mazus reptans **I**
O. cappadocica, O. verna navelwort **PP**
Origanum vulgare 'Aureum' golden oregano **I**

Penstemon procerus **PP**
Persicaria (Polygonum) affinis border jewel, Himalayan fleeceflower **L**
Phalaris arundinacea 'Picta' ribbon grass, gardener's garters **I**, 'Feezey's Form' doesn't run
Phlox divaricata sweet William phlox
Phlox stolonifera creeping phlox
Pulmonaria lungwort, soldiers and sailors
Raoulia vegetable sheep **L**
Rumex scutatus
Sagina subulata Irish moss
Saponaria officinalis bouncing Bet **I, L**
Sedum acre, S. album, S. kamtschaticum, S. nevii, S. ternatum stonecrop
Symphytum grandiflorum, S. rubrum lesser comfrey
Thymus pseudolanuginosus woolly thyme **L**
Thymus serpyllum 'Minus' tiny creeping thyme **L**
Tiarella cordifolia foamflower
Veronica filiformis, V. repens bird's eye veronica **I**
Vinca minor periwinkle, vinca
Viola violet some are **I**
Waldsteinia fragarioides, W. ternata barren strawberry

▲ Astilbe chinensis *'Pumila'*.
▼ Tiarella cordifolia, *foamflower*.

▲ Trillium erectum, *ferns, Lenten rose*.
▼ Lilium henryi.

▲ Astrantia major *'Rosea'*, Hattie's pincushion.
▼ Erythronium grandiflorum *'Pagoda'*.

PERENNIALS FOR DRY SHADE

Cross-reference these with the above list for information on invasive behavior.

Anaphalis pearly everlasting L
Antennaria pussytoes L, PP
Artemisia ludoviciana L
Aster divaricatus wood aster
Bergenia pigsqueak L
Brunnera macrophylla Siberian bugloss
Campanula carpatica Carpathian bellflower L
Campanula poscharskyana L
Campanula punctata
Chimaphila maculata pipsissewa
Corydalis lutea yellow fumitory
Crucianella stylosa crosswort
Deschampsia tufted hair grass
Duchesnea indica false strawberry
Epimedium barrenwort
Eupatorium rugosum white snakeroot
Ferula communis giant fennel L
Galium odoratum sweet woodruff
Geranium macrorrhizum creeping geranium
Geranium sanguineum L
Geranium x *cantabrigiense* L
Glechoma hederacea ground ivy
Hedera helix ivy
Helleborus foetidus
Hemerocallis daylily L
Heuchera coralbells L
Hypericum St. John's wort
Iberis sempervirens candytuft L
Lamiastrum galeobdolon, 'Herman's Pride' yellow archangel
Lychnis coronaria rose campion L
Malva moschata musk mallow L, PP
Mertensia lanceolata narrowleaf chiming bells
Origanum vulgare 'Aureum' golden oregano
Paeonia mlokosewitschii Mollie the witch L, PP
Paeonia tenuifolia fernleaf peony L
Penstemon digitalis L, PP
Penstemon hirsutus var. *pygmaeus* L
Penstemon procerus L, PP
Penstemon richardsonii L
Penstemon smallii L
Penstemon virens L
Persicaria (Polygonum) affinis border jewel, Himalayan fleeceflower L
Phlox bifida sand phlox L
Phlox douglasii L
Phlox subulata moss phlox L
Prunella selfheal L
Pulmonaria soldiers and sailors, lungwort
Pulsatilla pasqueflower L
Rumex scutatus creeping sorrel
Salvia bulleyana
Salvia forskaohlei
Salvia glutinosa
Salvia haematodes

Sedum acre, S. album, S. kamtschaticum, S. nevii, S. spurium, S. ternatum stonecrop
Stachys byzantina lamb's ear L
Stachys grandiflora showy betony L
Symphytum grandiflorum lesser comfrey
Tanacetum (Chrysanthemum) parthenium feverfew PP
Thymus pseudolanuginosus woolly thyme L
Vinca minor periwinkle
Viola violet some
Waldsteinia fragarioides, W. ternata barren strawberry
Xerophyllum turkeybeard, bear grass

▲ *Delphinium and lily in light shade.*

▲ Lonicera periclymenum *'Graham Thomas', honeysuckle vine.*

▲ *Tufted hair grass, cutleaf selfheal, bergenia.*

▼ Cercis canadensis, *eastern redbud.*

▲ Stachys grandiflora, *showy betony.*
▼ Silene fimbriata, *purple sweet rocket.*

SHRUBS FOR SHADE

Berberis thunbergii 'Aurea' L
Cornus alba 'Elegantissima', 'Argenteomarginata' variegated dogwood
Daphne daphne L
Holodiscus dumosus rock spiraea L
Hydrangea arborescens 'Annabelle' PP
Hypericum St. John's wort L
Jamesia americana waxflower
Juniperus communis ground pine
Juniperus squamata 'Blue Star' L
Ligustrum privet L
Lonicera honeysuckle L
Mahonia grape holly
Microbiota decussata
Paxistima canbyi mountain lover
Philadelphus mock orange L
Physocarpus monogynus mountain ninebark
Rhododendron prinophyllum/roseum
Rhododendron x 'Northern Lights'
Rhodotypos scandens jetbead
Rhus aromatica fragrant sumac L
Ribes wild currant
Rosa eglanteria sweetbriar rose L
Rubus deliciosus boulder raspberry L, PP
Sambucus canadensis 'Aurea' golden elder
Sorbaria sorbifolia ashleaf spiraea L
Symphoricarpos snowberry
Symplocos sapphireberry L
Taxus cuspidata Japanese yew
Vaccinium blueberry

SMALL TREES FOR LIGHT SHADE

Acanthopanax sieboldianus, 'Variegatus'
Amelanchier serviceberry, shadblow
Aralia elata
Cercis canadensis redbud
Chionanthus virginicus fringe tree
Cornus alternifolia pagoda dogwood
Cornus florida flowering dogwood
Cornus mas, C. officinalis
Hamamelis vernalis, H. virginiana witch hazel
Hydrangea paniculata 'Grandiflora', 'Tardiva' peegee hydrangea
Picea abies dwarf forms Norway spruce L
Picea omorika 'Nana' dwarf Serbian spruce L
Ptelea trifoliata, 'Aurea' hops tree
Tsuga canadensis dwarf forms hemlock

VINES

Aristolochia durior Dutchman's pipe
Clematis paniculata/maximowicziana sweet autumn clematis L
Hedera helix ivy
Humulus lupulus hops vine PP
Lathyrus latifolius perennial pea L, PP
Lonicera honeysuckle L
Parthenocissus quinquefolia Virginia creeper, Englemann ivy
Polygonum aubertii silver lace vine L

BULBS

Anemone blanda Grecian windflower L
Arisaema Jack-in-the-pulpit
Arum italicum lords and ladies
Chionodoxa glory of the snow
Colchicum L
Cyclamen
Endymion wood hyacinth
Eranthis winter aconite PP
Erythronium troutlily, dogtooth violet, avalanche lily
Fritillaria meleagris checker lily, guinea hen L
Galanthus snowdrop
Leucojum snowflake
Lilium canadense, L. grayi, L. hansonii, L. henryi, L. martagon, L. philadelphicum, L. pumilum, L. pyrenaicum, L. speciosum, L. superbum, L. tigrinum L
Lycoris squamigera naked ladies L
Muscari grape hyacinth L
Narcissus daffodil
Ornithogalum umbellatum star of Bethlehem L
Puschkinia scilloides
Scilla squill
Trillium wake robin
Zigadenus death camas L

ANNUALS AND BIENNIALS/SHORT-LIVED PERENNIALS

Ageratum houstonianum
Angelica archangelica B
Asperula orientalis blue woodruff
Begonia
Bellis B
Borago officinalis borage L
Browallia speciosa
Caladium tender bulb
Catharanthus roseus Madagascar periwinkle
Ceratotheca triloba
Coleus x *hybridus*
Collinsia
Conium maculatum poison hemlock B
Cynoglossum amabile hound's tongue L, PP
Digitalis purpurea great foxglove B
Heracleum cow parsnip, cartwheel flower B
Hypoestes phyllostachya polkadot plant
Impatiens balsam, busy Lizzie
Isatis tinctoria woad B
Limnanthes douglasii butter and eggs L
Lobelia erinus lobelia

Lobularia maritima sweet alyssum L
Lunaria annua moneyplant
Meconopsis cambrica Welsh poppy
Mimulus x *hybridus* monkey flower
Moluccella laevis bells of Ireland
Myosotis sylvestris forget-me-not B
Nemophila baby blue-eyes, five-spot L
Nicotiana flowering tobacco
Pelargonium peltatum ivy geranium
Pentas lanceolata star flower
Rehmannia angulata
Reseda odorata mignonette L
Schizanthus poor man's orchid, butterfly flower L
Smyrnium perfoliatum B
Tanacetum (Chrysanthemum) parthenium feverfew PP
Thunbergia alata black-eyed Susan vine
Torenia fournieri wishbone flower
Viola cornuta viola B
Viola tricolor Johnny-jump-up
Viola x *wittrockiana* pansy

PERENNIALS

Acaena New Zealand burr L
Acanthus bear's breeches L
Aconitum monkshood, wolfsbane
Actaea baneberry
Adenophora ladybells L
Adonis
Aegopodium podagraria 'Variegata' goutweed
Ajuga carpet bugle
Alchemilla lady's mantle L
Amsonia blue star L
Anaphalis pearly everlasting L
Androsace rock jasmine L
Anemonella thalictroides rue anemone
Anemone canadensis wood anemone
Anemone nemorosa wood anemone
Anemone sylvestris wood anemone
Anemone tomentosa Japanese anemone
Anemone x *hybrida* Japanese anemone
Antennaria pussytoes L, PP
Anthriscus sylvestris
Aquilegia columbine L
Arabis rock cress L
Arrhenatherum elatius 'Variegatus' bulbous oat grass
Artemisia lactiflora ghostplant L
Artemisia ludoviciana L
Aruncus goatsbeard
Asarum wild ginger
Aster divaricatus white wood aster
Astilbe false spirea
Astrantia Hattie's pincushion

Asyneuma canescens
Baptisia L
Bergenia pigsqueak
Bolax glebaria plastic plant
Borago laxiflora L
Brunnera macrophylla Siberian bugloss
Caltha marsh marigold L
Campanula bellflower L
Carex sedge
Caulophyllum thalictroides blue cohosh
Ceratostigma plumbaginoides false plumbago, leadwort
Chelone turtlehead
Chimaphila pipsissewa, wintergreen
Chrysogonum virginianum green and gold
Cimicifuga bugbane, snakeroot
Clematis recta L
Clintonia
Convalaria majalis lily-of-the-valley
Cornus canadensis bunchberry
Cortusa
Corydalis fumitory
Crucianella stylosa crosswort
Cynoglossum nervosum hound's tongue L, PP
Cypripedium lady's slipper orchid
Darmera peltata (aka *Peltiphyllum*) umbrella plant
Dentaria toothwort
Deschampsia hair grass
Dicentra bleeding heart
Digitalis foxglove
Dodecatheon shooting star
Doronicum L
Epigaea repens mayflower, trailing arbutus
Epilobium angustifolium fireweed, willow herb L, PP
Epimedium barrenwort
Eupatorium coelestinum perennial ageratum
Eupatorium rugosum white snakeroot
ferns
Ferula giant fennel L
Filipendula hexapetala dropwort L
Fragaria vesca strawberry L
Galax urceolata fairy wand
Galega officinalis goat's rue L
Galium odoratum sweet woodruff
Gaultheria
Gentiana asclepiadea willow gentian
Geranium L
Geum L
Gillenia trifoliata (aka *Porteranthus trifoliatus*) bowman's root L
Glaucidium palmatum
Hacquetia epipactis
Hakonechloa macra, 'Aureola'
Hedera helix ivy
Helleborus hellebore

Hemerocallis daylily L
Hepatica liverleaf
Heracleum cartwheel flower, hogweed, cow parsnip
Hesperis matronalis sweet rocket
Heuchera coralbells L
Heucherella tiarelloides L
Hosta plantain lily, funkia
Houttuynia cordata
Iberis sempervirens candytuft L
Iris cristata, I. douglasiana, I. ensata, I. forrestii, I. gracilipes, I. graminea, I. pseudacorus, I. setosa, I. sibirica I. tectorum, I. tenax, I, verna
Jeffersonia diphylla, J. dubia twinleaf
Lamiastrum galeobdolon, 'Herman's Pride' yellow archangel
Lamium maculatum dead nettle
Lathyrus vernus spring vetchling L
Leucanthemum vulgare oxeye daisy L
Lewisia L
Ligularia
Linnaea borealis twinflower
Lobelia
Luzula wood rush
Lychnis coronaria rose campion L
Lychnis x arkwrightii orange campion
Lysimachia nummularia creeping Jenny, moneywort
Macleaya plume poppy L
Maianthemum false lily-of-the-valley
Malva moschata musk mallow L, PP
Mazus reptans
Melissa officinalis lemon balm L
Mentha mint L
Mertensia chiming bells
Meum athamanticum
Milium effusum 'Aureum' millet grass
Mimulus monkey flower
Mitchella repens partridge berry
Mitella miterwort
Moltkia L
Monarda L
Myosotis sylvatica forget-me-not
Nepeta govaniana
Omphalodes cappadocica, O. verna PP
Onosma L
Origanum vulgare 'Aureum Compactum'
Pachysandra
Paeonia mlokosewitschii Mollie the witch L
Paeonia tenuifolia fernleaf peony L
Paris polyphylla
Patrinia
Penstemon digitalis, P. hirsutus v. pygmaeus, P. procerus P. richardsonii, P. smallii, P. virens L
Persicaria (Polygonum) affinis border jewel L
Phalaris arundinacea 'Picta' gardener's

garters, ribbon grass
Phlox bifida sand phlox L
Phlox divaricata sweet William phlox
Phlox douglasii
Phlox stolonifera creeping phlox
Phlox subulata moss phlox L
Phlox x procumbens
Physostegia virginiana obedient plant L
Pimpinella major
Podophyllum mayapple
Polemonium Jacob's ladder
Polygala milkwort
Polygonatum Solomon's seal
Primula PP
Prunella selfheal L
Pulmonaria soldiers and sailors, lungwort
Pyrola wintergreen
Raoulia vegetable sheep L
Rheum palmatum ornamental rhubarb L
Rodgersia
Ruellia humilis wild petunia L
Rumex scutatus
Sagina subulata Irish moss
Salvia bulleyana, S. forskaohlei, S. glutinosa, S. haematodes sage L
Sanguinaria canadensis bloodroot
Sanguisorba burnet L
Saxifraga saxifrage
Sedum stonecrop
Selinum carvifolium, S. tenuifolium
Shortia fringebells
Silene fimbriata, S. virginica L
Smilacina false Solomon's seal
Solidago goldenrod L
Stachys grandiflora showy betony L
Stokesia laevis Stokes' aster L
Stylophorum celandine poppy
Symphytum comfrey PP
Synthyris PP
Telekia speciosa (aka *Bupthalmum*) L
Tellima grandiflora fringecups
Thalictrum meadow rue
Thymus serpyllum thyme L
Tiarella cordifolia, Tiarella wherryi foamflower
Tradescantia spiderwort L
Tricyrtis toadlily
Trollius L
Uvularia merrybells
Valeriana officinalis valerian L
Veratrum green gentian L
Verbascum phoeniceum purple mullein L
Veronica filiformis, V. gentianoides, V. repens L
Veronicastrum virginicum Culver's root L
Vinca minor periwinkle
Viola viola, violet
Waldsteinia barren strawberry
Xerophyllum beargrass, turkeybeard L

▲   The leaves of silver Scots thistle, red orach, blue avena grass, striped iris and sea kale add color, form and motion to the flowers of yellow dyer's broom, Grecian foxglove and red hot poker.

◀   Leaves can create beauty without a single flower: California poppy and red orach, two lovely annuals.

visual rush, but if I had to look at it day after day, I would soon become slightly insane from overstimulation and then lapse into interminable boredom. With the new excitement about foliage, most gardeners have focused on foliage color, jamming way too many oddly hued plants into small spaces. Due to the sad but inescapable fact that most of us don't have the aesthetic talent and know-how of a Burle Marx, the results are at best highly unrestful and at worst the equivalent of a bad hallucination. I have found that conservative use of unusually colored foliage and more emphasis on the form and texture of the leaves promises a better effect.

Variegated and Golden Leaves

 Brilliant foliage color rarely acts as a backdrop. One should place it as one would a dramatic flower, with softer tones and textures surrounding it much like the charismatic partygoer is surrounded by mesmerized quieter types. Perhaps the most common foliage color variations are variegation and gold- or chartreuse-leaved forms of plants. Some gardeners are so fond of these, they will go to all lengths to acquire the most obscure, odd-looking variegated version of a plant. There is even a special plant society established for lovers of these plants. I would like to say "beware." The line between attractive and sickly looking is fine, and many variegated plants cross over into the latter, either by overuse, poor siting—too much sun will often burn these pale leaves—or, by the nature of the variegation itself. Some plants have refined, pale cream edges while others are haphazardly blotched, as if by a sloppy painter, or more sinisterly, by a virulent disease, as with variegated lemon balm (*Melissa officinalis* 'Variegata'). While some plants glow softly chartreuse—*Hosta* 'Kabitan' unfurling its shoots in a shady corner in spring, golden feverfew (*Tanacetum parthenium* 'Aureum') adding freshness to a somber scene—others, especially when given too much sun, turn a violent, sick yellow. One of the ugliest plantings I see all too often is a group of pallid, pathetic golden barberries in full sun, frying above a musty brown layer of bark mulch. This same barberry, surrounded by green and given a little shade from the ferocity of the afternoon sun, is transformed.

Almost all these pale plants prefer light shade and are at their best early in the season when they are fresh and bright. The more vigorous plants, like ribbon grass (*Phalaris arundinacea* 'Picta') or *Lamium maculatum*, can be cut back with impunity when they begin to look tired and tattered in the summer. They will resprout clean new foliage to boost the garden's looks for fall. Many, however, are slower growing and less hardy than their green counterparts, and need extra pampering. With a little extra care and good placement, golden and variegated plants become sublime additions, adding luminosity, like spots of sunlight, to a green scene. I especially like them in an informal setting, such as a woodland garden, where their interesting leaves add much to the endless green after the spring flower flush is finished. Somehow, in more formal settings, they can easily look self-conscious and contrived. The variegated strawberry (*Fragaria vesca* 'Variegata') creeps across the garden floor, in and out of larger plants, spreading a light, creamy carpet as it goes. Pale *Kerria japonica* 'Picta', a shrub of fine-textured, arching grace, makes an airy focal point.

I combine bulbs that prefer cooler, moister soil and some shade in the summer with emerging variegated and golden ground covers. Golden creeping Jenny (*Lysimachia nummularia* 'Aurea') and oregano (*Origanum vulgare* 'Aureum Compactum') make good companions to early pale blue *Puschkinia scilloides*, *Scilla siberica* or *Chionodoxa luciliae* and *C. sardensis*. The ground covers are just beginning to show traces of luminescent color when the bulbs bloom, but soon thereafter, their chartreuse-yellow carpets mask the dying foliage. Powder blue woodland phloxes *Phlox divaricata* and *P. stolonifera* 'Blue Ridge', as well as deeper lavender-blue, shade-tolerant *Penstemon procerus*, bloom in mid-spring, mingling with the golden ground covers just as their foliage is at its best. For a cooler look, I combine white 'Thalia' daffodils, small enough not to make heaps of dying foliage, with the pale blue bells and silver-spotted leaves of 'Roy Davidson' lungwort, my favorite of the many *Pulmonaria saccharata* cultivars.

In full sun, only a handful of these unusually toned foliage plants thrive. A popular choice for a well-drained, sunny garden are the golden or silver variegated *Iris pallida* forms. I combine the silver-striped linear leaves of the form 'Argentea Variegata' with peonies. The peonies' deep green, glossy mounds of foliage and plate-sized pink and crimson flowers make ideal companions to the iris, contrasting and harmonizing in color, form and texture. The more vigorous golden-striped form of the iris is paired in a bolder manner, with the blue leaves of sea kale (*Crambe maritima*) and blue avena grass (*Helictotrichon sempervirens*), and yellow-flowered dyer's broom, *Genista tinctoria*.

Golden-leaved sage (*Salvia officinalis* 'Aureovariegata') grows with natives blue flax (*Linum perenne* ssp. *lewisii*) and yellow Ozark sundrop (*Oenothera macrocarpa*), and several tufts of blue fescue in a similarly sunny, well-drained part of my garden.

 In contrast to the needs of variegated plants, red, bronze, copper and purple foliage plants require a good deal of sunlight to be most effective. The addition of purple leaves to the garden enrichens colors. With pastels, it makes them stand out; feathery, anise-scented bronze fennel frames white floribunda rose 'Iceberg'; purple-leaved sage (*Salvia officinalis* 'Purpurea') pairs with pastel sunrose *Helianthemum nummularium* 'Wisley Pink'.

Leaves with Red Tones

The real garden coup, however, happens when these richly toned foliage plants are mixed with hot colors—the reds and oranges. Two superb examples of this are the red garden at Hidcote in England and the northeast corner of the flower garden at Wave Hill in the Bronx. What makes this color marriage so successful is that the jarring

effect of green, the color that contrasts most fiercely with the reds and oranges, is mitigated by bronze, copper and purple. One needn't devote a whole area of the garden to the reds and oranges to enjoy this beautiful effect, however. I have seen this done beautifully on a smaller scale with just a few plants: crimson roses with purple smokebush (*Cotinus coggygria* 'Royal Purple') in a shrub border; red tulips with the emerging burgundy foliage of *Lysimachia ciliata* 'Rubra', which later turns green; bronze-purple *Heuchera micrantha* 'Palace Purple' with orange crocosmia flowers in late summer.

I go whole-hog for this effect in our German four-square garden, an area roughly thirty-five feet by thirty-five feet that my husband fenced in to protect from the ravages of three dogs. Here we grow all things for table and vase. The colors are bright and garish—red tomatoes mingling with pink cosmos, curly bronze lettuce with crimson pyrethrum daisies, purple and magenta China asters with golden rudbeckias. The garden is divided into four equal squares, a traditional German kitchen garden layout and a fun reprieve from the boring rows so commonly resorted to when growing these kinds of plants. The paths around the perimeter and crisscrossing between the squares are sodded in tall fescue, a tough, quite drought-tolerant, hardy grass that takes a lot of foot traffic. The paths allow access to all sides of the four twelve-foot by twelve-foot squares. I edge the tomato square in basil and signet marigolds, the tiny single-flowered ones, mixing the purple-leaved basil varieties 'Dark Opal' and 'Purple Ruffles' in

with the better-tasting green varieties and the tiny orange 'Tangerine Gem' marigolds. Thus a richly hued, fragrant girdle embellishes the lanky tomato plants.

In the cooler, partly shaded square where we grow snap peas, flowering sweet peas, radishes and lettuce, I grow the lovely, tender-leaved lettuce 'Red Sails', adding a burgundy note to a sea of green. In the cut flower square, a generous helping of bronze-leaved beefsteak plant (*Perilla frutescens*), supposedly edible but so far I've only used it to grace garden or vase, ties together the brilliant cacophony of orange zinnias, gold and maroon calliopsis (*Coreopsis tinctoria*), purple statice, magenta globe amaranth and indigo blue mealy-cup sage and larkspur.

Blue Leaves Another color commonly found in foliage is blue. This can vary from the gray-blue of some dianthus species, to the greenish blue of columbine and thalictrum leaves to an almost turquoise color, like that of some of the hostas. Blue, contrary to variegation and the sumptuous reds and purples, is a cool, quiet color, refreshing but never demanding more than its fair share of attention. There is little danger in its overuse or in unusual color combinations with it. The lacy blue foliage of rue (*Ruta graveolens*) is indispensable, whether softening brilliant red and orange gaillardias and rudbeckias of a hot midsummer garden, or framing the heavy trusses of pale pink cabbage roses in the traditional marriage of old garden roses with herbs. I use rue, fine tufts of blue sheep's fescue and the architectural fountains of blue avena grass throughout the sunnier parts of the garden. They act as foils to almost every color imaginable. What I like so much about these three plants, aside from their soft tones, is their wonderful form and texture. I remove their scrawny flowers when they appear; these are foliage plants par excellence.

The color combination that most appeals to me using these pale blues is orange. Three poppy family members create this effect all by themselves, with rosettes of glaucous blue foliage and flowers in various shades of orange, honey apricot and peach: ferny-leaved California poppies, coarse biennial horned poppy (*Glaucium* spp., the most scalloped foliage is that of *G. corniculatum*), and one of my all-time favorite plants, biennial *Papaver triniifolium*. This latter plant is not well known, yet it is easy to grow in any sunny, well-drained spot. Each flower lasts but an afternoon, yet the parade of peach-orange, four-petaled blossoms is unstoppable. The plant seeds like there's no tomorrow, and the hairy, convoluted, ice blue foliage rosettes that spring forth are evergreen. I've let it all but take over one of the hot, baked strips between the sidewalk and the street, where it mingles with blue flax, yellow sunrose, the lavender-blue spikes of *Salvia jurisicii* and purple-spired biennial *Dracocephalum nutans*. The other sun-loving blue-foliaged plant I'm partial to is donkey-tail spurge, *Euphorbia myrsinites*. Its stems of whorled, waxy blue leaves coil prostrately on the ground; from this writhing habit probably sprang forth the other common name, snakeweed. Some people are strongly allergic to its milky sap and should wear gloves when handling the plant. This nasty trait benefits the plant, however, in that no insects ever set a leg or proboscis on it. The plant is virtually problem free. Self-sown seedlings can rapidly colonize an area, so deadheading is advised to control the plant's spread. It also remains evergreen through most of the winter. Then, just at that juncture when winter and spring melt together, the donkey-tails bud and open into large chartreuse-yellow clusters of flowers and bracts. Early *Tulipa batalinii* 'Apricot Gem' or the more vibrant red species *T. wilsoniana* sprouting from between the blue drape of the spurge make for a wonderful start to the blooming season. For a different effect, I've combined the chartreuse spurge flowers with purple-flowering rock cress (*Aubrieta deltoidea*) at a dry corner near my garden gate. It is perhaps the most psychologically effective combination in the garden, setting the mood for advancing spring, filling me with delight and anticipation each time I go in and out of the otherwise still dormant garden.

Blue foliage plants are more versatile than many of their other unusually hued cousins in that both sun and shade lovers abound. The aforementioned delicate columbines and meadow rues thrive in light, dappled shade or in an eastern exposure. Their delicate flowers last longer when protected from the hot sun, the pastel tones of their petals show better in the soft light of a partly shaded situation and their wonderful foliage will remain fresh longer into the heat of the summer given this protection. Little *Aquilegia flabellata* is shorter and plumper than its graceful long-spurred hybrid relatives. In blue or white, the squat plant blooms a good three weeks before the more common hybrids begin. Its foliage is the bluest, waxiest and most pest resistant of all the species and hybrids I've grown. I've never known a miner to blemish a leaf. It blooms alongside soft yellow oxslip primroses (*Primula elatior*) in mid-spring. While the pretty flowers last only two weeks, a much shorter bloom period than the taller species and varieties, the foliage is so attractive that the flowers aren't greatly missed.

The bluest of the meadow rues is *Thalictrum speciosissimum*, which sends up sulphur yellow powder-puff flowers in early summer for a few weeks. If it never bloomed, it would still deserve a place in the shaded garden, for the delicate blue leaves are one of the finest of any plant. With the oval, almost tropical-looking foliage of some of the larger hostas like the sieboldianas, who needs flowers?

The palette of drought-tolerant shade plants is quite limited, but three good blue-leaved individuals stand out. Perhaps the blue leaves, due to a waxy coating, are in large part responsible for these plants' success in drier situations, helping them conserve moisture by preventing evaporation from the leaf surface. All three plants are small, about six inches tall and a bit wider in spread. *Silene vulgaris* ssp. *maritima* grows along seashores throughout Europe. Its dense, blue-green mats thrive in part shade here in the fierce, sunny, continental climate of Colorado. It blooms heavily in late spring—frilly white flowers with large,

▶ *Blue* Veronica incana *and orange cowboy's delight,* Sphaeralcea coccinea, *share pewter-toned foliage.*

(facing page) In Kelly Grummons' garden, silver Artemisia stellerana *sprawls over Mexican evening primrose;* Verbena 'Homestead Purple' *tumbles from above, while dwarf Colorado spruce and 'Blue Star' juniper calm the chaos.*

▼ Aquilegia flabellata 'Alba'.

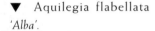

▼ Papaver triniifolium *foliage.*

papery, pale green calyces. I grow it in front of rose-pink coral bells at the edge of the path; the coralbells nod airily forward, and their dark green, mottled foliage looks good with the silene's once the flowers are spent. Both plants remain evergreen for most of the winter.

Another shade-loving blue plant I grow is *Allium senescens* 'Glaucum', a late-blooming bulb that quickly forms a dense clump in light shade. Come late August or early September, pale rose-lavender umbels of flowers grace the leaves. Throughout the spring and summer, the curiously curled, grasslike foliage is a soft, unusual blue accent among the greens of the shaded garden.

My other blue-leaved shade denizen, *Rumex scutatus*, garden sorrel, is a scrambling, spreading plant, excellent for hiding dying daffodil foliage under trees. Its leaves are gray-blue, shaped like an odd, blunted arrowhead; the flowers are useless except for collecting seed. The dry shade where I grow this plant doesn't allow daffodils to thrive, yet naked ladies (*Lycoris squamigera*) do fine. These old-fashioned bulbous beauties need a ground cover from which their naked stems are to rise in late summer. More prudish gardeners are known to call them surprise lilies, for indeed their eighteen-inch stems topped with a cluster of large pink flowers in August rise from the ground unannounced. The foliage they grow in the spring has long since died back and been forgotten. A retired farmer's wife in my town tends her huge vegetable patch with great care. She must hoe it every other day; I've never seen a weed in the perfectly aligned rows of beans, rhubarb, dill and beets. Late the first summer I had moved to our town, I was driving past this geometrical garden when I did a

double take. There, in three perfect rows a good fifty feet long each, were thousands upon thousands of naked ladies. If this woman only knew she were sitting on a gold mine. When I think of what mail-order companies charge per bulb, it makes me weak in the knees. In my garden, since I haven't gotten up the nerve to ask the lady if I could buy some of her prodigious bounty, I have to be satisfied by a dozen or so of the lovely pink bulbs. With blue-gray garden sorrel as an underplanting, I'm quite pleased, although a few hundred more of the bulbs couldn't hurt.

The last of the foliage colors I want to mention are green and gray. They can add more to the overall appeal of a garden than any of the others. As with other foliage colors, good form and texture and combinations must be taken into account, but with green and gray, this is all the more important since more such plants are used and the color itself is not as dominant an attribute. First off, the plants' leaves must in and of themselves be attractive for most of the season—that old cardinal rule. Then one needs to consider how to place them so that their attributes will be noticed. Contrast is the best way of accomplishing this: Bold, rounded peony, bergenia or brunnera leaves look their best combined with finer or more vertical leaves like the ferny foliage of Jacob's ladder, *Polemonium foliosissimum,* or the linear foliage of daylilies, Siberian iris and, of course, many of the ornamental grasses.

One can think of plants as personalities. Are they bold, the life of the party, grabbing for attention every time one walks in the garden? Or are they supportive, stepping back and complementing those around them while drawing little attention to themselves? A party full of bold extroverts would drive most guests crazy—the same with a garden full of bold "focal" plants. But a party of listeners and agreers would be as dull as boiled zucchini; likewise a garden of "filler" plants. What a garden needs is a balance of both personalities.

Green Leaves The interplay of green foliage is the backbone of all but the driest gardens, where gray and silver take the place of green. The importance of both green and gray foliage should never be underestimated. These colors soothe an otherwise jarring cacophony of foliage and flower colors. They separate colors that would otherwise do deadly battle, and at the same time unify the composition, drawing in the colors beyond the narrow confines of the garden—the natural flora, bark, water, stone and sky. This is what happens in the mad burst of color that is a rock garden in spring. The rocks, generally muted tones of gray, and the foliage—greens, grays and silvers—prevent the brilliant flower colors from clashing and overpowering the picture. Imagine a flower bed without foliage; well, actually, one need only go to a test garden or to a park planting of annuals. These poor plants have been so perverted by breeding that their flowers literally cover all remnants of foliage. A rectangle of red impatiens, with not even the slightest snippet of green to break up the sea of color, is not my idea of good gardening or color sense.

Gardeners take green for granted; it is ubiquitous in any nonarid landscape. The role of green is probably the most important in the garden. It is no accident that green has been used in such seemingly divergent ways as the walls of mental institutions and on the undersides of baseball cap visors. In both cases, the soothing properties of the color are being called forth. Similar in effect, gray, in the language of color theory, has neither complement nor opposite, so it creates a sense of balance and equilibrium in and of itself. Gray has been associated with peace, neutrality and quiet.

All-green gardens, as are many woodland gardens after the flowering flush of spring and early summer has passed, may at first glance seem not a garden at all. Given time for contemplation, one begins to drink in the serenity, to notice the play of light and shadow, the infinite variety of leaf form and texture. In a few quiet moments, what was at first hastily judged as boring becomes a Garden of Eden. In southeastern Pennsylvania where I grew up, I remember a low stream bank untouched by gardeners' hands: a sea of feathery horsetail, a beautiful but highly invasive prehistoric plant, grew among a handsome group of young, vase-shaped skunk cabbage plants. Neither of these plants is particularly gardenworthy, but the sculptural quality of the skunk cabbage in that froth of green was an early lesson in garden design.

 In a dryland garden, the dominant role of green is taken over by gray-green and gray. In a good third of the North American continent, the predominant color of the native plants is not the lush green of the coastal and eastern forests, rather the sages and silvers of mountains, vast steppes and deserts. Plants adapted to these conditions, whether native plants, old friends from the Mediterranean region—the lavenders, sages, thymes and santolinas, or newer discoveries from Central Asia and the colder regions of Australia and South Africa, make for good, tough garden choices in the interior West. They also look right, much more harmonious and aesthetically appropriate than square after square of green lawn.

Silver and Gray

Yet all-gray-and-silver gardens rarely are as successful as an all-green garden. This is mainly due to the fact that so many plants of these hues are hopelessly similar in form and texture. They have developed similar adaptations to some of the world's harshest climates. Native to deserts, rocky cliffs, wind-whipped mountain tops and battered seashores, these tough survivors have developed their characteristic coloring to combat the relentless sun, wind, drought and extremes of heat and cold. This is why so many of them are happily at home in gardens subject to harsh continental climates. Winter hardiness is less of a problem for many than moist soil and lack of sunshine in winter or heavy humidity in summer. Dry air, strong sunlight, heat and a well-drained mineral soil low in organic matter are what most of these lovely plants require. By means of white, silver or gray hairs, or a waxy coating on the surface of their leaves, they reflect the sun to cool themselves and trap

A miniature foliage garden fills this square foot: Penstemon teucrioides, chocolate Geranium sessiliflorum 'Nigricans', silver 'McClintock' pussytoes, gun-metal Veronica incana and the greens of Turkish veronica and buffalo rose.

▼ Stachys byzantina 'Helene von Stein' and 'Silver Carpet', two non-flowering forms of lamb's ear.

▲ Tanacetum densum *var.* amani, *partridge feather.*

moisture escaping from the leaf to reduce water loss. These water-saving characteristics, along with small leaves and fine, twiggy or matlike form, tend toward busy texture. The dearth of larger forms makes an all-silver garden seem flat.

Just add a touch of green foliage and white and cream flowers, still basically leaving the monochromatic idea alone, and suddenly a masterpiece results. These successful pale gardens, such as the much-loved white garden at Sissinghurst Castle in England and many moon or twilight gardens, allow the whites, grays and silvers to take on their most luminous, ethereal qualities thanks to deeper greens and varied textures and forms that add complexity and depth. Gray foliage softens the harsh contrast of dark green with white, making the white less flat and glaring, and texture more apparent. I tried this by mixing shimmering gray Artemisia x 'Valerie Finnis' with the pure white flowers of 'Miss Lingard' phlox and creamy blossoms of feverfew. The whites become more delicate and their forms more defined. They look less like bleached-out blurs and more like the gracefully formed blossoms that they are.

Gray and silver foliage consorts well with not only white and cream, but just about any color. In fact, silver and gray plants are perhaps the most versatile for achieving varied design effects. They can make pale colors—white and the pastels—glow more brightly, while dark colors like the purples and blues seem richer and deeper in their company. Similar colors, such as pink and purple or blue and green, appear more distinct when combined with gray and silver. Yet when many colors are mixed, the addition of silver and gray ties them together and gives the eye a needed rest. I learned this from an old, abandoned fencerow in northern Connecticut near the farm where I worked. At one time, a creative gardener had lovingly planted a narrow strip of perennials along the fence. What remained

▲ *Silver 'Valerie Finnis' artemisia, feverfew and white* Phlox maculata *'Miss Lingard' make a cool, ethereal composition.*

▶ *Some foliage needs no flowers: cardoon, blue avena grass and low-growing* Lamium maculatum *'White Nancy'.*

▼ Scabiosa graminifolia.

was an odd assortment of thistle, grasses and a few stalwart remnants of past glory. The strongest of these, the aggressive wormwood, *Artemisia ludoviciana*, ran ribbons of silver in and out of all the others. In early summer it gleamed alongside the white faces of oxeye daisies. By the Fourth of July, orange and deep red daylilies sent up their starry fireworks above the silver carpet. Then came the rose spikes of loosestrife (*Lythrum salicaria*), and as the nights grew chilly, purple asters and goldenrod finished the season, still embellished by a silver spray.

Versatile silver enhances virtually any color. It can separate or unify, depending on the colors it accompanies. Put gray and silver with one or two very strong colors, such as orange or bright red, and the effect is intensified. Take for example *Lychnis coronaria*, whose white-felted stems and leaves make the strong magenta flowers glow even more brightly. For these multifaceted qualities in garden combinations, gray and silver plants have rightfully been called social facilitators.

Silver and gray plants can also make an area appear larger. At the end of an herbaceous border, a group of gray plants shimmers and melts ethereally into the hazy distance. But when placed in front of a dark, somber object—an evergreen or a dark wall, for instance— the plant's effect is quite the opposite: instead of receding and fading, the luminous spot advances and highlights its surroundings. Plants with gray and silver tones, mirroring similar tones in the non-living landscape—stone, bark, water, sky—help tie these "hard" elements in with the rest of the garden. In my wild and woolly cottage garden, I let several low-growing silver plants such as 'Wisley Pink' sunrose, *Veronica incana*, lamb's ear and the featherlike foliage of *Tanacetum densum* var. *amani* spill out onto the gray sidewalk and peach-mauve sandstone paths. They are tough enough to take the reflected heat, and add a shimmering, undulating wave that softens the demarcation between cement, stone and living garden.

Threading more of the same silver and gray through the garden gives unity to even the most seemingly loose, wild, chaotic abundance of plants. I learned this from what I consider the finest public garden in America (where I was fortunate enough to have worked), Wave Hill in New York City, and I have used the same principle in my garden. I call on two favorite artemisias, 'Valerie Finnis', almost white, a foot tall and a bit invasive, and 'Powis Castle', a surprisingly hardy four-foot perennial, its pewter filigree well behaved and shrublike, to mingle with the larger perennials and shrubs. I've experimented with nearly a dozen species and cultivars of this classic foliage genus, the artemisias, many of which made themselves altogether too comfortable in the garden (I'm still pulling out pieces of 'Silver King' when I thought I had dethroned him over two years ago). Famed *Artemisia schmidtiana* 'Silver Mound' is lovely the first two or three months of the growing season, then after the first heavy summer thundershowers or the all-too-common run-in with hail, it is pretty much ruined, open and woody in the center, formless and bedraggled-looking.

The native silver shrub *Artemisia tridentata* is also a bit weak in the form department, but I've been pruning it for shape here and there, eager to have a large woody silver plant to add some size and dimension. Biennial silver six-foot giants *Verbascum bombyciferum* (woolly mullein) and *Onopordum acanthium* (Scottish thistle), the first soft and benign, the second a spiny warrior, are living statues, lending their bold, architectural lines to the garden while I impatiently wait for the woodies to catch up.

For lower-growing yet bold rosettes of white-felted leaves, *Salvia argentea* is peerless. Its flowers, loosely arranged on weak stems, are an utter disappointment and candidates for premature removal. The best use of this fabulous foliage plant I've seen is in the Rock Alpine Garden at the Denver Botanic Gardens. On a slope next to a granite outcrop sparkling with mica, the silver sage rosettes are interplanted with the small but profuse pink flowers of cascading rock soapwort (*Saponaria ocymoides*). The planting is perfection of form, color and texture. *Salvia aethiopsis*, another bold-leaved biennial, is a more uncommon choice for a similar effect; its leaves are cut wavy in outline like those of an oak.

Bright pink and silver are always good bedfellows, whether on the same plant, as in the case of the lovely *Stachys inflata*, a relatively new plant with almost pure white foliage and stems and hot pink flowers, or in combining plants. I pair the gray, wrinkled leaves of *Marrubium incanum* with bright *Penstemon barbatus* 'Elfin Pink'. Lavender and blue are also natural companions to silver and gray foliage. *Nepeta phyllochlamys*, the whitest catmint I know of, grows almost prostrately next to tussocks of blue sheep's fescue, creating a soft harmony without the help of a single blossom. This catmint blooms modestly; the foliage is its best feature. *Scabiosa graminifolia*, on the other hand, blends gunmetal foliage with showy lavender pincushion flowers.

In light shade, fewer silver and gray plants thrive, yet many appreciate the cooler temperatures, as long as the light is still bright. A tiny, very silver form of pussytoes (*Antennaria parvifolia* 'McClintock') thrives between the cracks of the sandstone path on the bright but shaded north side of our house, as does the gleaming metallic rosette of *Onosma sericeum*, whose drooping yellow flowers hang gently into the path.

Silver and gray can also be paired with deeper and brighter tones, but for my taste, it is among the whites and pastels that they work best. Here, without conscious intent, one can extend the beauty of the outdoors by several hours each summer day. I remember hurtling down Highway 6 though western Utah and Nevada on the way to California one night. There, stretching for miles and miles, was a natural moon garden. The white salt flats and the silver sagebrush-covered hills glowed ghostlike in the moonlight. Deserts and other harsh regions of the world brim with these wonderful light-reflecting silver and gray plants. They sparkle in the sun, and shimmer under the moon. There's no reason why they can't cast their magic in the garden in the same way. The pale colors of foliage and pastel flowers become luminous at dusk, creating a personal twilight or moon garden. I plant pale fragrant plants such as lilies, old-fashioned flowering tobacco (*Nicotiana alata*, not the many stubby, scentless modern varieties), pink and lavender night-blooming stock (*Matthiola longipetala* ssp. *bicornis*), sweet alyssum and my two favorite evening primroses, *Oenothera biennis* 'Grandiflora', a five-foot biennial with huge, scented, sulphur yellow flowers and the lovely, low-growing Western native *Oenothera caespitosa*, with delicately fragrant three-inch white flowers that fade to pink as they age. As the light fades, these plants become more and more prominent, as if emanating a light from within. The garden is transformed; large tawny hawk moths appear, eager to drink from the nectar of the fragrant flowers. The cats rise from their late-afternoon naps, refreshed and ready to stalk the enticing moths. The dreamlike, sensual atmosphere of the colors and fragrances keeps me out in the garden until the mosquitoes finally break the spell. A twilight garden is truly the finest reason for bringing silver and gray foliage plants into the garden.

Whatever the color, form or texture of a leaf, its ability to bring beauty to the garden is far greater than the showiest flower, for leaves have staying power that most flowers don't. While leaves aren't meant to take the place of flowers, and due to that ephemeral quality of flowers, will never be seen as special as the fleeting beauty of most blossoms, they should be given a great deal of consideration when planning and planting a garden. I can honestly say that while different spots of the garden capture my eye as the year goes by and flowers wax and wane, the single most effective combination in the garden, for its pure staying power, is that of three foliage plants on the right side of my front door. There, in an area less than four feet square, the giant pewter rosette of a cardoon (*Cynara cardunculus*, grown as an annual here), a more silver and jagged-leaved version of the artichoke, stands guard over a grassy mound of blue avena grass. At the base of this pair, green and silver variegated *Lamium maculatum* 'White Nancy' spills onto the mauve sandstone path. Every day as I come and go, these three plants serve to remind me that foliage is what truly makes a garden.

(left) In the Rock Alpine Garden at Denver Botanic Gardens, avant-garde curator Panayoti Kelaidis allows giant ornamental rhubarb, Rheum palmatum, a place under aspens and spruce.

(right) Artemisia stellerana and Sedum spurium 'Dragon's Blood' tangle and twine together.

▲ Epimedium x rubrum, *barrenwort*

▲ Bloodroot; Athyrium nipponicum *'Pictum'*,
Japanese painted fern.

▶ *Sempervivum;* Geranium
sessiliflorum *'Nigricans'.*

▲ *Unfurling* Crambe maritima, *sea kale.*

◀ *Tricolor* Houttuynia cordata *'Chameleon'.*

▶ *Pasqueflower seedheads;* Sedum x *'Vera
Jameson'.*

PERENNIALS WITH GOOD FOLIAGE

No woody plants are included here because generally we expect them to have attractive leaves—it is
in our beds and borders where good foliage is most needed.

KEY

B: biennial.

PP: featured in plant portrait section.

**Bold—dramatic focal points,
architectural, tropical-looking**

Acanthus bear's breech
Anemone hupehensis, A. tomentosa, A. vitifolia
   A. x hybrida, Japanese anemone
Aruncus dioicus/sylvester goatsbeard
Bergenia pigsqueak
Brunnera macrophylla Siberian forget-me-not
Caltha palustris marsh marigold
Cimicifuga racemosa snakeroot, bugbane
Clematis heracleifolia davidiana
Crambe sea kale **PP**

Darmera peltata/Peltiphyllum peltatum
Filipendula rubra meadowsweet
Glaucidium palmatum
Helleborus
Heracleum cartwheel flower
Hosta
Inula magnifica, I. helenium
Kirengeshoma palmata
Ligularia
Limonium latifolium sea lavender
Macleaya plume poppy
Paeonia peony **PP**
Petasites
Phlomis russeliana **PP**
Podophyllum mayapple
Rheum palmatum ornamental rhubarb
Rodgersia

Salvia argentea silver sage
Silphium perfoliatum compass plant
Symphytum comfrey **PP**
Telekia/Bupthalmum speciosa
Trachystemon orientale
Veratrum

**FineTextured—fillers and
softeners**

Achillea yarrow
Adonis
Alyssum montanum mountain basket-of-gold
   PP
Anacyclus depressus Mt. Atlas daisy
Antennaria pussytoes **PP**
Anthemis marguerite
Aquilegia columbine

Artemisia wormwood
Aruncus dioicus 'Kneiffii' cutleaf goatsbeard
Astilbe false spiraea
Calamintha nepetoides
Cassia senna
Cerastium snow-in-summer
Chamaemelum nobile Roman chamomile
Coreopsis verticillata threadleaf coreopsis
Coronilla varia crown vetch
Corydalis fumitory
Crucianella (Phuopsis) stylosa crosswort
Dicentra bleeding heart
Epimedium barrenwort
Eryngium bourgatii sea holly
Euphorbia cyparissias cypress spurge
ferns, especially *Adiantum pedatum* and *Osmunda regalis*
Ferula
Filipendula hexapetala dropwort
Galega officinalis goat's rue
Galium odoratum sweet woodruff
Helianthemum sunrose
Lavandula lavender
Paeonia tenuifolia fernleaf peony
Penstemon caespitosus, P. linarioides, P. pinifolius
Perovskia Russian sage
Polemonium Jacob's ladder
Pulsatilla pasqueflower
Ruta graveolens rue
Salvia jurisicii upside-down sage **PP**
Sanguisorba burnet
Santolina lavender cotton
Scabiosa ochroleuca yellow pincushion flower **PP**
Selinum tenuifolium
Semiaquilegia ecalcarata **PP**
Tanacetum **PP**
Thalictrum meadow rue
Thymus thyme
Veronica many of the mat-forming species **PP**

Linear—dynamic motion, cascading or stiff
Armeria sea thrift
Asphodeline Jacob's rod
Dianthus pinks
Eryngium yuccifolium rattlesnake master
grasses, rushes, sedges
Hemerocallis daylily
Iris
Kniphofia red hot poker
Liatris prairie gayfeather
Yucca

Gold/Yellow/Chartreuse/Variegated
Aegopodium podagraria 'Variegata' goutweed

Ajuga reptans 'Variegata' carpet bugle
Alopecurus pratensis 'Aureus'
Arabis fernandi-coburgi 'Variegata'
Arrhenatherum elatius bulbosus 'Variegatus' bulbous oatgrass
Arum italicum 'Pictum' lords and ladies
Astrantia major 'Sunningdale Variegated' Hattie's pincushion
Aurinia saxatilis 'Dudley Neville' basket-of-gold
Brunnera macrophylla 'Hadspen Cream', 'Variegata', 'Langtrees' Siberian forget-me-not
Carex morrowii 'Variegata'
Convallaria majalis 'Variegata'
Cyclamen hederifolium
Disporum sessile 'Variegatum'
Eryngium variifolium sea holly
Filipendula ulmaria 'Aurea'
Fragaria vesca 'Variegata' strawberry
Glyceria maxima 'Variegata'
Hakonechloa macra 'Aureola'
Heuchera micrantha 'Dale's Variety' silver coralbells
Holcus mollis 'Variegatus'
Hosta many
Iris pallida variegated forms
Iris pseudacorus 'Variegatus' yellow flag
Lamiastrum galeobdolon, 'Herman's Pride' yellow archangel
Lamium maculatum dead nettle
Lunaria biennis 'Variegata' honesty **B**
Lysimachia nummularia 'Aurea' golden moneywort
Melissa officinalis 'Aurea', 'Variegata' lemonbalm
Milium effusum 'Aureum'
Miscanthus sinensis 'Strictus', 'Variegatus', 'Zebrinus' maiden grass, eulalia
Origanum vulgare 'Aureum' golden oregano
Phalaris arundinacea 'Picta' gardener's garters
Phlox paniculata 'Nora Leigh', 'Harlequin' garden phlox
Physostegia virginiana 'Variegata' obedient plant
Plantago lanceolata 'Streaker' striped plantain
Polygonatum odoratum 'Variegatum' Solomon's seal
Pulmonaria saccharata, P. longifolia lungwort
Salvia officinalis 'Icterina' culinary sage
Scrophularia aquatica 'Variegata'
Symphytum grandiflorum 'Variegatum' small comfrey
Symphytum x uplandicum 'Variegatum' giant comfrey **PP**

Tanacetum (Chrysanthemum) parthenium 'Aureum' feverfew **PP**
Thymus x citriodorus 'Argenteus', 'Gold Edge' thyme
Vinca minor 'Variegata' periwinkle
Yucca filamentosa 'Golden Sword', 'Bright Edge', 'Variegata'

Tricolor Variegation
Ajuga reptans 'Burgandy Glow' carpet bugle
Athyrium nipponicum 'Pictum' Japanese painted fern
Houttuynia cordata 'Chameleon'
Salvia officinalis 'Tricolor' tricolor garden sage
Sedum spurium 'Tricolor'

Red/Maroon/Bronze/Purple/Copper
Ajuga pyramidalis 'Metallica Crispa' carpet bugle
Ajuga reptans 'Bronze Beauty', 'Atropurpurea' carpet bugle
Astilbe x arendsii 'Fanal', 'Spine' false spiraea
Cimicifuga simplex ramosa 'Atropurpurea', 'Brunette', Braunlaub'
Clematis recta 'Purpurea'
Dryopteris erythrosora
Epimedium x rubrum barrenwort
Geranium sessiliflorum 'Nigricans'
Heuchera micrantha 'Garnet', 'Palace Purple'
Imperata cylindrica 'Red Baron' Japanese blood grass
Ligularia dentata 'Desdemona', 'Othello'
Lychnis x arkwrightii
Lysimachia ciliata 'Rubra' redleaf loosestrife
Penstemon digitalis 'Husker Red' **PP**
Plantago major 'Atropurpurea' red-leaf plantain
Ranunculus ficaria 'Brazen Hussy' celandine
Rheum palmatum 'Atrosanguineum' red-leaf rhubarb
Salvia officinalis 'Purpurea' purple culinary sage
Sedum maximum 'Atropurpureum'
Sedum spurium 'Red Carpet'
Sedum x 'Vera Jameson'
Sempervivum many forms hens and chicks
Tellima grandiflora 'Rubra' fringe cups
Viola labradorica

Silver/Gray
Achillea yarrow many
Allium karataviense
Alyssum montanum mountain basket-of-gold **PP**
Anaphalis pearly everlasting
Antennaria pussytoes **PP**

Anthemis biebersteiniana, A. cupaniana
   marguerite
Artemisia sage
Aurinia saxatilis basket-of-gold
Ballota
Cerastium snow-in-summer
Erodium chrysanthum silver storksbill
Eriogonum buckwheat many
Eriophyllum lanatum woolly sunflower
Helianthemum sunrose many
Helichrysum everlasting many
Hieracium lanatum silver hawksbeard
Lavandula lavender
Lychnis coronaria rose campion
Marrubium horehound **PP**
Mentha longifolia
Nepeta phyllochlamys
Onosma alboroseum, O. sericea
Perovskia Russian sage
Potentilla nivea silver cinquefoil
Psilostrophe paperflower
Raoulia vegetable sheep
Salvia argenta, S. cyanescens, S. dorrii,
   S. lavandulifolia, S. officinalis sage
Santolina lavender cotton
Scabiosa graminifolia
Sedum spathulifolium
Sideritis **PP**
Stachys betony many
Tanacetum densum var. *amani, T. niveum* **PP**
Teucrium marum, T. polium germander
Thymus mastichinus, T. pseudolanuginosus
   thyme
Veronica bombycina, V. cinerea,
   V. incana
Zauschneria California fuchsia some **PP**

Blue
Aethionema stone cress
Agave parryi century plant
Allium senescens 'Glaucum'
Aquilegia columbine many
Arundo donax giant reed grass
Asphodeline lutea Jacob's rod
Baptisia australis false blue indigo
Centranthus ruber Greek valerian
Crambe maritima sea kale **PP**
Dianthus pinks some
Dicentra eximia, D. 'Stuart Boothman'
   bleeding heart
Elymus arenarius/glaucus lyme grass
Eryngium maritimum sea holly
Euphorbia myrsinites, E. rigida, E. nicaensis
   spurge
Festuca ovina var. *glauca* sheep's fescue

Gypsophila baby's breath
Helictotrichon sempervirens blue avena
   grass
Hosta many
Hypericum cerastioides, H. olympicum
Iris germanica, I. pallida
Linaria genistifolia var. *dalmatica* yellow toadflax
Lysimachia ephemerum
Macleaya plume poppy
Mertensia asiatica, M. ciliata chiming bells
Rudbeckia maxima giant black-eyed Susan
Rumex scutatus creeping sorrel
Ruta graveolens rue
Sanguinaria canadensis bloodroot
Sedum some
Silene vulgaris ssp. *maritima* sea campion
Thalictrum minus T. speciosissimum, meadow rue

Glossy
Aconitum monkshood
Ajuga reptans carpet bugle
Asarum europaeum, A. hartwegii ginger
Astilbe false spiraea
Bergenia pigsqueak
Chelone turtlehead
Dictamnus albus gas plant
Helleborus orientalis Lenten rose
Paeonia peony
Patrinia
Polystichum acrostichoides Christmas fern
Ranunculus buttercup many
Sedum kamtschaticum
Sidalcea checkerbloom
Synthyris missurica **PP**
Vinca minor periwinkle
Waldsteinia ternata barren strawberry

Just Plain Pretty
Actaea baneberry
Alchemilla lady's mantle
Arisaema
Arum
Callirhoe buffalo rose **PP**
Centaurea bella, C. dealbata, C. hypoleuca,
   C. ruthenica knapweed
Cimicifuga snakeroot, bugbane
Echinops globe thistle
Erodium storksbill
Heucherella tiarelloides
Geranium cranesbill
Geum
Gillenia trifoliata bowman's root
Incarvillea olgae
Lathyrus vernus spring vetchling
Lavatera shrub mallow **PP**

Lupinus lupine
Malva mallow **PP**
Paris polyphylla
Potentilla cinquefoil
Smilacina false Solomon's seal
Thermopsis golden banner **PP**
Tiarella foam flower
Trillium wake robin
Trollius globe flower
Veronicastrum culver's root

Annuals, Biennials, Tender Plants
Angelica **B**
Asparagus densiflorus asparagus fern
Atriplex hortensis 'Rubra' red orach **PP**
Begonia
Beta swiss and ruby chard
Brassica ornamental kale
Caladium
Canna x *generalis*
Cirsium spinosissimum **B**
Coleus x *hybridus*
Colocasia esculenta elephant ear
Cynara cardoon
Dahlia x *hybrida* 'Bishop Llandaff'
Dolichos lablab hyacinth bean
Foeniculum vulgare 'Purpureum' purple fennel **PP**
Fuchsia several selections with reddish
   or variegated leaves
Glaucium horned poppy **B**
Helichrysum petiolatum, 'Mo's Gold' licorice plant
Hibiscus acetosella 'Coppertone' redleaf hibiscus
Hypoestes phyllostachya polkadot plant
Impatiens New Guinea strains
Ipomoea batatas 'Blackie' black sweet potato vine
Ipomoea quamoclit cypress vine
Lotus berthelotii lotus vine
Ocimum basilicum 'Purple Ruffles', 'Dark Opal'
Onopordum Scots thistle **B**
Papaver triniifolium Armenian poppy **B, PP**
Pelargonium geranium
Perilla frutescens beefsteak plant
Ricinus communis castor bean
Salvia aethiopis, S. argentea, S. microstegia,
   S. sclarea sage **B, PP** sage
Senecio cineraria dusty miller
Setcreasea pallida 'Purple Heart' purple
   wandering Jew
Silybum marianum milk thistle
Tropaeolum majus nasturtium
Verbascum mullein **B, PP**

IV

Roses for
Realists

It takes a cold, atrophied heart not to be swept away by the beauty of an opulent rose gar-den. Graceful swelling buds announce the beginning of the June flush, a magical time full of hope and high spirits: brides in white, graduates with great expectations and gardens spilling over with fragrant roses. Any rose grower knows, however, that there is much work behind each perfect blossom. I know, from three years of slavery to an estate planting of over four hundred hybrid teas, floribundas, climbers and miniatures, that rose growing is no picnic. While guests would stroll through the formal rose beds at twilight, pastel gowns rustling and cocktails in hand, I was home tending my scratches, showering off the sweat from hours spent encased in a nonbreathing moon suit spray-ing the prima donnas for black spot, powdery mildew, aphids, spider mites or whatever the insect or disease of the hour. The rose season would begin in the cold winds of April, with the removal of mounds of mulch from the bushes. Then came careful prun-ing of the canes, my chilled wrists eaten alive by thorns. Summer meant a rigid sched-ule of feeding, watering and spraying. Then there was late fall, just before the holidays, when several cold days were spent mounding mulch over the canes, mummifying climb-ers in burlap and performing miniature burial ceremonies on the tree roses. All this effort did indeed produce a lovely rose garden. To my surprise and relief, when I left that mid-Atlantic garden, I learned that growing roses is different here.

(preceding pages) 'William Lobb'
rose, also known as old velvet
moss, is joined by Geranium
pratense *'Mrs. Kendall Clarke'*
and perennial yellow foxglove,
Digitalis grandiflora.

First, fungal diseases like black spot, rust and powdery mildew are much less ram-pant in the dry, windy air of the continental West. I categorically do not spray any of my roses. While this costs me a few plants here and there, it is a far cry from what would happen had I opted for the same philosophy back in Pennsylvania. One particu-lar gallica rose did seem overly prone to mildew, so after two years I removed the weakling. The much-heralded new shrub rose 'Bonica' came down with black spot its first season in the garden and had severe dieback that winter, so out it went. All the others, so far, have been unmarred.

Second, there are no Japanese beetles to contend with here. These gluttonous me-tallic insects took up many of my summer mornings back in Philadelphia, when I would pace methodically up and down the rose beds, picking the sleeping orgiasts from what

▲ *Roses 'Louise Odier' and 'Windrush' share the garden with purple sweet rocket, blush pink cranesbill, Silene fimbriata and the spikes of white-flowered fireweed.*

remained of the blossoms and drowning them in a jar of kerosene. Walking up to what was a perfect six-inch 'Peace' rose blossom the day before, I would find it hanging in tatters, full of beetle frass, with a few lingering insects precariously copulating on the edge of the last untouched petal. This I don't miss in the least.

Aphids and spider mites are still with us out here on the prairie, however, as are earwigs, leaf-cutter bees, cane borers and other various and sundry pests. And the need to add compost to the soil and water, water, water is much more crucial than along the East Coast. The intense sun and dry air make it possible, in some cases even preferable—especially with pastel-colored roses—to grow roses where they receive afternoon shade. The east side of the house has worked out well for me—gentle morning sun until early afternoon, then a cooling respite for the rest of the day. Contrary to the west side, which is hotter and can cause more winterkill because the canes are warmed and brought out of dormancy earlier, the east side is ideal in many ways: It lessens the need for watering, keeps the spider mite population down, and helps the pale blossoms last longer without fading. Fragrance, intensified by humidity, returns to the rose garden once it is lightly shaded. In addition, many wonderful companion plants thrive in this more benign siting along with the roses.

The last and most important lesson I learned about rose growing in this harsh climate is that many of the modern roses I fussed over so diligently back East will succumb to the winters here, if not immediately, then after only a few years, no matter to what lengths the gardener goes. Nursery people won't let the cat out of the bag regarding this, because replacement rose bushes account for a lot of spring business. There's something utterly relieving about having fate make a decision for you. I had already decided more or less that I was more interested in growing tough, easy roses—shrub roses, species roses, many of the old garden roses—but I was elated to be forced out of even contemplating the possibility of planting a garden full of hybrid teas and floribundas. I still grow a few of my very favorite modern roses—those that offer a particular color I crave, and those that are tougher than the rest of the pack and still can give me those four months of indefatigable bloom. At the heart of my ever-growing rose garden is a vision of the most beautiful and toughest roses grown with a profusion of perennials, herbs and annuals, a far cry from the ungainly, pesticide-drenched, stilted stick figures raising huge ungainly flower pompoms in the air over a thick carpet of brown bark mulch. Yuck.

While a majority of the hardiest roses bloom only once a year, causing many gardeners to ignore them outright, their shrublike, fuller, lusher forms make them an asset to the garden long after they have dropped the last petal to the ground. Unlike the gawky, stiff, sparsely leaved canes of hybrid teas and many of the floribundas, shrub, species and old garden roses look and act like good old-fashioned shrubs in the garden. Spiraea, mock orange and lilacs are all allowed to bloom only once, so why not the rose? Roses actually have much better foliage than these three old favorites, and some offer attractive fall color or fruit to boot. Many have exceptionally good form as well—arching, drooping, cascading or just making a dense, well-formed shrub. Reblooming roses, of course, are to be sought out; this I can't deny. But most certainly I have made and will continue to make room for the one-time bloomers. They are too wonderful to do without.

Species Roses

The first roses to bloom in my garden are several of the species roses: large, shrubby and demonically prickly in demeanor yet so demure when in flower. They are truly no-care roses. When I planted them, bare-root in late April in most cases, I made a two-foot wide, eighteen-inch-deep hole and mixed the soil with compost and old horse manure. Other than that and a few sporadic waterings in midsummer when I feel particularly motherly, have watering can in hand and the cisterns are full, they have been left totally to their own devices. Pruning after several years—the twiggiest, weakest growth and the oldest, least vigorous canes—will do them some good but is not necessary. Winter protection is a waste of time; they don't need it, and even if they did, how does one protect a six-foot by five-foot thorny mass of canes?

I grow most of my species roses out behind the house rather than in the so-called rose area, for several reasons. One, they are dog-proof, and the backyard desperately needs some ornamental plants that can't be chewed on, jumped in or just plain run over. Two, they are the most drought resistant group of roses, which goes along with the no-care philosophy of the back, a yard rather than a garden. Finally, these species roses are very large and bloom only once, so they would take up too much precious space, handsome though they are, in the more densely planted, smaller, more floriferous rose area on the east side of the house.

The first to bloom is the Father Hugo rose, *Rosa hugonis*, whose arching, ferny foliaged burgundy canes become smothered in primrose yellow single blossoms. I planted this large but graceful, fine-textured rose next to a hedge of lilacs, which bloom at the same time. The soft lavender trusses of the lilacs combine beautifully with the simple pale yellow faces of the rose. Sky blue forget-me-not flowers of *Brunnera macrophylla* or the periwinkle-blue spikes of the bulbous Spanish bluebell, *Hyacinthoides hispanica* (aka *Endymion hispanicus*) would make good underplantings in areas not ravaged by cavorting animals.

A totally different color effect takes place just a week or so after Father Hugo has finished. Then the Austrian copper rose, *Rosa foetida bicolor*, begins to flower. While its form is not the best, the lovely two-inch copper-orange single blossoms are the star of the garden in mid- to late May. If it weren't for the dogs, I would plant it with several crimson pygmy barberries and an underplanting of late orange and red tulips and chartreuse lady's mantle to enhance the brilliant orange flowers, which are such an unusual color for this time of year.

I received my Father Hugo rose accidentally, instead of Harison's yellow rose, which is what I had ordered. After two years of searching, I finally got a piece of this latter rose from an old shrub in Denver and am hoping it will grow quickly and start flowering. For me, *Rosa* x *harisonii* is perhaps the most romantic rose. Rather than the frou-frou stories of jealous court battles, rose petal baths and corsetted ladies that go along with the beautiful French garden roses of the eighteenth and nineteenth centuries, I like the pioneer past of Harison's yellow rose. It grows stalwartly among the broken and bleached split rails and sagging clapboards of countless abandoned farmsteads and ranches throughout the Midwest, Texas and the Great Plains. One of the finest specimens I've seen grows next to the abandoned Prairie Country Store on the border between South Dakota and Wyoming in the Black Hills where I made a pitstop one June. Two outhouses, marked Buffalo Bill and Calamity Jane, beckoned to this desperate traveler. But the masses of semidouble flowers the color of sunshine against the deep blue prairie sky stopped me on the way to my mission. Back home and paired with five-foot, azure blue *Anchusa azurea*, a short-lived perennial that thrives in full sun and relatively dry soil, this tough rose is a much anticipated and welcome addition to the garden of this recent western transplant.

▲ *Pinks, bronze fennel and* Tanacetum niveum *frame the hardy modern rose 'Iceberg'.*

Rugosa Roses

▲ *David Austin rose 'Mary Rose'.*

▲ Rosa rugosa *Blanc Double de Coubert'.*

The next group of roses to bloom are the rugosas, long the stepchild of the rose world. Their full, vigorous growth, exceptional disease resistance and hardiness must have made them suspect in the over-refined minds of the movers and shakers in rose circles. Anything that comes too easily is often considered proletarian; let those snobs spray and fuss to their hearts' delight. Rugosa roses are fabulous—aside from being easy to grow, they are fragrant, repeat-blooming, often have a golden- or burgundy-touched fall color and many form the largest, showiest fruits, called hips, in the rose kingdom. Tolerance of drought and poor soil conditions—clay or sand—and resistance to strong, drying winds (and to dogs) complete their long list of desirable attributes. Their name "rugosa" refers to the wrinkled or rugose appearance of the leaves; I like to think it also refers to rugged. I grow five varieties of this rose right now; I would like to grow many more but they are generally quite large, and space is getting scarcer all the time.

Rosa rugosa 'Alba' is a six-foot by six-foot, lush behemoth with charmingly simple, large single flowers of pristine white surrounding a dense cluster of golden stamens. Hips the size and color of cherry tomatoes begin to form by midsummer, appearing simultaneously with the later flowers. A bit smaller and with showier, semidouble white blossoms is 'Blanc Double de Coubert', unfortunately fruitless. Both these shrubs mingle well with purple smokebush or the ethereal pink sprays of the small tree *Tamarix ramosissimum*, also called saltspray cedar. Deep maroon hollyhocks and pink and white

▲ Harison's yellow rose graces an abandoned store in South Dakota.

▼ Rosa rugosa 'Agnes'.

▲ 'Windrush' rose blends with white spires of Campanula latifolia and fireweed.

cleome and cosmos might add a nice note of contrasting color and texture, and contribute extra flower power in midsummer when the roses are slowing down a bit.

Many rugosa rose selections come in strong shades of fuchsia, magenta, crimson and reddish purple. One might combine them with similarly toned fireweed (*Epilobium angustifolium*) in an area that gets average moisture. The invasive character of the fireweed isn't a problem in a large shrub border. In fact, I think of it as an asset; the graceful flower spikes of this perennial look wonderful let loose to wander in and out of large shrubs. Similarly huge, aggressive plume poppy (*Macleaya cordata*, not *M. microcarpa*—the former has creamy white panicles of flowers while the latter has dirty tan ones, reminiscent of the ugliest shade of cheap nylons) can be let loose among the shrubs. Its beautiful wavy-edged blue-green leaves show silvery undersides when they turn in the wind.

I prefer to grow the clearer pink cultivars of *Rosa rugos*a. 'Jens Munk', a five-foot by five-foot beauty developed in the prolific hardy rose breeding program in Ottawa, blooms all summer. Its semidouble flowers are one of the most well formed of the sometimes coarse-looking rugosa blossoms and a good medium pink. It produces relatively few hips but of a good red color. The other pink rugosa I grow is 'Fru Dagmar Hastrup', which can be easily accommodated in smaller gardens due to its compact three-foot by three-foot dimensions. This rose is the epitome of all the best of the species: large, single, blush-pink flowers waft a delicious fragrance into the air from early June until October; huge red hips and golden fall color grace the plant as the season draws to a close.

The last rugosa I grow at this time acts more like a species rose in the garden in that it only blooms once for me. I had to have it, though, for its color and lovely ruffled flower shape. 'Agnes' is a tall, coarse rugosa shrub, but makes up for its lack of year-round appeal during the three weeks it blooms. I am a fool for yellow-flowered roses of all kinds, and 'Agnes' has the most perfect, nonacid yellow color, tawny and warm like butterscotch and cream. With some giant lavender drumstick onions (*Allium aflatunense*, much prettier and more dependable than the ungainly *A. giganteum*) rising through and beside it, 'Agnes' is a sight to behold.

Hardy Roses from Canada

The Canadians have done a great deal of work producing ever-blooming, tough, hardy roses this century. Unfortunately, many of these fine roses are unavailable in the United States. There are two new introductions that have me contemplating a run for the border. 'John Davis' is a bone-hardy, ever-blooming large shrub rose of great promise. Its semidouble, soft rose-pink flowers are the most finely formed of any new hardy rose I have seen. They rival the old garden roses for charm. This rose, from all photographs and descriptions, has more elegance and less coarseness than any with similarly tough constitutions. The plant is tall enough to double as a climber or pillar rose. I thought I had to relegate all those lush, fragrant rose trellises to my maritime memories.

Growing climbing roses in this climate is a real game of Russian roulette. Unless they are laid flat on the ground and covered, or bundled with several layers of burlap or polystyrene in the winter, chances are slim that the vigorous canes produced the year before, which bear next year's flowers, will come through unscathed.

The other rose I crave is 'J. P. Connell', a hardy, double yellow, repeat-blooming shrub rose. The flowers start off deep yellow in graceful, pointed buds, open lemon and fade to cream. Need I say more? Visions of this yellow beauty with the narrow lavender-blue spikes of ladybells (*Adenophora* spp.), or mounds of *Geranium* x 'Johnson's Blue' spilling out from beneath, like the sugar plums greedy children dream of the night before Christmas, are dancing in my head.

The east side of our house, a strip approximately thirty feet long and fifteen feet wide, has become my rose garden. Here I have jammed nearly a dozen old garden roses and a few modern, ever-blooming roses in with perennials, annuals and herbs. The area was parched, overfertilized, underwatered bluegrass when we moved here in late summer. I let the grass dry out completely to weaken it, and then turned it under with a spade over a period of two months in late fall and early winter, before the ground froze solid. We spread several pickup loads of old horse manure on top, about six to eight inches worth over the entire area. This was then tilled in the spring by my husband—I'm desperately afraid of Rototillers after having been dragged behind one that ran amuck early in my gardening career. I laid black rubber soaker hoses lengthwise down the area, at two-foot intervals, and then got down to the fun part over the next two years—planting and experimenting with combinations in this part of the garden, the most traditional area in terms of culture, style and plant choice. Its soft demeanor—billowing roses, heady fragrances, pastel tones—reminds me of those wonderful gardens of the British Isles that have inspired so many gardeners, for better or worse, on this side of the Atlantic.

 Europeans have mingled roses with other plants since the dawn of gardening there, in monastery gardens where herbs, flowers and the apothecary rose, *Rosa gallica officinalis*, were allowed to consort. Herbs remain a superb choice for companion plantings to roses. Their fragrances attract the gardener while in many cases repelling insects and other pests, and the often fine-textured flowers and foliage make a perfect foil for the more voluptuous, attention-getting blossoms of the roses. Lacy blue leaves of rue; the licorice-scented, ferny, maroon-tinted foliage of bronze fennel and the pewter filigree of my favorite artemisia, 'Powis Castle', all blend well with the larger roses toward the back of the garden. These roses are dominated by the albas, dependably hardy and easy-care old garden roses that only bloom once, for a good month in early summer, with sweetly fragrant cabbage-like flowers in white and shades of blush and soft pink.

Old Garden Roses and Companions

▲ *In late spring, red-leaf and 'Frühlingsgold' roses mingle with yellow biennial woad, Isatis tinctoria.*

I grow four albas in the east-facing garden: All are full bushes with little or no cane dieback in winter, and covered with blemish-free, gray-green leaves during the growing season. This great foliage sets off the pale flowers to perfection. 'Celestial', shell pink and semidouble; 'Félicité Parmentier', the smallest of the four, with fully double, blush pink flowers; 'Madame Plantier', covered with extremely double white flowers; and 'Königin von Dänemark', with the classic quartered petal arrangement to its full soft pink flowers, all take up the rear part of this long garden bed. With the rich manure-amended soil, supplemental watering and the relief of cool shade in the afternoon, this part of the garden suits two short-lived, rather persnickety plants well: Both the tall spikes of delphinium hybrids in pale lavender, white, rose and sky blue, and the massive trusses of rose and white foxgloves (*Digitalis purpurea*) complement the color and form of the alba roses.

I also grow three gallica roses, hardy and tough and with a long history. The origin of this group of roses, with intensely fragrant and richly hued crimson, purple or maroon flowers, is the French or apothecary rose, *Rosa gallica officinalis*, which has been used for medicine and perfume for centuries. The petals of the gallicas are so fragrant, fresh or dried, that they make the best

100

▲ *Blue Chinese forget-me-not,* Cynoglossum amabile, *enhances Austin rose 'Bredon'.*

▼ Rosa foetida *'Persiana' and gold-tipped juniper make a gilded pair.*

▲ Rosa hugonis, *Father Hugo rose.*

▲ Rosa rugosa *'Roseraie de l'Haÿ'.*

▲ Rosa *'Sea Foam'.*

▲ Rosa gallica *'Tuscany Superb'.*

▼ Rosa gallica *'Versicolor' aka* Rosa mundi.

potpourri of any rose as well as having more esoteric uses such as wine, jam and syrup. Gallicas have lush, full foliage and grow into a dense bush. The leaves are dull green and have a characteristic "hang dog" appearance, with the oval, pointed leaflets drooping slightly. The gallicas are slightly smaller than the albas and take up the middle tier of roses in the bed along with their historical partners, a bevy of attractive herbs. 'Belle de Crécy' has double flowers that start off purplish pink, fading to violet and almost gray-lavender. 'Charles de Mills' blends crimson, maroon and purple in its full, flat blossoms, while 'Cardinal de Richelieu' sports large, evenly deep, ruffly purple flowers. With white sprays of double-flowered feverfew, the airy, fragrant white cymes of valerian (*Valeriana officinalis*), and the opalescent spikes of clary sage (*Salvia sclarea*), the tradition of herbs and roses lives on in this garden. Annual purple basil, the chartreuse foam of lady's mantle and the misty blue flowers of borage and catmint (*Nepeta* x *faassenii*) complete the picture.

Once the old-fashioned albas and gallicas have finished flowering, I depend on other plants to take up the flowering slack. Several annuals are worked in every year, many without my help but with my gratitude, thanks to their self-sowing ways, as is the case with tall but delicate-looking purple *Verbena bonariensis*, spikes of blue, lavender and pink larkspur (*Consolida ambigua*) and the frothy ground-covering sweet alyssum, blue *Asperula orientalis* and jaunty purple Johnny-jump-ups (*Viola tricolor* 'Helen Mount' and 'King Henry'). Other annuals require that I grow them every year from seed and then place them about the garden. Fragrant white *Nicotiana sylvestris* is the largest, at five feet to six feet, and so needs careful placement. The graceful, unhybridized white *N. alata*, which opens in the evening, is also usually included. A compact variety of cosmos, 'Sonata', with a never-ending parade of fresh white daisy-like flowers, mingles in the middle of the bed. There are many other annuals that might consort well with roses; the key is to avoid the flashiest, most overbearing ones and seek out airy, soft-colored species with smaller flowers than the newest hybrids. These same attributes are desired in perennial companions to roses—the roses should take center stage. Fragrant annuals and perennials can turn a rose garden into a paradise for the senses.

Modern Roses and Companions

Although I am incurably smitten by the charms of old garden roses, the fact that most bloom for only a few short weeks in early summer makes it necessary to look into the ever-expanding realm of modern roses to get the desired long season of rose bloom. Of these, I demand the hardiest, most disease resistant hybrids, and also those with the fullest growth habit. Two ever-blooming floribundas have proven themselves. 'Iceberg' is a leafy, robust shrub bearing a profusion of white semidouble to double flowers whose daintiness belies the ugly name, which should have been translated 'Snow White' from the original German 'Schneewitchen'. The other, another German import with an ungainly name—'Gruss An Aachen'—is a smaller plant with larger, ruffly double cream flowers blushed peach and flesh pink. Both these roses combine well with deep bronze-purple. The foliage of *Heuchera micrantha* 'Palace Purple' and both the flowers and leaves of bee balm 'Prairie Night' are wonderful companions to these two pale floribunda roses, giving four months of good color contrast.

The modern roses that have really taken my breath away these past few years are the so-called English garden roses, creations of the fine British hybridizer David Austin. This man, astute to the charms of old garden roses, sought to combine their graceful flower form, full shrubby growth and dependable fragrance with the ever-blooming qualities and peach, apricot and soft yellow tones found only in the modern hybrids. A great number of roses have come from this prolific and successful breeding program. While most are not as hardy as the albas or gallicas, they nevertheless are much tougher than your standard-issue hybrid tea. I neither spray nor prune them, but after a hard winter where most of their canes died almost to the ground, I now take the trouble to mound a foot of bark mulch over their crowns in early December. The beauty, unusual colors and long season of bloom they give my rose garden makes the little extra effort worthwhile. From a choice of several dozen in all shades known to the rose kingdom, I concentrated on the peach, buff, creamy yellow and flesh pink tones, an antidote to the preponderance of lavender-pink, crimson and purple old garden roses. They are clustered on one end of the bed to avoid an otherwise awful color clash. The largest and hardiest, 'Windrush', a single to semidouble creamy yellow number, stands well in the back, requiring no winter mulch and growing fuller every year. It is surrounded by the dangling lime bells of annual *Nicotiana langsdorfii* and perennials yellow columbine and blue *Campanula persicifolia*.

Closer to the middle and front of the bed I have planted 'Perdita', a double soft apricot; 'Belle Story', semidouble and peach-pink; buff 'Bredon' and peach 'English Garden'. Blue Chinese forget-me-not (*Cynoglossum amabile*), much tougher than its namesake, lime nicotiana hybrids and old-fashioned eighteen-inch ageratum 'Cut Wonder' make up the annual companions. A group of softly colored and textured perennials whose seed I collected while in Ireland finish the composition. Pale lavender-blue striped *Geranium pratense* 'Mrs. Kendall Clarke', the similarly toned spikes of *Salvia pratensis* 'Sky Blue', delicate pale yellow flower sprays of *Nepeta govaniana* and the fringed white blossoms of *Silene fimbriata*, with chartreuse calyces, all manage to evoke nostalgia while making perfect bedfellows for the similarly romantic and evocative Austin roses.

These are but a few combinations possible in a good-size rose garden. Just as a true queen is enhanced by an attractive court, the queen of flowers—the rose—deserves companions other than mulch. Spike forms, misty lacelike umbels and cymes and fine textures in both flowers and foliage are companion-plant traits that guarantee to please. Pale lavender blues go well with the softest pastels and the richest, brightest scarlets and oranges. With the best of the hardiest roses and the best companions, a garden in the harsh continental interior can have the nostalgic delicacy of the finest European rose garden.

▲ White-flowered fireweed, Epilobium angustifolium *'Album'*, leans casually on Bourbon rose *'Louise Odier'*.

◄ The intricate blossoms of columbine and Rosa *'Variegata di Bologna'* grow side by side.

► One of David Austin's first roses, *'Constance Spry'*, rises from a carpet of cranesbill and catmint.

GREAT HARDY ROSES

SPECIES ROSES
Rosa eglanteria sweetbriar rose, pink
Rosa foetida bicolor Austrian copper rose,
    orange **PP**
Rosa foetida persiana, yellow
Rosa glauca red-leaf rose, pink **PP**
Rosa hugonis Father Hugo rose, yellow
Rosa moyesii 'Geranium' red, 'Highdownensis'
    cerise
Rosa nitida rose
Rosa primula yellow
Rosa spinossissima burnet rose 'Altaica',
    'Hispida', Stanwell Perpetual' white
Rosa virginiana pink
Rosa woodsii woods rose, pink
Rosa x harisonii Harison's yellow rose

RUGOSA HYBRIDS
'Agnes' yellow
'Alba' white
'Blanc Double de Coubert' white
'Fimbriata' blush white
'Fru Dagmar Hastrup' pink
'Hansa' rose-purple
'Hunter' red

'Jens Munk' pink
'Max Graf' rose
'Mrs. Anthony Waterer' rose-purple
'Roseraie de L'Häy' rose-purple
'Ruskin' red
'Scabrosa' rose-purple
'Schneezwerg' white
'Thérèse Bugnet' pink

RECENT EVER-BLOOMING HYBRIDS
'Applejack' pink/red blend
'Ballerina' blush pink
'Charles Albanel' red
'Cuthbert Grant' red
'David Thompson' red
'Goldbusch' yellow
'Henry Hudson' blush white
'Martin Frobisher' blush pink
'Morden Blush' blush pink
'Nearly Wild' pink
'Prairie Dawn' pink
'Prairie Princess' pink
'Prairie Star' white
'Sea Foam' white
'Sparrieshoop' pink
'The Fairy' pink

CLIMBERS FOR HARSH CLIMATES
'Captain Samuel Holland' red
'Constance Spry' pink

'John Davis' pink
'Louis Jolliet' pink
'William Baffin' rose
'William Lobb' rose-purple

ROSA GALLICA SELECTIONS
'Belle de Crécy' pink
'Cardinal de Richelieu' rose-purple
'Charles de Mills' rose
'Ipsilanté' pink
'Tuscany Superb' burgundy
'Versicolor' aka *Rosa mundi* striped rose
    and white

ROSA X ALBA SELECTIONS
'Celestial' pink
'Félicité Parmentier' pink
'Königin von Dänemark' pink
'Madame Legras de St. Germain' white
'Madame Plantier' white
'Maiden's Blush' pink
'Semiplena' white **PP**

OTHER HARDY OLD GARDEN ROSES
'Comte de Chambord' pink
'Louise Odier' pink
'Madame Hardy' white
'Rose de Rescht' rose-purple
'Tour de Malakoff' ('Black Jack') rose-
    purple

COMPANIONS FOR ROSES

SPIKE FORMS
Adenophora ladybells
Consolida ambigua annual larkspur
Delphinium
Dictamnus albus gas plant
Digitalis foxglove
Epilobium angustifolium fireweed **PP**
Galega officinalis goat's rue
Liatris gayfeather
Linaria toadflax
Lythrum salicaria purple loosestrife
Nepeta sibirica **PP**
Penstemon—moisture-tolerant ones like
    P. digitalis 'Husker Red' **PP**
Phlomis russeliana **PP**
Physostegia virginiana obedient plant
Salvia pratensis, S. sclarea **PP**, *Salvia x*
    superba sage
Sidalcea checker mallow

Stachys byzantina, S. grandiflora lamb's ears,
    betony
Veronica

LACY AND PUFFY FORMS— UMBELS AND CYMES
Ageratum houstonianum tall forms,
    annual
Ammi majus annual Queen Anne's lace
Anthriscus sylvestris
Asperula orientalis annual, blue woodruff
Cleome hasslerana annual, spider flower
Conium maculatum biennial, poison
    hemlock
Crucianella stylosa/Phuopsis stylosa
    crosswort
Daucus carota biennial Queen Anne's
    lace
Galium odoratum sweet woodruff

Monarda didyma, M. fistulosa bee balm
Pimpinella
Trachymene caerulea (aka *Didiscus*) annual,
    blue lace flower
Valeriana officinalis valerian
Verbena rigida annual, **PP**, *V. bonariensis*,
    annual

MISTY, FROTHY, AIRY FLOWERS
Alchemilla mollis lady's mantle
Aster ericoides heath aster **PP**
Campanula lactiflora milky bellflower
Gillenia trifoliata/Porteranthus trifoliatus
    bowman's root
Heuchera sanguinea coralbells
Heucherella tiarelloides 'Bridget Bloom'
Lobularia maritima annual, sweet alyssum
Nepeta govaniana, N. x faassenii catmint
Tanacetum (Chrysanthemum) parthenium
    feverfew **PP**

GROUND COVERS FOR ROSES

Alchemilla mollis lady's mantle
Asperula orientalis blue woodruff, annual
Campanula poscharskyana creeping bell
    flower
Cerastium tomentosum snow-in-summer
Crucianella stylosa/Phuopsis stylosa
    crosswort
Galium odoratum sweet woodruff
Geranium macrorrhizum, G. x cantabrigiense
Lobularia maritima annual, sweet alyssum
Nepeta x faassenii catmint
Nigella damascena annual, love-in-a-mist
Symphytum grandiflorum lesser comfrey
Veronica
Viola tricolor reseeding annual, Johnny-
    jump-up

HERBS

Artemisia wormwood
Atriplex hortensis 'Rubra' annual, red orach **PP**
Borago officinalis annual, borage
Foeniculum vulgare 'Purpureum' annual,
    bronze fennel **PP**
Galium odoratum sweet woodruff
Hyssopus officinalis hyssop
Lavandula angustifolia lavender
Ocimum basilicum, purple forms especially,
    annual, basil
Perilla frutescens annual, beefsteak plant
Ruta graveolens rue
Salvia officinalis, S. sclarea **PP** biennial,
    sage
Symphytum comfrey **PP**
Tanacetum (Chrysanthemum) parthenium
    feverfew **PP**
Valeriana officinalis valerian

FOLIAGES

Alchemilla mollis lady's mantle
Artemisia wormwood
Atriplex hortensis 'Rubra' annual, red orach **PP**
Cynara cardunculus annual, cardoon
Foeniculum vulgare 'Purpureum' annual,
    bronze fennel **PP**
Galium odoratum sweet woodruff
Hibiscus acetosella 'Red Shield' annual
Ocimum basilicum purple forms, annual,
    basil
Perilla frutescens annual, beefsteak plant
Ruta graveolens rue
Senecio cineraria annual, dusty miller

Stachys byzantina lamb's ears
Symphytum x uplandicum 'Variegatum'
    comfrey **PP**

BOLD PLANTS FOR LARGER ROSE PLANTINGS

Acanthus spinosissimus bear's breeches
Alcea rosea, A. rugosa hollyhock **PP**
Allium aflatunense ornamental onion
Anchusa italica alkanet
Anemone x hybrida Japanese anemone
Cleome hasslerana annual, spider flower
Cosmos bipinnatus annual
Cynara cardunculus cardoon, annual
Delphinium
Digitalis purpurea foxglove
Epilobium angustifolium fireweed **PP**
Lactuca bourgaei
Lavatera thuringiaca shrub mallow **PP**
Lilium lily **PP**
Lycoris squamigera naked ladies, surprise lily
Macleaya cordata plume poppy
Nicotiana sylvestris annual, flowering
    tobacco
Salvia sclarea clary sage, biennial **PP**

OTHER GOOD COMPANIONS

Aquilegia columbine
Campanula carpatica, C. persicifolia
    bellflower
Clematis integrifolia **PP**
Eryngium sea holly **PP**
Geranium grandiflorum 'Plenum', *G. pratense,*
    G. sanguineum var. *striatum, G. x*
    'Johnson's Blue', *G. x magnificum*
Knautia macedonica **PP**
Lychnis coronaria rose campion
Malva alcea 'Fastigiata', *M. moschata*
    mallow **PP**
Monarda didyma bee balm
Saponaria ocymoides, S. officinalis soapwort
Silene fimbriata

ANNUALS

Ageratum houstonianum tall forms
Asperula orientalis reseeding, blue
    woodruff
Atriplex hortensis 'Rubra' red orach,
    reseeding **PP**
Borago officinalis reseeding, borage
Cleome hasslerana reseeding, spider
    flower

Consolida ambigua reseeding, larkspur
Cosmos bipinnatus, 'Sonata Series' shorter,
    reseeding
Cynara cardunculus cardoon
Cynoglossum amabile Chinese
    forget-me-not, reseeding **PP**
Digitalis purpurea biennial
Foeniculum vulgare 'Purpureum', reseeding **PP**
Gomphrena globosa globe amaranth
Hibiscus acetosella 'Red Shield'
Lavatera trimestris rose mallow
Lobularia maritima reseeding, sweet
    alyssum
Moluccella laevis reseeding, bells of Ireland
Nicotiana reseeding, flowering tobacco
Nigella damascena reseeding,
    love-in-a-mist
Ocimum basilicum purple forms, basil
Perilla frutescens reseeding, beefsteak
    plant
Salvia farinacea mealy-cup sage
Senecio cineraria dusty miller
Trachymene caerulea (aka *Didiscus*) blue
    lace flower
Verbena bonariensis reseeding, *V. rigida* **PP**
Viola cornuta, V. tricolor viola, Johnny-
    jump-up, reseeding

SHRUBS FOR CONTRAST

Berberis thunbergii 'Atropurpurea',
    'Atropurpurea Nana' crimson
    barberry
Berberis thunbergii 'Aurea' golden
    barberry
Cornus alba 'Elegantissima' variegated dog
    wood
Cotinus coggygria purple varieties purple
    smokebush
Prunus x cistena purple plum shrub

V

Hail

My first encounter with hail was a traumatic few minutes that felt like a lifetime when, as a child, I buried my head in my mother's lap as we waited out a rare pounding in our car during a Philadelphia summer thunderstorm. The din was unearthly, like being inside a tin drum. It reminded me of the time I took refuge in a metal trash can during a particularly nasty, rock-throwing neighborhood skirmish. It's a good thing that at the time I didn't know I would settle in an area where hail regularly breaks windows, gives cars a bad case of acne, bankrupts farmers and leaves gardeners in tears.

There is nothing like the sound of a hailstorm for beating the sense of smallness and vulnerability into a person. When I first moved to Colorado, I earned a living tending an acre and a half of greenhouse roses for the cut flower trade. June hailstorms turned the idyllic maze of fragrant rose rows beneath the fiberglass into deafening tunnels.

Hail damage varies with the size and hardness—the colder, the harder—of the individual stones, the force and angle of the wind driving them, the number of stones and the duration of the onslaught. In the garden, initial damage is most noticeable early in the season, when plants are lush with tender new growth and the summer heat, wind and drought have not hardened off the stems and leaves. Overwatered, overfertilized gardens suffer from this same soft-and-weak syndrome at any time of the year. Gardens hit in spring, while initially more devastated, recover more quickly. The plants are physiologically revved to grow foliage at this time of the year, and new leaves soon replace the hail-damaged ones.

Midsummer gardens hit by hail need extra water and fertilizer to recover. The main problem at this time of the year is the potential for insect and disease problems. I am convinced that most plants can fight off virtually any invader (except on a bad grasshopper year) provided they are healthy to start with and stress-free. So often I have seen a group of plants where one of the bunch is being eaten or attacked while the others are fine. In each case, this particular plant is stressed by a particular environmental factor that the others have avoided. A group of shrubby potentillas I observed on a bank illustrates this—the individuals highest on the bank were drought stressed (*Potentilla fruticosa* is not particularly drought tolerant, contrary to popular opinion) and

(preceding pages) A group of hail-tolerant perennials glows in the late-afternoon sun: silver Helichrysum trilineatum, *yellow* Alyssoides graeca, *dwarf bearded iris, red* Aquilegia formosa *and a small golden broom.*

infested with mites. Conversely, in my garden, a group of dry-loving hardy cacti thrive on the baked strip between the sidewalk and the street, while the few cacti I had planted close to the sidewalk, where water runoff seeps in, began to rot and were attacked by mealybugs.

Flea beetles, tomato hornworms, spider mites, grasshoppers, slugs, powdery mildew, anthracnose and on and on, all come flying, running, hopping, sliding and crawling to a post-hail garden like vultures to a corpse. Careful cutting back and cleaning up, prudent watering and some quick-release fertilizer will help the midsummer garden stave off these opportunistic intruders. Too much water can cause rotting, spread infections and help a burgeoning population of slugs. Watering at night fosters some fungal and bacterial infections. Watering during the heat of the day wastes water through evaporation and can increase root rot—warm, wet soils are favored by some pathogens. Watering in the morning is ideal. Mixing in a water-diluted general fertilizer with balanced nutrients like 10-10-10 with the irrigation completes two tasks in one. It acts as much as a foliar feeding as a root feeding, giving the plants an extra boost for regrowth. I am not a big advocate of fertilizers, especially inorganic ones. Most midwestern and interior western soils are quite rich in nutrients; what some, especially those farther west, lack is organic matter and nitrogen. Soluble salts coming to the surface and rendering soil unplantable are becoming a problem in many places just through irrigation practices. Adding more of these seems downright stupid. I think hail damage, however, is a justifiable reason to use fertilizers, at least for the first week or two after the storm.

The most devastating hailstorms are those that occur late in the season, from mid-July on. Most plants have finished their main foliage growth by this time. To shift back into the leaf-growth mode this late in the year makes them susceptible to early frosts and winterkill. Instead of hardening off and shifting to root growth and food storage, the plants are forced to grow new tops. These tops, in turn, have not had time to toughen, and the plants themselves have been compromised by not following their typical cycle to ready themselves for winter and dormancy. My first really bad hailstorm happened the last weekend in July. I had spring flowers—moss phlox, pasqueflowers, rock cress—blooming in October. Several things died that winter, probably due to this confused timetable and their not being hardened off. Tree, shrub and rose branches were injured and showed much disease and winter dieback. Because of this, I suggest that for late hail damage, only cleanup, not severe cutting back, should be attempted. Even tattered leaves and bare stems should be left, unless they are totally broken. The plants should have enough strength from a healthy first half of the growing season to get by. I'd prefer they went into winter ugly and a little punier but hardened off than unprotected, lush and fat with new leaves.

▲ *The hot-colored, sunny west side of the garden is planted so densely that hail damage is minimized.*

▼ *Some hailstorms are so severe that even dense plantings are pummelled, as in this thirty-minute late-July siege.*

Farmers and longtime residents of hail-prone regions can forecast hail pretty well. Hail can occur anytime of the day or night, but it often hits in the afternoon or evening when thunderstorms have had all day to brew and reach maximum force. Late spring until midsummer are peak times. I have grown accustomed to daily thunderstorms rolling in around midafternoon during these months. At first, the mere sight of ominous gray clouds in the west made me uneasy. Now I know the depth of charcoal gray they need to be for serious consideration.

Then there are clouds that are cause for real alarm. The out-and-out funnel should be recognizable to anyone, even an East Coast novice (unless for some inexplicable reason one has never seen *The Wizard of Oz*). Then it's time to hit the basement. Hail clouds, while not as dangerous, are accompanied by a strong chill, both to the body and to the psyche. A cold wind, an ominously

▶ *Hail-belt natives penstemon and buffalo grass can hold their own in bad weather; here they grow happily together at the North Platte Horticultural Experiment Station in central Nebraska.*

dark sky and often the presence of mammary clouds—my veterinarian husband says it's like being under countless gray cow udders—mean it's time to pull the car into the garage, haul in the container plants and do whatever else you can before the ice hits.

My neighbor, an ingenious retired German farmer, has a small but impeccable vegetable and fruit patch. After a particularly vicious pelting a few years ago, he built hail covers for his tomatoes—square wood frames covered with two layers of thick plastic—which he places over the tomato cages when he feels hail is imminent. Unfortunately, covering my third-of-an-acre garden isn't feasible, though we have considered ideas such as a pull-out tarpaulin rolled up against the side of the house, much like a huge awning.

Instead of diving into a costly engineering project of dubious outcome, I have found other ways of coping with hail. They involve a few strategies of plant placement, plant choice, garden management and recovery rituals.

As is to be expected, plants native to regions fraught with hail have evolved in ways to minimize damage. Some plants have fine, wiry leaves that most hailstones fall through; others have tough leaves that resist impact, or bend with it rather than ripping and shattering. Some plants appear devastated but have amazingly fast rates of regrowth and recovery. This adaptation is just one more reason I am constantly on the lookout for more garden-worthy native plants.

Most plants, unless the storm is particularly late in the season, recover enough to make the garden presentable again in about three or four weeks. While some may not bloom that season, the foliage is attractive and the garden is full. I have often been criticized, mainly by rock gardeners and landscape architects, for planting too closely. A friend says my garden looks like New York City at rush hour, with plants climbing over plants in horticultural chaos. There are pros and cons to both sides of the issue of planting space. In humid climates, close planting invites disease; here, with ample sunshine, wind and dry air, my crowded ways have not caused any disease. The plants also serve as their own mulch, cooling the soil and cutting down on moisture loss.

Aesthetically, certain gardeners prefer each plant to have its own place, to be allowed to develop fully and have a boundary to give it presence. Many rock gardeners feel this way. Some native plant enthusiasts, especially those interested in dryland and desert gardening, plant widely spaced to emulate the way plants grow in these difficult conditions in the wild, where competition for extremely limited resources forces their population to be so scanty. I garden to change nature in ways that I find attractive. If I love a particular plant, say purple prairie gayfeather, *Liatris punctata*, I want to triple its *oompf* in my garden. So I may see three clumps of the lovely late-bloomer in the grasses by the roadside; in my grassland area, I will plant ten.

The whole reason this subject came up is that there is really no right and wrong in terms of how closely one plants—it's a matter of personal preference, except when it comes to hail. My closely planted garden fares much better than do those with more widely spaced plants. The first year of my garden, when nothing had filled in yet, hail did the worst damage. Now plants shelter each other, bend over each other, cushion each others' fall. And the naked weeks that follow the cutting back and cleanup are shortened by virtue of the lesser damage and by the fact that it takes less growth for the plants to flesh out the garden once again. Through the garden tragedy of hail, my plant-stuffing ways are finally vindicated.

There are a few favorite plants that take unreasonably badly to hail. I haven't yet banned them from the garden, but I am considering a few of my neighbor's hail covers and other drastic measures to protect them. All these plants have growth patterns that make them particularly susceptible to lasting, sometimes fatal, hail damage. First, there are the peonies and the lilies. They put out all their buds and foliage in a few short weeks in spring and cannot repeat the performance until the following year. That one set of leaves is their food factory for the duration of the growing season; they cannot grow new ones until the next spring.

In a best-case scenario, a leaf-stripped lily stalk or peony clump will stand gawky and ugly until it dies down for winter. Its lack of leaves will weaken the plant and compromise next year's display. The second year, barring any more hail, the plant will return to normal. However, things can go rapidly downhill shortly after the hail. The damaged stalks are an invitation for infection, which can easily travel down the stem and into the bulb or roots. This means death. Be sure to remove all broken stem and leaf parts; this prevents the dying tissue, prime target of disease, from infecting the healthy parts. Some people apply a fungicide weekly for the first month while the plant heals and toughens up. I'm not much of a chemical user, so I take my chances. I've lost a few lilies; most have survived. My peonies refused to bloom the following year but otherwise were unscathed.

My main annoyance is the lackluster appearance of these plants for the whole season following hail. Are they worth a place when one foul swoop from the sky can render them aesthetically useless in a matter of minutes? Two out of three years, I had no lilies to speak of and miserable gaps where the glossy green foliage of peonies was desired. My answer, at this point, is to plant them where they are sheltered. Our local hail usually is driven by a northwesterly wind. The southeastern side of the house often has several feet of garden untouched. Another solution, thanks to our bright sunlight, is the possibility of growing lilies and peonies under the protection of a tall tree. The light shade still lets through enough light for good flowering, and the leaf canopy serves as a buffer, receiving the wrath of the hailstones before they hit the plants beneath.

My answers for hail protection of two other much loved plants aren't as simple. I am seriously considering hail covers for these. Both are woody plants, whose recovery is measured in years, not months. They are the roses and dwarf conifers. The latter, especially, represent a large time and dollar investment. I have lost two dwarf conifers to hail damage—a week after the storm, they turned brown and lost most of their needles. They may have lived, but chances are slim, and even if they had, their form would have been ruined. Their form is the reason I grow them in the first place, so out they went. Others are limping along, their tops needleless and their new shoots brown.

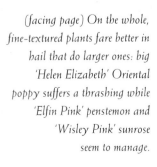

I watch vigilantly for spider mites, aphids and whatever other pest might find them and dine on them in their sorry state.

Roses suffer from the leaf loss that accompanies hail but are quick to refoliate. Food and water are vital in this effort. Flowering will be lessened that season; in fact, for the good of the plant, it should be discouraged. The big problem is cane damage. Canker infections abound in the bruised tissue. Winter-killed canes are the result of the compromised condition they were in the summer and fall before. Putting out many new canes is a great drain on a rose, and it will be a year or two before strength and vigor are up to snuff. An ongoing regimen of feeding and watering is necessary if the rose is expected to recover.

The big question facing the gardener when he or she stands amid the wasteland of the hail-stricken garden is what to do first. From the kitchen I have watched my delphiniums fall like soldiers in hand-to-hand combat, one by one—truly a masochistic torture for a gardener. Some people can dive in and begin cleanup right after the disaster, perhaps so as not to have time to reflect and be overwhelmed. I did that one year and found it not to be the wisest thing. Right after the storm, it is hard to tell damaged parts from the healthy. Everything is still fresh. I'll never forget the surreal feeling of wading into a bed of ice and green slush, dizzy from denial and a few self-pitying drinks too many, still in my summer sandals. The smell of the plants was intoxicating—all that sap flowing. The crushed herbs, the rose petals, all wafting in the humid air, were wonderful with eyes closed. As I began cutting and scooping up, I grew more and more angry. Soon I was mowing down everything in my path, damaged or not. While this may not be a typical reaction, it is another reason to wait a day or two.

The day after the storm, damaged plant parts will begin to wilt, and it is easier to determine what to remove, how hard to cut back and so on. With annuals, one needs to decide which to feed and which to forget. Since they are only around for this one season, their chance of recovering and creating the beauty, whether floral or foliar, they were intended to must be assessed. If it is early in the season, and they are very small, it may be wiser to pull them out and replant them while replacements are still available.

Mid-season hail means these individuals are the ones you are stuck with, so either pull them or pamper them. I have great faith in the recovering abilities of most annuals. Most are damaged severely, being lush and rapid of growth by nature. Yet since they are programmed to live, reproduce and die in a single season, they can regrow faster than most perennials. To further the cause of giving annuals a chance, no matter how battered, is the fact that having a late flush of annual bloom in the fall is, contrary to perennials, of no detriment to their future, since they are going to die anyway. I had nicotiana, verbena, feverfew, tall ageratum, snapdragons, alyssum, petunia and California poppy back blooming a month after the hail, fresher looking than they had been before. A delusioned optimist (not a bad way to be in times like these) might think of a hailstorm as a forced pinching that actually enhances the late-season annual display.

The past three years have been abnormally hail-ish, and from this burdensome occurrence has arisen a large, by no means complete, yet useful body of combined knowledge and experience. Certain plants fare poorly, others start off badly and recover well and yet others resist damage altogether. There are patterns but no hard and fast rules for predicting how wimpy a plant will be. Most large-leaved plants such as hosta, borage and caladium take it on the ear. Yet the sizeable foliage of bergenia, hellebores and redbud is hardly scathed. Many shade lovers, with their softer, more lush composition, turn quickly to slush, notably bleeding heart, impatiens, lamium and coleus. Soft sun lovers—mainly those with hairy leaves—are also badly pummeled. Fine-textured plants generally fare better, especially drought-tolerant ones like moss phlox, blue flax and rue. Just to ruin the formula, most species of artemisia, portulaca, dill, fennel and California poppies are thrashed to smithereens. All the gardeners I have met since I've lived in Colorado have been hailed out at one point or another. My thanks to all these people for helping me compile these lists and for holding my hand during my first bouts with a then-unfamiliar weather phenomenon.

For the gardener who has had it and is ready for a hail-proof garden, the following lists may be of use. While I am not ready to give up on peonies, dwarf conifers and the like, I am looking more and more to native plants. After all, these rugged beauties don't get a dousing of Peter's 20-20-20 after a hailstorm on the prairie, so I think they've earned their garden space. With careful selection of plants, sheltered placement of delicate individuals, a strategy for what to do when hail hits and a strong belief that it can't happen every year, everyone gardening in the hail belts of this continent can continue to do so with impunity and little psychological trauma. One needs to remember that the damage can be put to good use—it makes great compost to feed next year's garden, which will of course be much better.

▲ *Orange cowboy's delight and indigo* Dracocephalum nutans *make a vibrant, hail-tolerant pair.*

▼ *Exotic beauty* Tamarix ramosissima *takes hail, heat and cold and has made itself a bit too comfortable along some riverbeds in the arid West.*

▲ *This hail-resistant triumvirate features stone cress* (Aethionema grandiflorum), Dracocephalum botryoides *and western native whiplash daisy*, Erigeron flagellaris.

PLANT RESPONSE TO HAIL

The following information deals with damage surveyed after five separate hailstorms over a period of four years. All the storms were serious; the damage was surveyed in three different gardens.

PLANTS SUFFERING SEVERE DAMAGE

Achillea millefolium yarrow **R**
Ajuga **R**
Alcea hollyhock **R**
Annuals—most—notably resistant ones listed below
Arabis rock cress **R**
Aubrieta rock cress **R**
Aurinia saxatilis basket-of-gold **R**
Brunnera macrophylla Siberian bugloss **R**
Buddleya butterfly bush
Catalpa speciosa
Cerastium snow-in-summer **R**
Cheiranthus allionii Siberian wallflower
Chrysanthemum zawadskii
Clematis
Crambe **R**
Cynara cardoon
Delphinium
Dicentra bleeding heart
Digitalis foxglove
Echinacea purpurea purple coneflower **R**
Echinops globe thistle
Elaeagnus angustifolia Russian olive **R**
Eriogonum buckwheat
fern—most species
Gaillardia Indian blanket **R**
Galium odoratum sweet woodruff **R**
Galega officinalis goat's rue **R**
Gaura lindheimeri apple blossom grass
Geranium cranesbill larger species **R**
Geum **R**
Glaucium horned poppy
Gypsophila baby's breath **R**
Helichrysum everlasting most
Heliopsis summer sun
Hemerocallis daylily **R**
Hesperis matronalis sweet rocket
Heuchera coralbells
Hosta
Hydrangea arborescens 'Annabelle'
Inula helenium

Lamium maculatum dead nettle **R**
Lathyrus latifolius perennial pea
Lavatera shrub mallow
Leucanthemum vulgare oxeye daisy
Leucanthemum x *superbum* Shasta daisy
Lilium lily
Limonium sea lavender
Lychnis chalcedonica Maltese cross
Lychnis coronaria rose campion
Malus crabapple
Marrubium horehound **R**
Monarda didyma bee balm
Nepeta x *faassenii* catmint **R**
Onopordum Scots thistle
Papaver orientale Oriental poppy
Phlomis russeliana **R**
Phlox carolina, P. maculata, P. paniculata tall garden phlox
Plantago major 'Atropurpurea' red-leaf plantain **R**
Potentilla megalantha
Primula primrose
Pulmonaria lungwort **R**
Rheum palmatum ornamental rhubarb **R**
Rhus typhina staghorn sumac
Rudbeckia black-eyed Susan
Salvia aethiopsis, S. argentea, S. sclarea
Saponaria soapwort **R**
Sedum
Sideritis except *S. byssopifolia* **R**
Stachys betony **R**
Tanacetum densum var. *amani* **R**
Tiarella foamflower
Trollius europaeus globe flower
vegetables—most
Verbascum mullein
Verbena bipinnatifida **R**
Zauschneria California fuchsia

HAIL-RESISTANT PLANTS

In the worst batterings, however, even these plants will succumb.
Acaena New Zealand bur
Acantholimon spikethrift
Achillea yarrow all but *A. millefolium*
Aconitum monkshood
Aethionema stone cress

Alchemilla lady's mantle
Allium senescens 'Glaucum'
Alyssoides graeca
Alyssum montanum mountain basket-of-gold
Amelanchier serviceberry
Amorpha canescens leadplant
Amsonia blue stars
Anacyclus depressus Mt. Atlas daisy
Andryala agardhii
annuals:
    Cleome serrulata plains spider flower
    Consolida ambigua larkspur
    Coreopsis tinctoria
    Cosmos bipinnatus
    Diascia twinspur
    Dyssodia tenuiloba Dahlberg daisy
    Nigella love-in-a-mist
    Salvia farinacea mealy-cup sage
    Salvia greggii cherry sage
    Tagetes marigold
    Thelesperma greenthread
Antennaria pussytoes
Aquilegia columbine
Arenaria montana sandwort
Argemone prickly poppy
Armeria maritima sea thrift
Artemisia sage
Asclepias tuberosa butterfly weed
Aster
Baptisia australis wild blue indigo
Bergenia pigsqueak
cactus
Callirhoe buffalo rose
Campanula bellflower
Catananche caerulea Cupid's dart
Centaurea knapweed
Centranthus ruber Greek valerian
Cephalaria alpina giant pincushion flower
Cercis canadensis redbud
Chamaebatiaria millefolium fernbush
Chrysothamnus rabbit brush
Cirsium spinosissimum
Coreopsis tickseed
Corydalis lutea fumitory
Cotinus smokebush

Cytisus broom
Daphne
Delosperma iceplant
Dianthus pinks
Dracocephalum dragonshead
Ephedra joint fir
Epimedium barrenwort
Erigeron fleabane
Erodium storksbill
Eryngium sea holly
Euphorbia spurge
Fallugia paradoxa Apache plume
Festuca ovina var. *glauca* sheep's fescue
Genista broom
Geranium small, mounded species
Gillenia/Porteranthus trifoliata bowman's root
Goniolimon statice
grasses
Gutierrezia sarothrae broomweed
Helianthemum sunrose
Helictotrichon sempervirens blue avena grass
Helleborus
Hypericum St. John's wort
Hyssopus officinalis hyssop
Incarvillea olgae
Iris
Knautia macedonica red pincushion flower

Kniphofia red hot poker
Lavandula lavender
Lesquerella bladderpod
Liatris prairie gayfeather
Linaria toadflax
Linum flax
Lithospermum incisum puccoon
Lychnis viscaria catchfly
Lysimachia clethroides gooseneck loosestrife
Lysimachia nummularium moneywort
Malva mallow
Mirabilis multiflora desert four o'clock
Nepeta catmint all but *N.* x *faassenii*
Oenothera evening primrose
Origanum oregano
Oxytropis locoweed
Papaver triniifolium Armenian poppy
Penstemon beardtongue
Persicaria (Polygonum) affinis border jewel
Phlox all but the large garden phloxes
Physaria bladderpod
Physostegia virginiana obedient plant
Platycodon grandiflorus balloon flower
Polemonium Jacob's ladder
Potentilla fruticosa shrubby potentilla
Prunus tomentosa Nanking cherry
Pulsatilla pasqueflower

Quercus oak
Ratibida prairie coneflower
Rhus trilobata squaw bush
Rosa all species roses and *R.* x *alba*
Rubus deliciosus boulder raspberry
Ruta graveolens rue
Salvia azurea azure sage
Salvia jurisicii upside-down sage
Salvia lavandulifolia
Salvia officinalis culinary sage
Salvia x *superba* garden sage
Santolina lavender cotton
Scabiosa pincushion flower
Scutellaria skullcap
Sempervivum hens and chicks
Senecio longilobus silver groundsel
Shepherdia argentea buffaloberry
Sidalcea checkerbloom
Sideritis hyssopifolia
Solidago goldenrod
Sphaeralcea cowboy's delight
Spiraea
Syringa lilac
Tamarix ramosissima salt cedar
Tanacetum niveum snow daisy
Thymus thyme
Veronica

VI

Annuals:
Season-Spanners
Worth the Effort

According to the movers and shakers of the gardening world, annuals rank along with leisure suits and Naugahyde furniture. Ever since William Robinson and Gertrude Jekyll berated the carpet-bedding craze of Victorian England, "tasteful" gardeners have spurned all but the most subtle or unusual annuals and even these are used with restraint, never allowing them to steal the limelight from supposedly more worthy perennials.

Some purists reject annuals altogether. I remember sitting in the drawing room of a famous English plantswoman, nervously balancing a bone-china teacup on my knees. I had just remarked on how many unusual and lovely annuals were making their way into the traditional English herbaceous border. "My dear," she replied in a condescending tone made all the more so with the help of an upper-class British accent, "as you grow in sophistication, your interest in annuals will wane."

In less self-conscious gardening circles, much-maligned annuals are permitted and the results are often wonderful. As far as I'm concerned, annuals are as garden-worthy or disappointing as any other group of plants. Beauty and toughness are what count. Where they really shine is in the continuity of color they offer, something that few other plants can guarantee. As the blooms of perennials, bulbs and flowering trees and shrubs come and go with the seasons, annuals tie the garden together. Their dependable, cheerful blossoms are the colorful glue that keeps the gardener from mourning the passing of June's frothy flush. They move on to brighten the tired green of late July doldrums. And many annuals face the early frosts of fall with a brilliant burst of color like the multiple fireworks that signal the end of an Independence Day display.

Annuals, however, require work. Unusual ones often must be grown from seed; few nurseries and garden centers carry the variety of annuals they do perennials. Most annuals must be planted yearly. Even the so-called perennial annuals, those that self-sow dependably, often don't plant themselves exactly where they are wanted. Most annuals also need regular deadheading to continue flowering and remain vigorous and attractive. Otherwise, they will put their efforts into seed production and let their looks go to pot. And the appeal of annuals in the winters of cold regions, except for the few that have interesting dried forms and seedheads, is literally and figuratively a dead issue. Given these drawbacks, they still deserve space in the garden.

(preceding pages) 'Fairy Wings' poppy reseeds faithfully, promising to grace the garden with many diaphanous blossoms each summer.

Annuals are often planted all by themselves with no attempt made to integrate them with plants that have more interesting foliage or winter form. Maybe this is why they fell out of favor in the first place. Annual beds are colorful and dependable, yet they become dull after the first month of bloom. The coming and going of different flowers is one of the pleasures of gardening. A garden stultifies when there is no change. How unnatural and boring a sea of purple petunias; a velvety purple petunia may have its place in a garden, but the unchanging sameness of a canvas of only purple petunias, all the same height, the same texture, the same color, speaks little more of the beauty and diversity of the natural world than does a blank wall. Be they large plantings in parks and outside malls or small circles and strips on front lawns, there's no excuse for such monotony. From October until June, the beds remain bare earth; from June until October, they switch from brown to red, or perhaps white or yellow. That is all that changes.

Both extremes—a monoculture of annuals and a snobbish disdain for these good plants—do gardening and the gardener a disservice. Tough, adaptable, beautiful annuals should be integrated with the other plants in a garden. This takes sensitivity; certain annuals, especially some of the most popular, can quickly become overbearing and dominate more subtle plants much like a loud drunk draws attention at a party.

Sadly, it seems the annuals chosen by breeders as most worthy of selection work and promotion are beginning to look more and more alike. With the emphasis on developing strains that are more compact, floriferous, brightly colored and with larger and larger flowers, it's becoming increasingly hard to determine whether that sprawling amoeba of color over in the park is petunias or geraniums, zinnias or marigolds.

The most effective annuals for a diverse yet harmonious garden have not lost all sense of natural proportion. Foliage is visible beneath the flowers. Rather than all equally squat and ungraceful, some are so airy as to appear to float above and between more substantive plants: Tall, flat-topped purple flowers of *Verbena bonariensis* hover over hefty golden daylilies, attracting eager butterflies; brilliant scarlet spikes of Texas native *Salvia coccinea* dress the blue needles of a dwarf Colorado spruce.

Flower arrangers and dried flower enthusiasts don't need to be told the value of annuals. The gardener attempting to create a full, floriferous first-year garden should also give annuals a serious look. While woody plants and herbaceous perennials are still puny, there's a lot of bare earth or mulch to be seen. Aside from being ugly, the unplanted areas are hotter and drier than if they were planted, and often become occupied by a host of unwelcome weeds by the end of the season.

I leaned heavily on large, luxurious yet tough annuals the first two years in my present garden. Between purple-leaved smokebush (*Cotinus coggygria* 'Royal Purple'), creamy, chocolate-centered daisies of 'Italian White' sunflower stood tall. White and pink cleome and cosmos softened the sunny, dry, raw-looking area by the new fence.

▶ Lavatera trimestris 'Mont Blanc' and 'Snow Crystals' alyssum are two annuals with the grace and proportion of perennials.

▲ 'Italian White' sunflower.

▲ Dyssodia tenuiloba, *Dahlberg daisy.*

(facing page) Self-sowing red orach adds depth to a monochromatic yarrow and daylily combination.

The massive, fresh green foliage and fragrant white flower clusters of *Nicotiana sylvestris* filled the gaps between still small shrub roses on the moister, partly shaded east side of the house.

I regret that there is less and less room for these as the perennials and shrubs fill in. I have grown so fond of them that I've left a few bare spaces originally slated for more permanent plants, to be filled every year with these favorite annual giants.

Self-Sowers The most enjoyable annuals are those that seed themselves and are small or airy enough not to usurp space. They find the most unlikely places to grow— mulched patches under bushes, bare spots under a fence, unfriendly cracks between stones in paths or walls. These opportunists not only relieve the gardener of having to buy or raise them from seed, they also add a playful disorder to what can easily become an overstudied display of plant combinations. I'm usually quite daring with color, but self-sown annuals have taken me beyond what I ever would have tried intentionally: orange California poppies mingle with shocking pink *Silene armeria* in a gay, drought-tolerant jamboree; purple *Verbena rigida* battles for attention with the fiery, black-stemmed spikes of Texas scarlet sage. These unpredictable gypsies bring a carefree spirit into the garden.

Few gardens are not improved by introducing some hearty and hardy self-sowers. One needs to let go a little, to accept that not every seedling will be perfectly placed. One also needs to be ruthless when seedlings threaten the appearance or health of a more permanent plant. In early May, coinciding with my dogs' yearly shedding of their winter undercoats, I pull larkspur and nigella out in equally impressive clumps. If left, the feathery green seedlings would certainly form the closest thing I have resembling a lawn. Annuals grow much faster than most perennials, so to think the two are equally matched and to let annual seedlings and perennials fight it out with no intervention will probably result in an all-annual garden in a short period of time.

Smaller self-sowing annuals can do wonders to soften the harsh lines of stone walls, railroad-tie edges, sidewalks and such. Unless the look desired is one of sleek formality, strong lines formed by the "hard landscape"—the nonplant elements—can dominate and diminish the impact of the plants.

The environment a plant must tolerate when growing near a hard landscape element can be severe. Stone, brick, wood and concrete all absorb and radiate heat. Sometimes, as with a wall, less air circulates, amplifying the heat and encouraging pests and diseases, especially grasshoppers and spider mites. On the plus side, the hard elements of the landscape can serve as a mulch to give plants a cooler, moister root run. Anyone traveling the Great Plains in mid- and late summer is treated to mile after mile of road lined with annual sunflowers. The edge of the highway blacktop captures water runoff, enabling a host of plants to thrive there. This is why many self-sown annuals seem to find these spots on their own. It is the luck of the draw that some seeds land in a such a spot, unless the gardener intervenes, as I do, and does a little pod shaking and seed sprinkling in desired areas. It is not divine providence, however, that the seeds germinate and grow— sweet alyssum and Johnny-jump-ups graciously reappear every year between the bricks of a walk because they like it there.

I let several other self-sowing annuals colonize various harsh spots throughout the garden. In the driest areas, California native *Phacelia campanularia*, the purest navy blue, fights it out with a yellow Texan, Dahlberg daisy (*Dyssodia tenuiloba*). Both stay under six inches. Orange California poppies and fiesta-colored moss rose sometimes join in. Moss rose can get a bit bossy, seemingly tripling in size overnight after a rain, so I leave only a few seedlings each year, pulling out the ones in the wrong places and those whose colors jar with neighboring plants. Pure white moss rose is a lovely thing; with its yellow center and fresh green foliage, it goes well anywhere. As soon as other color strains are introduced, though, seedlings become undependable; strong fuchsia and orange ones pop up among pastel flowers, and the whole thing gets out of hand. Yet they are welcomed in an area where brilliant colors mix unbridled.

California poppies usually come in orange, a color few people rank among their favorites. Near the end of October and November, the general populace goes through a period of benevolence toward the maligned color and does a bit of seasonal decorating with it. When it represents a winning sports team's colors, a similar spurt of interest may surface, but otherwise orange is shunned. I have come to appreciate orange, through the colors with which it combines well. California poppies led the way. These carefree annuals are rare among their kind in being blessed with foliage as lovely as their flowers. Most annuals suffer in the foliage department, making up for this shortcoming by smothering themselves in flowers as if hoping the gardener won't notice their dowdy leaves. California poppies, from early spring until after the frosts of autumn, keep lush, finely cut blue-green leaves. Eager to introduce crimson, purple, pink, cream and double forms into the garden, I went on a purge of the few orange poppies that had made themselves at home. While the softer-toned varieties blended well in the pastel areas of the garden, in most other areas, I sorely missed the vibrancy of the orange ones.

The crimsons, reds and frilly doubles failed to impress at all. I did like the creamy white and dusky plum varieties. In the final analysis, however, none of the fancy types truly compared; those orange petals are without question the perfect match for the blue-toned foliage. Luckily my mistake was soon erased by the dominance of the orange genes over the carefully bred pastels. Orange seedlings popped up everywhere. The ensuing combinations, for which I could take no credit, taught me about orange. Poppies grew through sky-blue flax and veronicas, next to purple salvias and verbenas, alongside yellow evening primroses, making mockery of my feeble attempts to improve the color coordination of the garden. I promised to include orange from here on.

For sunny, dry rock gardens or any areas devoted to smaller, neatly growing perennials, few self-sowers should be allowed to take hold, for their boisterous nature can quickly overcome the more refined denizens of such gardens. Some smaller, better-behaved self-sowers should be considered for these areas. The first, *Talinum mengesii*,

▲ *Western natives prickly poppy* (Argemone platyceras) *and California poppy fight off invasive perennial 'Silver King' artemisia.*

▲ *Bright pink annual catchfly, red orach and California poppy bring color and spontaneity to a subdued planting of* Salvia aethiopsis, *'Silver Mound' artemisia, Grecian foxglove and German statice.*

native to the Southwest and perennial in warm climates but annual in my garden, is a petite, well-behaved cousin of the weedier, fleshier moss rose. Its small rose-pink flowers open daily all summer on threadlike, almost invisible stems above a succulent tuft of leaves. A succession of fecund, beadlike seeds ensures its presence in the garden the following year. It especially likes a gravel mulch and its airiness makes it a fine companion to alpine bun and cushion plants or hardy cacti.

The second well-behaved, diminutive self-sower is the Corsican violet, one of the finest plants I have ever grown. It has permanently cured me of any yearnings for the grotesquely large-flowered pansies to which it is related. Sometimes perennial and always in bloom—it flowers every month of the year, even December and January—*Viola corsica* has a deep purple, one- to one-and-a-half-inch face with irregular violalike petals that give it spry character the overbred pansies lack. Corsican violet rarely grows taller than four inches and thrives in almost any soil in full sun. Dry gardens with gravel mulch suit it ideally. It is at its best in early spring with pink and white mats of moss phlox or among miniature dwarf bearded irises. Late summer and fall bring on renewed vigor and the deep purple flowers enhance dwarf goldenrod and magenta colchicums.

Finally, for gardens where summers are cool, fragrant Iceland poppies (*Papaver nudicaule*), in shades of yellow, orange, peach, pink and white, are welcome wanderers. In my hot plains garden they have never amounted to much, but I have seen their diaphanous beauty grace many a mountain garden. They are so gentle of demeanor that they accompany just about any color without jarring.

In the lovely chaos of a cottage garden, the larger self-sowing poppies find a place. The opium poppy, which I refer to as sleepy poppy whenever I am feeling particularly paranoid, is a *planta non grata* with the U.S. government for its role in the production of opium. Strictly speaking, it is illegal to grow, yet it has flourished in century-old farmyard gardens in some of the most law-abiding, pious parts of this country. Few regions of this continent offer a climate suitable for producing the latex in the seedpod that is required for making the drug, so there is no real threat anyway. The seeds, however, find wholesome use on many delicious baked goods, especially of central and eastern European origin. I introduced opium poppies to my first garden by picking them off the top of a bagel. Apparently baking hadn't done them in, because I was rewarded by many gray-green seedlings that followed with lovely, ephemeral, single pink blossoms.

As with most taprooted poppies, sowing seed directly into the garden and then letting the plants reseed themselves rather than starting them in pots and transplanting

▲ *The orange of California poppies is to revel in, not to be squelched; cowboy's delight and* Veronica incana *join in.*

them is the best way to handle opium poppies. Extremely double, so-called peony-flowered forms have more substance and last longer in the garden than the singles but lack their grace. The things I love most about poppies—their tissue-like petals and prominent ring of stamens—are lost in the translation from single flower to double. Red, pink, salmon, purple and white forms exist, some with contrasting black centers, some with fringed petals.

A smaller, legal version of these ethereal plants is a group of poppies of unknown parentage called 'Fairy Wings'. Their opalescent colors of smoky lavender, dusky pink, white and pale apricot are welcome throughout a soft-toned, sunny garden. They have politely filled gaps between my faded bearded iris and mingled with the midsummer lavender-blue spikes of ladybells, *Adenophora lilifolia*. The one drawback of both these poppies is that, unlike most annuals, they only bloom for a few weeks. But they are so narrow that once they set seed and die down, a process they dutifully perform in a few short weeks, they leave no noticeable gaping hole. Rather, they leave the garden with a whisper and a legacy of seed full of promise for the coming year. Their curious salt-shaker pods rattle in the wind, spreading thousands of tiny seeds.

As far as seedpods go, love-in-a-mist (*Nigella damascena* and *N. hispanica*) has one of the best. *Nigella* blooms for a good six weeks in early summer, and then develops maroon-striped, papery pods with tufted horns which must have given rise to its other common name, devil-in-the-bush. It self-sows immodestly and tolerates almost any soil. Early blooming lavender, rose, white or blue starry flowers and fresh green feathery foliage look good meandering through all but the tidiest gardens. My favorite variety is 'Miss Jekyll'; though English in origin, it mirrors the color of Colorado skies. It's great with the mauve and burgundy bearded iris 'Wine and Roses' or duking it out with a fellow annual, the orange California poppy.

Several headstrong giants such as sunflowers, cleome and cosmos leave more than their share of offspring every year which I ruthlessly remove, but one tall annual will always find a home with me: larkspur (*Consolida ambigua*). Its fine texture counteracts the three to four feet it sometimes reaches. In the hottest, driest parts of the garden, larkspur survives, dwarfed to a foot but still carrying those intensely blue-purple flowers. In the lightly shaded east garden, the well-watered home of primadonnas lily, delphinium and rose, larkspur stretches to almost four feet, toppling over and breaking after a heavy downpour. A sunny, relatively dry garden produces the best larkspur—lean, tough and full of flowers.

Each year, as I watch slugs, hail and grasshoppers take turns with the hybrid delphiniums, I vow to let larkspur loose among those overbred weaklings. Each year, a few more delphiniums die and a few more larkspur take hold. In the coolest mountain gardens and farther north, delphiniums grow like weeds. But in areas scorched by dry, hot summers, larkspur, with its six to eight weeks of color and dependable self-sowing, plus its more slender, graceful flower spike, is the plant of choice for vertical spires in the summer garden. Given less water, no staking is needed, a practice too often with uglier results than what it was trying to avert in the first place. Only the lushest, most well-leafed plants can be staked with impunity. Leaner, scantily leaved plants like larkspur that thrive in more rigorous climates look absolutely ridiculous with even the most masterful staking job. The moral of the story is if the plant needs staking, it is growing in too windy a site for its structure and should be relocated, or it is being spoiled rotten with water and food. With larkspur, the gardener can take heart even if it topples, for then it can be cut and brought into the house. It lasts a long time in a vase and also dries well.

Given the choice, I prefer to let larkspur spread its beauty around outside. As with all spiked flowers, the best companions are round or flat-topped blossoms. The deep blue-purple form springs up among golden yarrow, orange butterflyweed (*Asclepias tuberosa*) and the large red daisies of *Gaillardia* x *grandiflora* 'Burgundy'. Pastel varieties of larkspur, in pink, white and lavender, mix with the white form of Greek valerian (*Centranthus ruber* 'Albus') and pink shrub mallow, *Lavatera thuringiaca*. I need to resow these every few years, otherwise the deeper tones soon dominate.

 While many annuals come from tropical or subtropical regions and are therefore accustomed to high humidity and a good deal of moisture, a few actually need dry air and soil and resent fertilizers, especially those high in nitrogen. This handful of annuals can be plunked in a hot, baked spot with no manure or compost added—only a bit of turning to lighten the soil prior to planting. As is the case with many plants native to harsh environments and humus-poor soils, the traditional gardening mantra of organic matter, organic matter and more organic matter can actually be a death sentence.

Daisies for Drought

I might even call these annuals low maintenance, although I hate the term. Members of the daisy family dominate this resilient group of annuals, their faces imitating the image of the fierce star in whose heat and light they revel. Annual Indian blanket, *Gaillardia pulchella*, is aptly named; its jagged-edged petals are striped in bold rust, red, orange and gold, resembling an Indian saddle blanket. Breeders have created more and more double forms of this lovely native, to the point that one can hardly discern that it was once a daisy. Hopefully, they will come to their senses soon and the caricatures will go by the wayside like nehru jackets and leisure suits.

The double forms of annual black-eyed Susan (*Rudbeckia hirta*), a midwesterner, are not nearly as grotesque as what Indian blanket has been subjected to. I still find the single form the prettiest, especially the popular selection 'Rustic Colors' where the

▲ Black-eyed Susan brightens perennials Russian sage and goldenrod in late summer.

▲ Vegetables, herbs and flowers for the house all mingle in a traditional German four-square garden, a fine example of blending function and aesthetics.

▲ Erigeron karvinskianus.

▲ Diascia sp., twinspur.

▶ Violas, desert bluebells (Phacelia campanularia) and California poppies self-sow with abandon in the gravel mulch of the unwatered hell strips, here next to yellow sunrose Helianthemum croceum.

petals are touched with brown and bronze. A few years back, feeling nostalgic for the time I spent gardening in Ireland, I grew the variety 'Irish Eyes', a single golden daisy with a chartreuse eye. What a disappointment. It was close to impossible trying to blend it with other colors in the garden—the green center cried out for soft pink, lavender, pale yellow and blue while the golden rays demanded bold, vibrant colors as accompaniment. It was a true case of color schizophrenia. Out went 'Irish Eyes'. I even hated it in a vase. While green and blue eyes are coveted by many, the black- and brown-eyed version of lovely Susan is best left as she is.

Both Indian blanket and black-eyed Susan bloom from early summer until after the first frosts, especially if kept deadheaded. Tahoka daisy (*Machaeranthera tanacetifolia*) begins a bit later. Pale lavender with a golden eye, the two-inch daisies native to the Great

Plains look fabulous with the more drought-tolerant species of goldenrod and prairie gayfeather.

All three of these daisies, probably due to their heritage, cry out to be planted with ornamental grasses. Perhaps the grasslands and meadows of summer and early autumn have entered our collective gardening subconscious. Daisies, be they perennial asters, boltonia, heliopsis, purple coneflower, the almost clichéd 'Goldsturm' rudbeckia, or these annual variants, are finding their way alongside grasses in more and more gardens. To steer clear of some of the more tender, water-consuming grasses, one might combine blue avena grass with annual Indian blanket, black-eyed Susan or Tahoka daisy. Blue and purple perennial sages, catmints or the plant that looks good with almost any other, Russian sage (*Perovskia*), all with vertical, more diffuse flowers, also show off the daisies to advantage.

*More
Water-Wise
Annuals*

Annual, sometimes perennial, southwestern *Salvia farinacea*, whose common name mealy-cup sage does it no justice, can take uncoddled garden conditions right along with the daisies and lend its fresh green foliage and navy blue spires to the scene. Once again, someone has seen fit to meddle with this plant, as fine as it is, and produced pale blue and white variants. These miserable shadows of the deep blue original have the bad habit of showing the dead flowers on their spikes as conspicuously as those in their prime. At any given time, half the spikes on a plant will be more brown than light blue or white. I remain true to the good old-fashioned blue.

For the most demanding conditions, desert marigold, *Baileya multiradiata*, is ideal. With any additional irrigation, it will flop on its side. Let this one bake itself senseless. Scant silver foliage gives rise to a succession of perfectly formed bright yellow daisies for several months. As a child, I was an incurable magpie for jewelry and would festoon myself with all sort of hideous faux baubles. My mother, sensing a budding Liz Taylor, felt the need to ingrain in me that silver and gold should never be worn together. Now that I have come to terms with the fact that my gardening lifestyle and wallet will never afford me jewelry, I'm more than happy to watch desert marigold mine its metallic colors from the poorest of soils in my garden. Silver and gold never looked so good.

Verbenas are also ideal for the hot, dry garden. I like them especially for their twining and twisting grace of habit that blends so well with perennials, lending a refined look to a harsh spot. The smallest, *Verbena tenuisecta/Glandularia tenuisecta* or moss verbena, is perennial in warmer climates, as are most of the others. Its finely dissected foliage and petite lavender or white flower heads belie its toughness. The more common hybrid verbenas, in a range of colors from vibrant purples and reds to pale pinks and peaches, are very showy, sometimes even to the point of garishness, and unfortunately are also irresistible to whitefly, spider mites and powdery mildew.

Rose vervain (*Verbena canadensis*), on the other hand, is an unplagued, enthusiastic ground cover. It blooms tirelessly from early summer deep into autumn. If it does over-winter, which happens as often as not, there's no reason to fear its rampant ways be-cause rose vervain spreads aboveground, not by sneaky stolons down below. This can't be said of *Verbena rigida*, which has become a beautiful pest in parts of the South but is reliably nonhardy north of Texas. I pulled its tentacle-like web of spreading roots, its valiant attempt at manhandling the garden, from the ground the following spring, thank-ing my lucky stars it was as dead as a doornail. The brilliant violet is an easy color to succumb to, blending especially well with the round yellow and golden faces of sum-mer- and fall-blooming perennial daisies—*Rudbeckia fulgida* var. *sullivantii* 'Goldsturm', *Heliopsis scabra* and the like. A pale lavender form, 'Lilacina' or 'Polaris', combines well with silver artemisias and German statice, *Goniolimon tataricum*, for a softer look.

Verbena tenera, in bright rose, white or picotee—var. *maonettii*—couples the brilliant, large flower clusters of the susceptible hybrids with the graceful, sprawling habit of *V. canadensis* and *V. tenuisecta*. Whether cascading from a neglected pot on a hot stoop or scrambling across baked soil in the garden, its jewel-like colors are a summertime treat.

In the cooler dry garden, also preferring poor soil, a different but equally attractive and resilient group of annuals can be left to their own devices. Yellow and white California native *Layia platyglossa* has the lovable common name tidy tips, for the yellow "petals," the ray flowers, are neatly edged in white. This foot-tall annual only tolerated my garden until late June, when the heat brought about a flurry of seed production followed by a rapid demise. In cooler climates it may bloom well into fall. Sky blue flax, a perennial that likes the same dry, infertile yet cool conditions, would combine well with the yellow and white flowers.

Another daisy perfect for such a life is *Erigeron karvinskianus*, perennial in its native Mexico and where winters are milder but a showy bloomer its first year from seed. I fell in love with this airy thing in Ireland, where it has naturalized in many gardens, avoid-ing the damp by growing in the cracks of old stone walls. Mexican fleabane (a real Beulah of a common name that probably will keep it from the popularity it deserves) grows more horizontally than tall, making a great filler for containers. Like its mois-ture-loving relative the English daisy (*Bellis perennis*), which is one of the most pictur-esque of lawn weeds, *Erigeron karvinskianus* is rose in bud, white in full bloom and rose once again as it fades and goes over. Small, meager foliage and wiry stems ensure that the profuse flowers get top billing. It serves as a pretty annual cover to the dying foli-age of smaller spring bulbs, continuing on to fill the gap the bulbs leave behind. A plant of it tucked in late spring wherever a clump of crocus or snow iris remnants lie limp on the ground, ugly but not ripe enough to remove, quietly and efficiently makes the gar-den more presentable. The smallest things, like removing spent flowers, trimming brown tips off leaves or masking old bulb foliage, do wonders for a garden's appearance.

One other daisy not to be forgotten is *Brachycome iberidifolia*, Swan River daisy, from Australia. It lasts only a month in the heat of my garden, but with some afternoon shade, its life is prolonged. In cool, sunny gardens, Swan River daisy will send forth threadlike, tumbling stems covered in tiny purple, lavender, pink or white daisies for many months. It looks very much like a pastel twin to yellow, heat-loving Dahlberg daisy. Perfect for softening the edges of paths, flowing from hanging baskets or adding summer color to plantings of small, spring-flowering perennials such as candytuft, rockcress or basket-of-gold, Swan River daisy should be grown more than it is.

Also from the drier regions of the Southern Hemisphere, this time from South Africa, comes twinspur, *Diascia* spp. Several species and crosses make up this genus, and more hybrids and selections appear every year. The English have fallen in love with the warm pink, dainty little jester-cap flowers. In cool, sunny gardens on the West Coast, twinspur has found a happy home, and it is now moving inland. Several species have shown signs of being perennial, but the jury is still out. Since they bloom so well the first year from seed and so much yet needs to be learned about them, I've decided to grow them as annuals, to be pleasantly surprised if they prove otherwise. The shrimp pink color of the flowers—a peach suffusion rather than a cool lavender one—has helped diascia pair well with yellows and apricot oranges. Usually I keep pinks away from the warmer tones, unless the pink tends toward strong rose, almost purple.

When I first grew twinspur, I tried it in containers. I had seen photographs of the plant, but I thought I'd better pair it with white petunias and lavender *Verbena tenuisecta* for safety. It looked nice, but my more adventurous combination the following year put it to shame. In a large terracotta pot, diascia tumbled over the edges with the apricot flowers of African daisy, *Arctotis breviscapa*. I watered the pot infrequently, being forgetful and not inclined to routine, but it flourished in spite of my lack of attention while others cried out, their wilted denizens limply drooped over the edges of their containers. I never fertilized it either, guessing correctly that the two plants would bloom best on a lean diet. A bit of deadheading kept them in flower for four months. That year I also grew twinspur in the garden and fried it, learning in no uncertain terms that it prefers a cooler spot than the one I had selected.

Indefatigable miniature snapdragon, *Linaria maroccana*, from North Africa, has naturalized in waste places in parts of North America. Selected varieties expand the color range from purple to an exotic mix of crimson, pink, orange and yellow, echoing the kaleidoscope of a Moroccan marketplace. Yet the flowers are so delicate, the foliage so threadlike that the brilliant colors never jar with one another. The more moisture and food it receives, the more *L. maroccana* will flop and the less it will flower.

Moss rose, *Portulaca grandiflora*, thrives in the most inhospitable places. My neighbor lets it self-sow in his dirt drive; the baked strip between the ruts of his car's tires

◀ A tiger swallowtail visits showy annual catchfly, Silene armeria, amid perennial pinks and buckwheat, Eriogonum jamesii, on the hot, dry hell strips.

becomes a jumble of jewel-like color. For cooler climates, moss rose should be substituted by equally worthy and not quite so aggressive a succulent—rock purslane, *Calandrinia umbellata*, a brilliant magenta gem small enough to fit comfortably in a rock garden. Threaded among white and pink dianthus, it is a lovely thing and will self-sow dependably.

Annuals for Light Shade

On the other end of the cultural spectrum, there is, of course, shade. There are no annuals, nor virtually anything else aside from ferns and moss, that can face the gloom of deep shade. Large, deciduous trees with greedy roots, even if their canopies create a benevolent, dappled shade, will outcompete annuals for food and water. Yet given part-day shade of a fence, a house or some other structure, or the bright shade of a well-behaved, small-leaved tree like honey locust, several annuals can brighten up the green patchwork of perennial foliage. In the warm, humid climate of East Coast summers, impatiens, begonias and coleus are paraded out each summer as dependably as barbeque grills and lawn chairs. In the continental West, cool night temperatures, humus-poor soils and lack of rain and humidity prevent these from being the tried and true fixes for the shaded garden that they are back East. They certainly can be grown, and in many cases very well, but not without a lot of artificial intervention. More often than not, they would best be left to pampered, peat-rich, well-watered containers. Shade gardens need to become more varied and interesting.

With an average amount of moisture, a good number of annuals—including standards like Johnny-jump-ups (*Viola tricolor*); pretty little *Lobelia erinus* in blue, lavender, rose and white; and powder blue flossflower, *Ageratum houstonianum*—thrive. Ageratum now comes in white and pink as well as dozens of hopelessly similar varieties of the

▲   *In light shade, 'Jersey Gem' viola adds a deep note to frosty 'Valerie Finnis' artemisia.*

▼   *In the shade of an arbor at Denver Botanic Gardens, a subtle selection of variegated scented geranium, white impatiens and silver lotus vine,* Lotus berthelotii, *lights up a spot.*

original lavender blue. The pinks and whites, however, have the dirty habit of showing brown, spent blossoms amid the fresh ones. The deadheading and preening needed to keep them looking fresh is an endless and frustrating bore.

I have fallen in love with the old, eighteen-inch-tall blue form and am leaving all the overly compact, cauliflower-like newcomers to others. The older, taller varieties like 'Cut Wonder' blend more naturally with perennials and shrubs. Periwinkle blue is a color made in matchmaker's heaven; it never clashes. The old-fashioned ageratum is lovely with pale daylilies, white and pink muskmallow, *Malva moschata*, or just about any color. Every year, I plant the misty blue flowers, along with several other annuals—similarly hued *Asperula orientalis*, sky-blue Chinese forget-me-not (*Cynoglossum amabile*), rose foxglove-like *Rehmannia elata* and pink, white and chartreuse flowering tobacco—in a casual manner among the perennials and shrubs of the watered east side of the house, where they get the soft morning light and afternoon shade they enjoy most.

Dry shade is perhaps the most difficult situation for gardening. In nature, these conditions harbor a limited selection of plants—dry pine woodlands or hardwood forests dominated by greedy-rooted plants like beech often have few plants growing beneath them. Leaf or needle litter extends across the barren scene. I looked forward to hikes in beech woods back in Pennsylvania because it meant less bushwacking. Leaf litter rustled under my feet. In the spring, trout lilies and bloodroot would spangle the ground for a short while, but that was about it for the season. What all this means is that the gardener has a very small selection of plants available to choose from that are adapted to dry shade. Bulbs and perennials offer the greatest selection, annuals the least. I have had success with three.

Night-blooming stock, *Matthiola longipetala* ssp. *bicornis*, a scruffy plant redeemed by its heady, velvety fragrance, can hack it in light shade with very little water. I grow it under the eaves where rain never reaches it, beneath the window of the living room so the perfume can waft into the house on summer evenings. Every now and then, when I remember, I give it a splash from the watering can, but it is pretty much on its own. A hard shearing in midsummer, as done to sweet alyssum, rejuvenates evening stock for a good fall flush. Self-sown seedlings often appear.

Feverfew (*Tanacetum parthenium*, also known as matricaria) is more often perennial than annual, yet blooms reliably the first year from seed and steadfastly continues all summer and into the fall. It grows most luxuriantly in a rich, well-watered, partly shaded garden, yet blooms less and tends to flop and open up in the center. Dry, light shade and a leaner soil keep it a foot in height and girth and full of flowers. An old garden plant with various medicinal uses, pungently fragrant leaves that repel most insects and a long vase life, feverfew is a most versatile plant. A form with golden foliage, 'Aureum', more chartreuse than gold when grown in the shade, glows amid the deep greens of the shaded garden. In spring, at its brightest and freshest, it combines with another dry-shade candidate, perennial *Brunnera macrophylla*, Siberian forget-me-not. The massive dark green, heart-shaped leaves of brunnera, along with its long-blooming spray of light blue flowers, are the perfect foil for golden feverfew. Feverfew, as so many other plants, has been subjected to a dwarfing process and now often masquerades as shrunken, ball-shaped specimens. I have seen these lined out to edge many an annual bed, like so many confused snowballs in midsummer. Old-fashioned feverfew, with its handsome foliage and long-lived sprays of white single or double flowers, similar to a refined mum, is a cinch from seed and is often perennial as well as self-sowing, securing its place in tomorrow's gardens as it did in those of yesteryear.

The other annual for dry shade, lotus vine (*Lotus berthelotii*), is perennial in warmer climates. While not truly a vine, it does grow more prostrate than upright, a delight in a hanging basket. Lotus vine supposedly has beautiful red flowers resembling a parrot's beak. Mine have never bloomed, which I don't begrudge them at all, for the foliage in and of itself makes the plant more than worthy. The arching branchlets are cloaked in tufts of needlelike yet soft gray foliage, resembling a silver-leaved larch. Trailing rather than climbing, lotus vine looks best given a slope or a wall from which to cascade. Out-of-doors, it rarely reaches more than a foot and a half in length before frost does it in, while plants overwintered in a greenhouse can become almost twice that size. Flashy yet tough bulbous companions in light shade and dryish soil, magenta-pink colchicums beg for a delicate gray skirt of lotus vine to cover their leafless late-summer and autumn flowers.

 As I've said before, the true key to a beautiful year-round garden is foliage. I can't think of any plant of which I'm particularly fond that doesn't have at least good-looking if not stunning leaves. Annuals have never been strong in the foliage department. Perhaps it is the selection process of evolution that favored showy bloom for dependable pollination and seed set at the expense of foliage; after all, they only have one growing season to be done with it. Like ladies of the night, annuals only have so much time to accomplish their mission, and flashy flowers, like flashy clothes, are a means to that end. Perhaps this is all farfetched, and it is the gardener's interminable greed for larger, more numerous, more showy blossoms that has created an artificial pool of annuals from which to choose at the expense of foliage. Whatever the reason, good foliage annuals are few and far between.

Many, in fact, have been borrowed by foliage-hungry gardeners from other realms of horticultural tradition, namely vegetable and herb gardening. Maroon arugula, red Swiss chard, silver artichoke and blue, purple and rose cabbage have jumped the fence

Annuals
for Foliage

from the vegetable patch to the purely ornamental garden. Purple basil, bronze fennel and burgundy beefsteak plant are borrowed from the herb garden. I remember a huge compost heap at a garden I worked in where these three red-hued foliage annuals, joined by equally ruddy red orach, *Atriplex hortensis* 'Rubra', had self-sown and grown to enormous proportions, drawing on the wealth within the compost heap from which they sprung. When the sun lit the leaves just so, they were as beautiful as any iris, rose or dahlia. I vowed to make room for them in my garden.

Purple basil, more bitter in taste than its green counterpart, is, however, just as aromatic and much more interesting to look at. Whether the glossy oval leaves of 'Dark Opal' or the wavy-edged 'Purple Ruffles', these basil varieties can mix as well with pink, white and rose flowers as with the orange, red and yellow end of the spectrum. Basil, sadly, is not very drought tolerant and not the slightest bit able to withstand early frost.

More often, I call on the feathery, licorice-scented bronze fennel, *Foeniculum vulgare* 'Purpureum' and purple beefsteak plant, *Perilla frutescens* 'Atropurpurea' and 'Crispa'. Bronze fennel, a perennial in mild winters, grows anywhere from two to four feet, depending on available moisture, while shorter yet more weighty perilla stays at about one-and-a-half to two feet. Again, as with purple basil, both pastels and hot colors are enhanced. An added attraction of these latter two, more drought-tolerant annuals is their affinity for silver foliage. Flowers are forgotten when purple perilla takes a place next to shimmering lambs ears, or bronze fennel pairs with silver verbascum rosettes.

My favorite of the red-leaved annuals is red orach, *Atriplex hortensis* 'Rubra'. It has more crimson a cast than the bronzier, browner tones of basil, perilla and fennel. Its tall spires of purple seed are as ornamental as the foliage preceding them, and self-sowing is virtually guaranteed. It thrives in average soils and survives high alkalinity. Coupled with the soft yellow flowers of daylilies and a tawny selection of yarrow, red orach serves as the richest of backdrops.

Castor bean (*Ricinus communis*), a poisonous giant of an annual, is best left to accent areas near the house, for its exotic, tropical appearance and great thirst preclude its integration with the more natural-looking, tough natives. Castor bean is a bold, beautiful plant with huge, palmate leaves, tinted maroon in several varieties, and spiny scarlet fruit capsules. It's one of those plants that captures the imagination yet is hard to succeed with because it jars with most plantings except the very lushest. A friend grew it in containers, a good move, for ample food and water could be administered to the gluttonous giants, and the containers created a sense of appropriate artificiality that helped integrate castor bean into the overall garden scene. Similarly showy, slightly overbearing and very thirsty red-leaved *Hibiscus acetosella* 'Red Shield' can be used effectively the same way.

Three annual vines round out the best of the foliage annuals. All have been grown not just for their looks but also for the sake of the palate—tart nasturtium foliage and

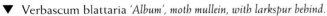

▲ Datura meteloides, *southwestern native angel's trumpet.*

▼ Verbascum blattaria 'Album', *moth mullein, with larkspur behind.*

▲ Nigella damascena, *love-in-a-mist.*

▲ Borago officinalis, *borage.*

▲ Pennisetum villosum, *feather top.*

▲ Delphinium grandiflorum.

▼ Cosmos bipinnatus 'Sonata White'.

flowers grace salads, hyacinth bean produces tasty pods and beans and golden hops plays a vital role in making beer. Nasturtiums grow best cool, dry and with little food. The most beautiful display I ever saw was at an aunt's home in Austria. There, instead of the legendary Rapunzel letting down her golden hair, it was trailing nasturtiums that tumbled in great gold, yellow and orange profusion from the third story balcony. I have tried to replicate that perfect scene more times than I care to admit. Unfortunately, not only human beings find nasturtiums tasty—rabbits, aphids and grasshoppers have acquired a taste for them as well. While it seems almost every other garden I visit, even the farmer's vegetable plot, is festooned with a carefree, healthy jumble of the plant, mine never amount to anything. Someday I will grow some decent nasturtiums. Anyway, the peculiar foliage is very beautiful: rounded, blue-green and with the leaf stalk joining in the center of the blade from which radiates a pale, spidery star of veins. Nonclimbing, pert little varieties now exist and are pushing the old-fashioned trailing ones out of the market. I want only the trailers, in bright oranges and yellows against the fresh foliage, and will keep looking for the seed and sowing them where they are to grow, which they prefer, and hoping that the critters will take pity on me and my poor plants and let me have a nasturtium Rapunzel.

Golden hops (*Humulus lupulus* 'Aureus'), also drought tolerant, brings light to a softly shaded area. It can be perennial in warmer climates. This select variety of the common green hops has chartreuse-yellow foliage shown to best advantage scampering up a dark fence or tree trunk.

Finally, there is the lovely hyacinth bean. This annual legume is the rare case where the botanical name is more colorful and enjoyable than the common name—irresistible *Dolichos lablab*. Every part of this plant is attractive, from the name on to the purple-backed leaves, from the pink flowers down to the glossy burgundy beanpods. Hyacinth bean needs full sun and average moisture to do well. It clothes itself sparsely, so should not be counted on to cover an unsightly cyclone fence or the like. Instead, allow it to ramble with other climbers—white morning glories, crimson clematis, golden-flowered honeysuckle.

Annuals, given a closer look, are much more varied than a quick peek at the nearest garden center in late spring would have one believe. Beyond marigolds, geraniums and petunias lies a whole world of diverse, unusual, beautiful plants waiting to find a cherished place in the garden. Annuals invite the experimental gardener, the adventurous colorist, the diehard seedgrower to give them a whirl. The key to happy results were brought graphically home to me one cool morning in early September. As I sleepily padded out the front door to retrieve the paper, I was greeted by an autumn scene I didn't remember ever having planned or visualized beforehand, or at any rate, never imagined in all its splendor: The bold pewter rosette of an artichoke set off scarlet spires of *Salvia coccinea*, while a cloud of purple perennial asters rose up behind. Here, in combination with other plants in the garden, marrying flower and foliage, color, form and texture, was the best of my annuals and the best of my garden.

ANNUALS WITH UNDAUNTED CHARACTERISTICS

KEY

B: biennial.

PP: featured in plant portrait.

SELF-SOWING ANNUALS AND BIENNIALS

Ammi majus annual Queen Anne's lace
Antirrhinum majus snapdragon
Asperula orientalis blue woodruff
Atriplex hortensis 'Rubra' red orach **PP**
Borago officinalis borage
Calandrinia umbellata rock purslane
Calendula officinalis pot marigold
Centaurea cyanus bachelor's button
Cheiranthus allionii Siberian wallflower **B**
Cirsium spinosissimum **B**
Cleome spider flower
Consolida ambigua larkspur
Coreopsis tinctoria calliopsis
Cosmos bipinnatus
Cynoglossum amabile Chinese forget-me-not **PP**
Delphinium grandiflorum annual delphinium
Dracocephalum nutans **B, PP**
Dyssodia tenuiloba Dahlberg daisy
Echium viper's bugloss
Erigeron karvinskianus Santa Barbara daisy
Eryngium giganteum silver sea holly **B, PP**
Eschscholzia California poppy
Euphorbia marginata snow on the mountain
Foeniculum vulgare 'Purpureum' bronze fennel **PP**
Gilia/Ipomopsis skyrocket **B**
Glaucium horned poppy **B**
Helianthus annuus sunflower
Hunnemannia fumariifolia Mexican poppy
Ipomoea purpurea morning glory
Layia tidy tips
Linaria maroccana
Linum grandiflorum annual flax
Lobularia maritima sweet alyssum

Machaeranthera Tahoka daisy
Malva sylvestris cheese mallow
Matricaria recutita German chamomile
Matthiola bicornis evening scented stock
Mentzelia blazing star some **B**
Moluccella laevis bells of Ireland
Nemophila baby blue-eyes, five-spot
Nicotiana flowering tobacco
Nigella love-in-a-mist
Papaver poppy **PP**
Perilla frutescens beefsteak plant
Petunia x *hybrida*
Phacelia campanularia desert bluebell
Portulaca grandiflora moss rose
Rudbeckia hirta black-eyed Susan
Rudbeckia triloba **B, PP**
Salvia coccinea Texas scarlet sage
Salvia sclarea clary sage **B, PP**
Salvia viridis
Silene armeria annual catchfly, none-so-pretty
Silybum marianum milk thistle **B**
Tagetes marigold—signet types
Talinum fame flower
Tanacetum parthenium feverfew **PP**
Verbascum **B, PP**
Verbena bonariensis, V. rigida **PP**
Viola corsica Corsican pansy **PP**
Viola tricolor Johnny-jump-up

ANNUALS THAT CAN TOLERATE LIGHT FROST (SPRING OR FALL)

Ammi majus annual Queen Anne's lace
Antirrhinum majus snapdragon
Arctotis African daisy
Atriplex hortensis 'Rubra' red orach **PP**
Baileya multiradiata desert marigold
Borago officinalis borage
Brachycome iberidifolia Swan River daisy
Brassica ornamental kale

Calendula officinalis pot marigold
Centaurea cyanus bachelor's button
Consolida ambigua larkspur
Coreopsis tinctoria calliopsis
Crepis rubra pink hawksbeard
Cynara cardoon
Cynoglossum amabile Chinese forget-me-not **PP**
Delphinium grandiflorum annual delphinium
Dianthus chinensis annual pinks
Diascia twinspur
Echium viper's bugloss
Erigeron karvinskianus Santa Barbara daisy
Eschscholzia California poppy
Foeniculum vulgare 'Purpureum' bronze fennel **PP**
Gaillardia pulchella annual Indian blanket
Gypsophila elegans annual baby's breath
Lathyrus odoratus sweet pea
Layia tidytips
Linaria maroccana
Linum grandiflorum annual flax
Lobularia maritima sweet alyssum
Matricaria recutita German chamomile
Matthiola bicornis evening scented stock
Moluccella laevis bells of Ireland
Nemophila baby blue-eyes, five-spot
Nicotiana flowering tobacco
Nigella love-in-a-mist
Papaver poppy **PP**
Petunia x *hybrida*
Phacelia campanularia desert bluebell
Rudbeckia black-eyed Susan **PP**
Salvia farinacea mealy-cup sage
Scabiosa atropurpurea pincushion flower
Senecio cineraria dusty miller
Silene armeria annual catchfly, none-so-pretty
Tanacetum parthenium feverfew **PP**
Tropaeolum majus nasturtium
Verbena **PP**
Viola pansy **PP**

*Flowers
With Fortitude:
Long-Blooming
Perennials*

Anyone who has worked in a nursery or garden center is well acquainted with that nonexistent plant all neophyte gardeners so desire: *Planta perfecta*—hardy, tough, maintenance-free, pest and disease resistant and, of course, blooming all season long. I include this chapter to make room for those plants I feel come closest to those characteristics, but for whatever reason did not fit into the other chapters. In other words, I write this out of duty to those star performers that happen not to be particularly dry loving or shade tolerant, nor are they annuals, which are expected to be relatively easy to grow, carefree and long-blooming. All these plants want is moderately fertile soil with average moisture, a decent amount of sunshine, and they will bloom dependably for at least a month, in many cases much longer. They are flowers with fortitude.

The family that represents the largest number of these desirable garden plants is the *Compositae*, or daisy tribe. Most are summer and early autumn flowering, the majority in cheery tones of yellow and white. Their simple, friendly faces can disarm even the most snobbish of horticulturists once the slow days of summer have set in. Drought-tolerant western natives Indian blanket, prairie coneflower (*Ratibida columnifera*), greenthread (*Thelesperma ambiguum*), paper flower (*Psilostrophe* spp.), Rocky Mountain zinnia (*Zinnia grandi-flora*), Blackfoot daisy (*Melampodium leucanthum*), chocolate flower (*Berlandiera lyrata*) and golden aster (*Chrysopsis* spp.) have already been mentioned earlier. So have water-thrifty *Tanacetum niveum* and *Achillea* x 'Moonshine', a cluster of daisies without the rays; the hardy *Chrysanthemum zawadskii* clan are given their due in chapter eight. The following deserve mention:

Coreopsis verticillata, threadleaf coreopsis, is a native, fine-textured golden daisy for all-summer bloom. The straight species reaches between two and three feet in height and is somewhat invasive. Average garden soil is best, sun or light shade. The plant is easy to divide. 'Moonbeam' is the famed pale yellow, shorter hybrid cultivar, blooming for four months; 'Zagreb' has the golden flowers of the species but is smaller—only a foot or so—and not as invasive.

Catananche caerulea, Cupid's dart, has a flower somewhere between a bachelor's button and chicory. The lavender-blue stars rise about fifteen inches or so above a small, flat rosette. As each flower goes over, it leaves behind a pretty pearl-like button made up of the papery calyx and seeds. Cupid's dart is short-lived but easy to grow from seed. Full sun and a well-drained soil is best.

Centaurea dealbata is a robust pink-flowered knapweed, with pretty ragged-edged flowers like a large bachelor's button. The bushy plant boasts large, incised green foliage with silvery undersides, remarkably lush for such a drought-tolerant plant. Pink knapweed grows two to three feet tall and wide, and thrives in full sun in both very dry and average garden soil. Easy from seed or division.

Echinacea purpurea, purple coneflower, is a rose-colored, heavy-textured daisy native to the prairie. The stiff orange-brown disk flowers, the "eye", attract bees and butterflies; the ray flowers often hang down from this prominent center. Rough green foliage clothes purple coneflower's two- to four-foot presence. Full sun and a good but well-drained garden soil are ideal. White forms 'Alba', 'White Lustre', 'White Swan' and selections with larger, less droopy flowers—'Magnus', 'The King'—are available. Easy from seed or division.

Rudbeckia spp., the gold and yellow black-eyed Susans of North America, are premier summer and fall flowers for the sunny garden with good soil. *Rudbeckia fulgida* var. *sullivantii* 'Goldsturm' is a stocky, extra floriferous eighteen-inch mass, quite in vogue as of late. *R. laciniata* is a giant five- to eight-foot plant with a crown of golden daisies, usually double pompoms of the more common cultivars such as 'Golden Glow'. *R. nitida* is similar; 'Herbstsonne', another German selection, has a cool green center. All these plants are easy to divide.

Helenium autumnale, Helen's flower, offers a profusion of little shuttlecock-like daisies in warm shades of gold, orange, copper and rust. Helen's flower needs a relatively moist soil in full sun; the plant grows three to five feet and needs the support of other plants close by or else it may flop over. Many good cultivars exist. Easy to divide.

Aster x *frikartii* has the largest flower of the asters, over two inches in diameter, over a two- to three-foot plant, quite gamely proportions for an aster. The flowers are a soft, glowing lavender. *Aster* x *frikartii* does best in light shade or morning sun, in average garden soil. 'Flora's Delight' is an extra compact cultivar, about half the height of the more commonly seen forms 'Mönch' and 'Wonder of Stäfa'. Divide carefully.

Anaphalis margaritacea and *A. triplinervis*, the gray-leaved, white-flowered pearly everlastings, are one of the few hairy, silver plants that prefer a bit of shade and not too dry a soil. They bloom late in the summer and fall. The larva of the painted lady butterfly can be a pest on the young developing shoots and buds but will not harm the plant. Hand picking and/or spraying the plant with *Bacillus thuringiensis* should clear up the problem. Pearly everlastings grow one to two feet tall and a bit wider. Easy to divide.

(facing page) Purple coneflower (Echinacea purpurea 'Bright Star') and sea lavender (Limonium latifolium) make a long-lasting late-summer picture with the waxy blue foliage of sea kale.

▶ Fleeting Oriental poppies glow against a backdrop of stalwart Salvia x superba 'Lubeca'.

▲ Aster x frikartii.

▲ Perovskia *sp., Russian sage.*

▲ Calamintha grandiflora *and* Geranium sanguineum.

Another family full of wonderful, dependable, long-blooming plants for daunting climates is the *Labiatae*, or mint family. Aromatic herbs, both medicinal and culinary, are disproportionately represented. Many labiates are drought tolerant and were mentioned in that context: Russian sage, the showy oreganos, lavender, some of the dragonsheads (*Dracocephalum* spp.), skullcaps (*Scutellaria* spp.) and catmint. Long-blooming labiates for the watered sunny garden include:

Prunella grandiflora 'Pinnatifida', or cutleaf selfheal is a fancy version of the common little European wildflower. Cutleaf selfheal does best with morning sun or light shade; in full sun, it wilts from the heat by midday. The dense, low, six- to eight-inch mound of purple-tinted, incised foliage is topped by many loose clusters of hooded rose-pink flowers in the summer. Easy to divide.

Salvia azurea, azure sage, grows wild in the central and southeastern states. A tall, floppy plant with little substance, its lax figure is redeemed by the fiercely true blue flowers it produces in late summer and autumn. Azure sage needs the support of other plants. Full sun and a soil on the dry side helps keep the plant more sturdy. Butterflies are attracted to the flowers. Easy from seed.

Salvia x *superba*, garden sage, is a stiffly upright clump of a plant bearing brilliant dark purple-blue flower spikes in late spring and early summer, often repeating the performance if cut back hard after the first flush. Full sun and an average garden soil produce the best flowering. 'Rose Queen' has deep pink flowers. Divide carefully.

Monarda didyma, bee balm, is a rangy perennial native to the eastern half of North America. Its showy, rounded flowerheads attract bees, butterflies and hummingbirds. The plant's form and foliage are sub-par—it is a lax, invasive clump of straggly,

unbranched stems and often mildew-infested leaves. Bee balm should be placed behind other plants so only the beautiful flowers can be seen. Moist soil and morning sun or light shade are best. Red, crimson, white, lavender, pink and purple cultivars are available. Easy to divide.

Nepeta sibirica. See plant portrait section.

Agastache barberi and *A. cana* are two giant hyssops with showy deep pink flowers for most of the second half of the summer and autumn. Hummingbirds cherish the flowers. *A. barberi* is taller and more elegant, with airy three- to four-foot spikes over mauve-tinted foliage. *Agastache cana*, named Double Bubble mint for the delectable fragrance of the flowers, leaves and seeds, is a foot or so shorter, with gray-green foliage and stouter flower spikes. Both giant hyssops do best in full sun with a well-drained soil on the dry side but not completely so. They should be grown from seed.

Regal lilies are surrounded by a long-flowering supporting cast of yellow Cephalaria alpina, Digitalis lutea, *pink* Lavatera thuringiaca *and white 'Miss Lingard' phlox, as fine-textured* Tanacetum niveum *finishes.*

Physostegia virginiana, obedient plant, carries tiered spikes of snoutlike pink or white flowers on square stems in late summer and autumn. The flowers can be moved and rearranged on the stem, hence the common name. An eastern native, obedient plant surprisingly prefers the climate of the continental West. The most strapping clumps with the finest foliage are those I've seen in Colorado. Obedient plant grows three to four feet tall and wide and is a bit invasive. A variegated form exists but always seems gnarled and twisted in the leaves, not particularly appealing to me. Easy to divide.

The bellflowers are so charming of flower shape and color that they are nearly impossible to dislike, except for the self-important, invasive ones like *Campanula rapunculoides*, a pretty thug deceitfully graceful and delicate in appearance, which the gardener usually doesn't learn to despise until it is too late. Many members of the *Campanulaceae* family are not only pretty, but also agreeable and long-flowering. Some of the smaller species do well in part shade with less water—*Campanula carpatica, Campanula portenschlagiana, Campanula poscharskyana*. Other easy-to-please bellflowers include:

Campanula glomerata, the clustered bellflower, is the least graceful of the bunch, but the flowers are so freely produced and so vivid a purple that one must forgive it. Clustered bellflower forms spreading patches of dense green foliage. The flowers rise up on stiff one- to two-foot stems in summer. Good garden soil and morning sun or light shade are best. 'Alba' is a commonly available white form. Easy to divide.

Campanula persicifolia, the peach-leaf bellflower, is the opposite of clustered bellflower— all grace and little *oompf*. Powder blue or white bells rise on thin but strong two to three-foot stems all summer. Peach-leaf bellflower wants the same conditions as its

coarser cousin. The double forms are unattractive balls, having lost all semblance of bells. 'Cup and Saucer', however, is a beautiful semidouble that is aptly named. This bellflower self-sows and can also be divided.

Asyneuma canescens bears narrow spikes of the daintiest deep purple stars in the summer. It has one of the most unusual flower shapes—the stars are so finely cut they almost appear drawn with a fine purple marker. It grows twelve to eighteen inches tall and prefers light shade. Easy from seed or division.

Platycodon grandiflorus, balloon flower, is so named for its puffy flower buds. These actually pop as the blossoms open, all summer long, into large, shallow bells of blue or white. Balloon flower is very late to emerge in the spring, and its form is not the best, a bit floppy at times and scant in the foliage department. The foliage does turn a good straw yellow in the fall, however. The plant prefers a good garden soil and some protection from the hottest sun. Pink, dwarf and double cultivars are now the rage; these are not nearly as appealing as the two-foot-tall plants with blue or white single flowers. Balloon flower grows easily from seed.

The delightful pincushion flowers include these four essential summer bloomers:

Scabiosa caucasica 'Butterfly Blue' is an airy plant, carrying misty blue pincushions all summer and into the fall. It grows about a foot in height; the sage green leaves are low and not very substantial, making the plant an excellent filler to squeeze in between plants. It does best with morning sun in a well-drained garden soil.

Scabiosa ochroleuca. See plant portrait section.

Knautia macedonica. See plant portrait section.

Cephalaria alpina, the giant pincushion flower, carries summer-blooming moonlight yellow flowers four to eight feet above a massive clump of incised green leaves. Sun or light shade and a well-drained but not completely dry soil is what the plant wants. Easy from seed.

The huge phlox clan, all natives of North America, can also be counted on for many weeks of bloom. The earliest, the drought-tolerant moss phloxes (*Phlox bifida, P. douglasii, P. subulata*) and the shade-loving sweet William phlox, *P. divaricata*, are already familiar from previous chapters. For gorgeous trusses of fragrant flowers from summer into early autumn in sun or light shade and good garden soil:

Phlox maculata is the earlier group to bloom, also not as tall, reaching two to three feet. The shiny leaves are quite mildew resistant. 'Miss Lingard' is pure white, 'Alpha' a warm pink and 'Omega' white with a dark eye.

Phlox paniculata, the old-fashioned garden phlox, is a tall stately clump of flowers, one of the classic border plants for late summer and fall. Mildew is its biggest problem, though more so in maritime climates; good air circulation is helpful. There are oodles of cultivars; some of the best include: 'Mt. Fuji' white, 'Franz Schubert' pale lavender, 'Antonia Mercer' lilac with purple eye, 'Starfire' deep red, 'Bright Eyes' blush pink with rose eye, 'Nora Leigh' lilac flowers and evenly variegated cream and green leaves, 'Dodo Hanbury Forbes' pink with dark eye.

My favorite group of tractable garden flowers is the mallows. They possess an elegance that enables them to slip easily into either supporting or leading roles in summer garden compositions. Quite drought tolerant yet blessed with good foliage, the mallows give a sunny garden on the dry side that lush, cottage feel without the water. I wouldn't be without any of the following:

Alcea rugosa. See plant portrait section.

Malva alcea, the hollyhock mallow, is a large three- to four-foot leafy mass studded with typical pink mallow flowers most of the summer and fall. 'Fastigiata' has more discernible spikes arising from the mound. Easy from seed.

Malva moschata. See plant portrait section.

Lavatera thuringiaca See plant portrait section.

Lavatera cachemiriana is a taller, more vertical and refined pale pink version of *L. thuringiaca*, with deeply notched flower petals giving the blossoms a starry look—a hollyhock that went to finishing school. Easy from seed.

Sidalcea malviflora, checkerbloom, makes a polished clump of rounded basal leaves, while the foliage that cloaks the flower stems is quite distinct and deeply cut. Satiny mallow flowers in all shades of pink and rose bloom on spikes most of the summer. Checkerbloom reaches two to four feet tall and grows from seed or careful division. Most of the cultivars are annoyingly similar; 'Elsie Heugh' stands apart for its pale pink flowers with frilly edges, and 'Nimmerdor', deep pink and up to six feet in height.

Hibiscus syriacus, rose-of-Sharon, is an old-fashioned large shrub or small tree, a so-called "trub." It looks best when allowed to form a leafy, casual multistemmed clump rather than trained stiffly into a poor excuse for a tree. Its coarse, vase-shaped growth habit is completely redeemed during the second half of the summer when the plant

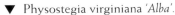

▲ Physostegia virginiana, *obedient plant.*

▼ Physostegia virginiana *'Alba'.*

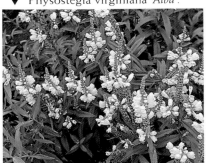

▲ Cutleaf selfheal and bergenia grow in light, dry shade.

▼ Lavatera thuringiaca *'Barnsley' and Russian sage in late summer.*

▼ Verbena bipinnatifida, *Dakota vervain, and violas in spring.*

▼ Fragrant Agastache cana, *Double Bubble mint,* and 'Clara Curtis' mum bloom well into autumn.

becomes an almost tropical vision of floral abundance. A multitude of named selections exist, with large flowers in shades of pink, lavender, red or white, either single or double blossoms, and some with contrasting dark eyes. Rose-of-Sharon does best in ordinary, well-drained but not completely dry garden soil in full sun. The larger flowered newer hybrids such as 'Diana' and 'Helene' are not quite as hardy.

Many of the drought-tolerant spring-flowering mustards, such as stone cress (*Aethionema* spp.), *Alyssum montanum* and basket-of-gold, as well as the more shade-desiring candytuft (*Iberis sempervirens*) and sweet rocket (*Hesperis matronalis*), can be counted on for a long show, as can all the mysterious foxgloves, most of which prefer some shade. Several evening primroses, dry-demanding *Oenothera serrulata*, *O. brachycarpa* and *O. caespitosa* and the more adaptable Ozark sundrop *O. macrocarpa* and pink *O. speciosa*, as well as their close relatives, the fireweeds or willow herbs, bloom for well over a month. The delicate fireweed, *Epilobium dodonaei*, is hardly known in gardening circles, yet at one and a half to two feet in height, with less invasive ways than its taller brethren but with the same glowing rose-purple flowers on graceful stems whorled with willowlike gray-green leaves, this plant deserves more popularity.

A beautiful garden doesn't necessarily mean slaving over finicky treasures. Just because a plant is easy doesn't mean it should be eschewed. The sense of accomplishment when a rare gentian settles in and begins to bloom, the anticipation of the short but spectacular bloom of peonies and bearded irises—both add dimensions to the pleasure of gardening. But for a pleasing year-round garden, one needs to combine a backdrop of good foliage, both deciduous and evergreen, a smattering of annuals and biennials, and then a large helping of these reliable, rewarding perennials: the flowers with fortitude.

(preceding page) In light shade, shimmering white musk mallow, Malva moschata 'Alba', feverfew and graceful yellow Aquilegia chrysantha bloom for well over a month.

PLANTS THAT BLOOM FOR MORE THAN A MONTH
This list does not include annuals.

KEY

D: tolerates dry conditions.

S: prefers some shade.

PP: featured in plant portrait.

PERENNIALS

Achillea millefolium yarrow D
Achillea x 'Moonshine' yarrow D
Aethionema stone cress D
Alcea rosea hollyhock D
Alcea rugosa hollyhock D, PP
Agastache giant hyssop D
Alchemilla lady's mantle S

Alyssum montanum mountain basket-of-gold D, PP
Anchusa azurea alkanet D
Anaphalis pearly everlasting
Anemone pulsatilla (aka *Pulsatilla vulgaris*) pasqueflower D
Anemone tomentosa Japanese anemone S
Anemone x *hybrida* Japanese anemone S
Anthemis tinctoria golden marguerite D
Aquilegia columbine S
Argemone prickly poppy D
Armeria sea thrift D
Aster x *frikartii*
Astrantia Hattie's pincushion S
Asyneuma canescens

Aurinia saxatilis basket-of-gold D
Berlandiera lyrata chocolate flower D
Brunnera macrophylla Siberian bugloss D, S
Calamintha
Callirhoe prairie winecup D, PP
Campanula carpatica Carpathian bellflower D, S
Campanula garganica D, S
Campanula glomerata clustered bellflower
Campanula persicifolia peach-leaf bellflower D, S
Campanula portenschlagiana D, S
Campanula poscharskyana creeping bellflower D, S
Campanula rotundifolia harebell

Catananche caerulea Cupid's dart **D**
Centaurea dealbata pink knapweed **D**
Centaurea hypoleuca pink knapweed **D**
Centranthus ruber Greek valerian **D**
Ceratostigma plumbaginoides false plumbago, leadwort **S**
Chrysanthemum zawadskii 'Clara Curtis'
Chrysogonum virginianum green-and-gold **S**
Chrysopsis golden aster **D**
Coreopsis **D**
Corydalis lutea yellow fumitory **S**
Delosperma cooperi purple iceplant **D**
Delphinium elatum
Dianthus pinks **D**
Dicentra eximia fringed bleeding heart **S**
Dicentra spectabilis old-fashioned bleeding heart **S**
Digitalis foxglove **S**
Dracocephalum botryoides **D**
Dracocephalum multicaule **D**
Dracocephalum nutans **D, PP**
Dracocephalum renatii **D**
Dracocephalum speciosum sapphire dragon-head **S**
Echinacea purple coneflower **D**
Epilobium angustifolium 'Album' white fireweed **PP**
Epilobium dodonaei small fireweed **D**
Eriogonum umbellatum sulphur flower **D, PP**
Erodium storksbill **D**
Euphorbia corollata flowering spurge
Gaillardia x grandiflora Indian blanket **D**
Gaura lindheimeri apple blossom grass **D**
Geranium cinereum 'Ballerina' **D**
Geranium endressii **S**
Geranium pratense meadow cranesbill
Geranium sanguineum **D**
Goniolimon statice **D**
Gypsophila paniculata baby's breath **D**
Helenium autumnale Helen's flower
Helianthemum sunrose
Heliopsis helianthoides summer sun **D**
Helleborus hellebore **S**
Hemerocallis 'Stella d'Oro', 'Happy Returns' **D**
Hesperis matronalis sweet rocket **S**
Heuchera sanguinea coralbells **D, S**
Heucherella tiarelloides **S**
Hibiscus moscheutos swamp mallow
Iberis sempervirens candytuft **D, S**
Knautia macedonica **D, PP**
Lamium maculatum dead nettle **S**
Lavandula angustifolia lavender **D**

Lavatera shrub mallow **D, PP**
Leucanthemum vulgare oxeye daisy
Leucanthemum x superbum shasta daisy
Limonium statice, sea lavender **D**
Linaria toadflax **D**
Linum flax **D, PP**
Lobelia cardinalis cardinal flower **S**
Lychnis coronaria rose campion **D, S**
Lythrum purple loosestrife
Malva mallow **PP**
Melampodium leucanthum Blackfoot daisy **D**
Mirabilis multiflora desert four o'clock **D**
Monarda beebalm, horsemint, oswego tea
Nepeta catmint **PP**
Oenothera brachycarpa desert sundrop **D, PP**
Oenothera caespitosa tufted evening primrose **D**
Oenothera macrocarpa (O. missouriensis) Ozark sundrop **D**
Oenothera serrulata **D**
Oenothera speciosa pink evening primrose **D**
Onosma **D**
Origanum showy oregano **D, PP**
Papaver rupifragum **D**
Papaver triniifolium **D, PP**
Penstemon ambiguus moth penstemon **D**
Penstemon barbatus scarlet bugler **D**
Penstemon digitalis
Penstemon pinifolius prairie fire penstemon **D**
Penstemon procerus **D, S, PP**
Penstemon richardsonii **D, S**
Perovskia Russian sage **D**
Persicaria (aka Polygonum) affinis border jewel **D**
Persicaria amplexicaulis
Petrorhagia (aka Tunica) saxifraga **D**
Phlox bifida sand phlox **D**
Phlox divaricata sweet William phlox **S**
Phlox douglasii moss phlox **D**
Phlox maculata garden phlox
Phlox paniculata (aka Phlox decussata) garden phlox
Phlox subulata moss phlox **D**
Physostegia virginiana obedient plant
Platycodon grandiflorus balloon flower
Polemonium caeruleum Jacob's ladder **S**
Prunella grandiflora selfheal
Psilostrophe paper flower **D**
Ratibida prairie coneflower **D**
Rudbeckia black-eyed Susan
Salvia azurea azure sage **D**
Salvia cyanescens **D**
Salvia forskaohlei **D, S**

Salvia sclarea **D, PP**
Salvia x superba **D**
Saponaria officinalis bouncing Bet, soapwort
Saponaria pamphylica **D**
Scabiosa pincushion flower **PP**
Scutellaria skullcap **D**
Sedum spectabile **D**
Sedum spurium **D, S**
Sedum x 'Autumn Joy' **D**
Sedum x 'Ruby Glow' **D**
Sidalcea malviflora checkerbloom
Sideritis hyssopifolia **D**
Stachys coccinea red betony
Tanacetum niveum **D, PP**
Tanacetum parthenium feverfew **PP**
Tellima grandiflora fringe cups **S**
Thalictrum delavayi late meadow rue **S**
Tiarella cordifolia v. collina (aka T. wherryi) foamflower **S**
Tradescantia spiderwort
Trillium grandiflorum wake robin **S**
Verbascum mullein **D, PP**
Verbena bipinnatifida **D**
Veronica incana 'Saraband' **D**
Veronica spicata 'Red Fox' **D**
Veronica x 'Sunny Border Blue'
Zauschneria **D, PP**
Zinnia grandiflora Rocky Mountain zinnia **D**

LONG-FLOWERING WOODY PLANTS

Buddleya butterfly bush **D**
Campsis radicans trumpet vine **D**
Caryopteris x clandonensis blue mist spirea **D**
Clematis
Cotinus smokebush **D**
Fallugia paradoxa Apache plume **D, PP**
Hibiscus syriacus rose-of-Sharon **D**
Hydrangea arborescens 'Annabelle' **S, PP**
Hydrangea paniculata peegee hygrangea
Hypericum calycinum St. John's wort
Hypericum patulum St. John's wort
Hypericum x moseranum St. John's wort
Polygonum aubertii silver lace vine **D**
Rosa mainly the modern shrub roses, hybrid teas, floribundas, grandifloras, miniatures, some of the old garden roses—hybrid perpetuals, Bourbons
Spiraea japonica
Spiraea x bumalda

VIII

Autumn in the Garden: The Reprise

Fresh, vibrant June passes to a languid, slow July. Then comes a turning point, when summer suddenly feels utterly tiresome. Some years, late summer weather is kind and merciful, indulging the gardener in a quick turn to cool nights and days filled with a mellow, amber sunlight that actually feels good on the face, totally unlike the prickling and piercing rays of high summer. Other years, the wait is interminable, summer's heat oozing on well into months traditionally autumnal.

Autumn has become my favorite time of the year. It took a while for negative associations with the beginning of the school year to wane, for the golden sunlight and foliage to stop conjuring up the intestinal butterflies that went along with similarly toned school buses lurching down the street. While some find spring with all its optimistic beginnings the finest season in the garden, I much prefer the unfrenzied pace of fall. In the spring, it is easy to feel overwhelmed by the sudden demands of the garden. A long winter has a way of creating such great yearnings and high expectations that I could almost say I feel a bit pressured by the new season, not to mention out of shape after a lazy winter spent fattening up by the fire. By autumn, I'm synchronized with the garden, lean and mean, realistic about my expectations. The garden requires much less of me—weeds are well under control and careful deadheading has long been abandoned. As a friend once described so well, the autumn garden is a machete garden. Anyone still trying to control or tame it in September is either hopelessly deluded or has a strange need to use large cutting tools from the jungle. The season transforms the garden and the gardener. While a similar scene in June might send one scrambling for stakes and twine, come September it is a wonderful sense of release to watch plants collapse slowly on each other, soft and heavy with the weight of a full season's growth. Leaves begin to yellow and brown. Flowers become seeds. Everything is soft, large, ripe. As I walk among the plants, they reflect my mood—placid and self-satisfied.

Fall isn't all retrospective mellowness. It is also a time for renewed activity. As the oppressive heat wanes, rediscovered energy can be put to great use, and not just for the traditional autumnal rite of bulb planting. Seed collecting kicks into high gear. Autumn is also the best time to assess the garden and decide which plants need to be

(preceding pages) A multitude of daisies celebrate autumn: asters, pink 'Clara Curtis' mum, 'Moonbeam' coreopsis (in bloom since June), with silver lamb's ear and airy purple Verbena bonariensis *rounding out the scene.*

166

moved, divided or tossed out altogether. Plants are at their largest, and crowding is painfully evident. A plant from which one waited patiently for some sign of beauty can now be given the old heave-ho without reservations if it has failed to perform. Integrating new plants is easier than ever; a full, live picture lies before the gardener, helping inspire good combinations as compared to the spring, when tiny, barely awakened leaf rosettes require calling upon strong imaging powers to visualize what may develop later. Most plants relish the chance to put out good roots without the competition of top growth and moisture-sapping heat. The soil stays warm much longer than the air, giving fall-planted individuals a long season of underground growth and establishment. If it weren't for the fact that some plants are not available in the fall, I would probably stop almost all my spring planting. Even small transplanted seedlings, given the benefit of some mulch around their base, have done remarkably well when planted in the fall.

Autumn is a time when warm color and rustling sounds resonate throughout the plant world. In the deciduous woodlands of the East and Midwest, winter spreads down the land from north to south, from highland to lowland, rolling a carpet of foliage color over the landscape before it. The land, so serenely green for all those months, suddenly looks like an infrared photograph. On the grasslands of the prairie and plains, the tired gray-green and buff of late summer take on richer amber, sienna and rust tones as the foliage and seedheads of the grasses ripen. Late-blooming wildflowers, predominantly deep golds and purples, attract sleepy butterflies and bees, while more energetic birds frenetically gorge themselves on seeds before the first snow cover blankets the land.

The sun arcs lower in the sky, softening and burnishing the light. All colors seem to emanate an inner warmth as if the heat of the summer were stored within them. The most mundane scenes—an empty concrete basketball court alive with whirling, wind-blown leaves, a chocolate-brown field spiked with tawny corn stubble—take on the qualities of gold leaf, the light of a Venetian Renaissance painting.

The lower sun also creates lovely lighting effects in the garden. While in summer it would be suppertime before any similar effect might be possible, now mid- and late afternoon becomes a time for backlit drama. Grass panicles glisten and shimmer when touched by the slanted light; foliage reds and golds are intensified as the sun passes through them; fragile petals resemble halos given this autumnal spotlight.

Just as fall is a time for letting go, for riding with the slow, melancholy yet beautiful decline toward the inevitability of winter, it is also a time for loosening up rigid color rules. What may jar in the May and June garden is a welcome sight in October. Colors have richened and deepened with the cooler temperatures and golden light. The sunlight of autumn softens the boundaries that in spring and summer define orange, red, magenta and purple. The gardener should soften as well. Just as a person living out his

▶ *Japanese anemone 'Honorine Jobert' catches the low afternoon sunlight of late autumn.*

(facing page) 'Goldsturm' rudbeckia takes center stage in this ripe autumnal scene, as the season's golden light gives the foliage of dyer's broom, sea kale, shiny sand cherry and irises a warm glow.

▲ The papery calyces of Acantholimon spp. and the late flowers of Eriogonum niveum give texture to Gwen Kelaidis' garden.

or her last years should be indulged some special extravagances and not judged harshly for them, so should an autumnal garden be allowed a grand finale of wild color fireworks without too many "tasteful" restraints. Nature combines cobalt skies, red and yellow leaves and purple asters; the gardener does well to take inspiration from these stunning scenes.

Form and texture take on their most important roles this time of the year—seedheads, flower stalks and the mature size of the plants create a sense of fullness, of tactile and visual abundance. Grasses hiss and rattle in the breezes like so many whispering crones. I chuckle thinking of the overexcited Halloweeners soon to pass by the ravenna grass and miscanthus clumps. Not only are the grasses large enough to hide a menacing creature, their wind-borne voices are sure to strike fear in the more imaginative and suggestible trick-or-treaters. The sweet civility of Christmas, with its parade of guests to kiss and horrible velvet jumpers to wear, scored a distant second on my childhood holiday rankings, far behind the front-runner, Halloween. Those seemingly interminable dark walks between houses, long before street-lit safety became an issue, were more adrenalizing than the mountains of candy filling the sack. Sadly Halloween, with our good-natured attempts to protect the little ones from the increasingly dangerous traffic and increasingly sick adults, has become an utter bore. Children show up listlessly at the door with parents in tow. Well-lit malls and gymnasiums filled with high-tech scary props that now often host the event will never equal those unchaperoned nights spent running from whispering, chattering, cackling plant life.

Back in the garden, a frosty morning transforms all things hairy, spiny, silver. Prickly pear, snowball and claret-cup cactus are caught in a crystalline net of hoary spines. Lambs ears, santolina and *Salvia argentea* glisten in the weak early sunlight. The artemisias, a frosty sight even in the heat of summer, take on an ethereal quality. *Artemisia*

caucasica, a four-inch shrublet, and huge four-foot *A*. x 'Powis Castle' are the laciest. Whitest are ground-hugging *A. stellerana* and 18-inch *A*. x 'Valerie Finnis'. Prettiest of all, though, is the sparkling silver skeleton of 'Silver King' artemisia's flower panicles. The foliage of this plant is nice, but I can find silver in many other plants less inclined to bossiness in the garden. The only reason I tolerate this spreading garden thug (and only in one small, isolated spot) is for those delicate flower stalks that appear late in the summer and remain until the first heavy snow flattens them. Their airy effect is intensified on those mornings when hoarfrost transforms the landscape and they look like white plumes of chilled breath from the garden.

Two very distinct autumn scenes dominate my garden. The east-facing rose garden offers lingering pastel perennials and frost-tolerant annuals among the last cabbagy heads of various peach, pink, yellow and white ever-blooming David Austin roses. On the other side of the house, in the warm western sun, grasses, late-blooming perennials and tough annuals in hot colors—indigo-blue, red, orange, gold, purple—burn brightly until well into November when a pummeling of successive hard frosts and snowy dustings finally extinguish them. The two areas couldn't be any more different in mood.

The Last of the Flowers

The rose garden acquiesces, its billowing denizens bowing slowly to the end of the season. Some of the rose blossoms tend to ball, not opening fully, yet their colors are deeper than any other time of the season. The gallica roses' foliage takes on burgundy overtones. Pearl-like buds of Japanese anemones—pink 'September Charm' and large white 'Honorine Jobert'—begin to open. These aristocrats of the fall-blooming perennials raise their flowers on sturdy yet wire-thin stems high above the lush, grapelike foliage. Their blossoms, so simple of face—a yellow center surrounded by five or so oblong petals just as a child would draw—have a charm unmatched by the most intricate orchid. Companion to them are the white bottlebrush spikes of foul-smelling *Cimicifuga simplex* 'White Pearl', placed well in the back between the larger rose shrubs. Seen and not smelled from a distance, the flowers resemble fine white tapers, slightly bent as if they had been stored in too hot a place over the summer.

Small patches of color appear here and there against the tangle of fading greens. A persistent panicle of white 'Miss Lingard' phlox, much appreciated for its long bloom and resistance to mildew, stands out, almost blindingly pristine, like a beacon from the muted background. A spangle of fluorescent pale yellow *Coreopsis verticillata* 'Moonbeam' daisies flirt with hardy ageratum (*Eupatorium coelestinum*), a tough, foot-tall spreader with fuzzy, periwinkle blue flower heads that, like 'Moonbeam' coreopsis, take on extra luminescence late in the day. Various nicotianas, surprisingly frost-tolerant given their leafy, tropical appearance, weave in and about the roses. Graceful white dusk-blooming *Nicotiana alata* attracts the last hawk- and hummingbird moths of the season to its fragrant, tubular flowers. Lanky *Nicotiana langsdorfii* dangles small lime green bells over a spray of apricot 'Bredon' roses. *N. sylvestris*, in all its bulk, still opens a few white blossoms in its starburst of a flowerhead, and the few solitary chartreuse stars of an unknown nicotiana seedling frame the last blooms of fragrant pink damask rose 'Comte de Chambord'.

While I appreciate these soft remnants of the lush, heady bloom that drew my attention to the rose garden in June, now I am drawn to the west side. Early shadows encase the east side; the warmth of the season lingers on the west. The plantings here are grown hotter and drier, staying smaller and less apt to tumble. Many perennials are still flowering or just peaking. Self-sown annuals abound, starting their bloom later than transplants and giving a prolonged show well into fall.

 The main players in this final act of the year are ornamental grasses and daisies. This isn't by coincidence. A large part of the North American continent revels in delightful autumn weather, unlike much of Europe where the summers are the peak of the season and fall means only cold drizzle and dreary, dark days. Little surprise then that a great many native grasses and composites—the sunflowers, goldenrods, asters of the North American flora—are as perfect for giving a glorious late flush in the garden as they are along roadsides, in a meadow or on the prairie. It has taken gardeners on this side of the Atlantic a lot longer to realize this and appreciate the bounty of native fall-blooming plants. The English and Germans have coveted our glorious autumnal flowers while we still considered them weeds and are to be thanked for having done a great deal of selecting, making some especially fine forms available for the newly enlightened gardener.

Grasses and Daisies

Ornamental grasses have risen from half a century of obscurity to the ranks of a fad in recent years. A horticulturally correct garden cannot afford to be without a token clump here or there. Many Japanese and German selections are introduced here annually, at exorbitant prices, only to be plunked clumsily by the nouveau gardener among plants with which they are not visually compatible. At least a few people are bold enough to admit they dislike grasses rather than make feeble half-hearted attempts at integrating them into their gardens. Grasses require more artistic attention than the average run-of-the-mill new perennial introduction. Their uninhibited wildness, their linear silhouettes, their lack of blooms in the traditional sense all demand creative placement. A gardener needs to understand the unkempt look of nature, the subtleties of texture and form. Grasses appeal to the less tidy, more dramatic and vivacious spirit. Perhaps that is why the Germans are so smitten by them—throughout history, their culture has romanticized the untamed side of nature, as if to counteract their need for order in the home and at work. Grasses in the garden offer the same release. I often wonder about artistic expressions of national spirit— why Italian and French cultures, considered more loose and sensual than the German or the English, gave rise to such controlled formality in the garden, and the English and the Germans

▼ Rudbeckia triloba; Aster novae-angliae *'Hella Lacy'*.

▲ Late October in the garden.

▼ Silken butterfly weed seedheads and asters.

▲ *Orange sand cherry leaves, blue California poppy and* Poa baldensis *foliage, silver pussytoes and chocolate rudbeckia seedheads make a perfect autumn vignette starring* Crocus speciosus.

have let plants grow with wild, romantic abandon, all the while watching their clocks and keeping everything else in line.

My mother, city-born and bred, taught me to love grasses. When we took hikes in the country, she would pick a small bouquet of wildflowers, always including delicate tassels of grasses. She said grasses were special; they had rhythm; they danced and sang in the breeze. From those small bouquets I also learned that the best companions to grasses were most certainly not roses, peonies or delphiniums. Aside from generally looking their very best later in the season, past the famous June flush, grasses call out for similarly natural, wild-looking companions. The wonderful array of native and exotic late-blooming composites are tailor-made for that role.

Since time immemorial, daisies have held a special place in people's hearts. The daisy chains of childhood give way to petal-plucking love-me-love-me-not sessions in adolescence and then a less abused role, petals and stems intact, in the wedding bouquet. There is something irresistible—sweet, unsophisticated, optimistic—in the simple round face of a daisy. Just when thoughts turn from blossoms to leaf raking, the garden responds with a multicolored explosion of these disarmingly pretty flowers.

The theme of daisies and grasses is replayed, in the most diverse ways, over and over throughout the fall garden. The classic combination of blue and gold can be created, mirroring the azure skies and warm yellow sunlight of the season. Shrubby blue mist spirea, *Caryopteris* x *clandonensis*, kept tight and full by severely cutting it to the ground early each spring, pairs with native golden aster, *Chrysopsis villosa*, both blooming for five to six weeks. Behind, tall yet stiff yellow *Rudbeckia nitida* 'Herbstsonne', one of those American plants that first went to Germany for refinement and came back with a Teutonic name that appropriately translates to 'Autumn Sun', helps hold up the lax, gentian blue spikes of *Salvia azurea*. The bamboo-like foliage of *Miscanthus sinensis* 'Strictus', called zebra grass for its green and gold cross-hatched leaf variegation, gives the composition needed weight and structure.

In an area where I want brilliant color all season long, I depend on two tough, self-sowing annuals for continuity: the leggy purple clusters of *Verbena bonariensis* and deep red flower spikes of Texas scarlet sage (*Salvia coccinea*), so much more graceful than the clumsy, artificial-looking red sage commonly grown in annual bedding schemes. The vibrant purple and red blooms continue faithfully well into autumn, when they are joined by my all-time favorite—black-eyed Susan, *Rudbeckia triloba*. This great plant has all but disappeared from the trade. I met it by accident, a last remnant of beauty in the wasteland that was our yard when we first moved in. An unassuming rosette of coarse leaves sat by the back porch all summer. I almost pulled it out, but thankfully was too busy removing more important items from the future garden, a legacy of neglect that included an old mattress, barbeque grill, rusty swing set and broken washing machine.

▲ *'Annabelle' hydrangea's dried flower heads add quiet elegance to Rob Proctor's garden in autumn.*

Suddenly in early September, these rosettes gave birth to a five-foot-tall stiff cloud of one-inch golden daisies with chocolate eyes. The sheer profusion reminded me of fairy tales in which a person down on his or her luck is suddenly showered by thousands of gold coins from the sky. I, the downtrodden gardener, after two months of trash hauling, weed pulling, and tree-stump hacking was suddenly beneficiary to this floral shower of gold. During times when I was more inclined to believe in providence, this was surely a sign to continue with the seemingly endless and unrewarding drudgery of starting a garden from less than zero. I have since collected seed and planted *Rudbeckia triloba* among the Texas scarlet sage and verbena. These heavy bloomers like it sunny and on the dry side, and though the

▲ *Dahlberg daisy and Zauschneria californica combine boldly in Gwen Kelaidis' garden.*

▶ *As winter approaches, hardy pampas grass, Erianthus ravennae, stands sentinel over Denver Botanic Gardens' Rock Alpine Garden.*

planting may be ephemeral, its intense colors are forever seared in my mind.

The most well-known of the daisies, as much a harbinger of autumn as pumpkins, football and turkey, is the mum. Whether one chooses to dress the autumn garden in tones of russet, gold and burgundy, or to keep the soft pink, white and lavender tones of the early season alive, mums can fit the bill. I do bear some resentment toward these popular flowers, however. For one, they have so dominated the fall flower scene that most people can't imagine anything else blooming at that time. This is partly the fault of nurseries and garden centers that jump lustily onto the mum bandwagon and fill

their displays with the showy plants, eager for some quick-selling, marginally hardy stuff to draw in the customers. Impoverished leftover potted perennials are pushed aside, and even those promoted for fall planting have a hard time competing with the floral fireworks that mums can pull off in the confines of a pot. Mums have pushed many other fall-blooming plants out of the limelight for too long.

Another reason for not seeing them as the end-all and be-all of the fall garden is that many have been so overbred that they look unnatural and contrived among the other plants in the garden (Do they have any leaves under all those flowers?). Also, to the disappointment of many misled buyers, the majority of chrysanthemums also have lost their ability to come back after a hard winter, or if they do, to come back with good vigor and strong blossoms. Perhaps they should be sold with the suggestion they remain quarantined in their pots rather than planted in the garden and kept near the doorway for a pretty, short-lived seasonal display, much like the poinsettia's role indoors a couple of months later.

There are, however, a number of tough mums with enough grace to deserve a place in even the most finely honed autumnal garden. An especially winsome cushion mum with the endearing name 'Grandchild' comes back dependably in Colorado gardens year after year. Its muted mauve-lavender consorts beautifully with the deep plum form of cherry sage (*Salvia greggii*), a semitender shrublet that blooms nonstop from early summer into November. The coppery maroon leaves of a clump of *Heuchera* 'Palace Purple' anchor the taller mum and sage, and wands bearing the last of the mothlike white flowers of *Gaura lindheimeri* rise airily in the background.

Chrysanthemum weyrichii is a shorter, one-foot-tall spreader with a tough constitution. In my sandy soil, it became overly zealous so I sadly had to ban it to the compost, yet in stiffer clays it remains a well-behaved clump for years. Two named varieties, unfortunately not baptized by the same person who thought of 'Grandchild', are the double forms 'White Bomb' and 'Pink Bomb'. The long-blooming perennial vervain, *Verbena bipinnatifida*, with its glowing rose-purple flower clusters, is lusty enough to stand up to the territorial mum. A fine tuft of blue sheep's fescue, always a good accompaniment to lower-growing plants in the sunny garden, would soften the dominating pink mum and rose verbena flowers. In the hottest part of my garden, along the ruddy flagstones of the path, a similar tuft of cool blue fescue graces the lingering warm yellow and gold daisies of drought-tolerant native annuals Dahlberg daisy (*Dyssodia tenuiloba*) and desert marigold (*Baileya multiradiata*).

The one other mum I can count on for hardiness and longevity is *Chrysanthemum zawadskii* and its selections. While these mums don't have the variety of flower forms that the fancier popular hybrids offer, they are equally floriferous. Their daisy-like flowers are actually an asset, more natural in appearance and therefore less overbearing in the garden. 'Mary Stoker' is a tawny amber, 'Duchess of Edinburgh' a coppery red; both are wonderful with smaller native grasses such as the fine-textured, rusty-panicled switch grass, *Panicum virgatum* 'Rehbraun' or the dangling bronze spikelets of sea oats, *Chasmanthium latifolium*. The most well-known and available of this deserving group of mums is 'Clara Curtis', an earlier bloomer with warm pink daisies. I pinch mine twice, in late May and late June, not so much to shorten the plant since it is quite sturdy and needs little if any help standing up straight, but to delay the onset of bloom. If left to its own devices, 'Clara Curtis' would start blooming in late July, on through August. With a pinching, I postpone it until September. Then it makes a soft autumn picture with the deep rose flowers and dusky purple foliage of *Sedum* 'Vera Jameson' and an unsung native daisy, *Aster ericoides*. This latter plant is also called the heath aster, for it is so tiny in flower and leaf that it resembles the delicate mesh of its namesake. I think of it as fall's answer to baby's breath; heath aster stands a good three feet tall unless pinched, yet is so diaphanous that it appears foamlike, almost without substance. The species is most commonly white, but pale pink and lavender forms are seen occasionally. Heath aster is also one of the more drought-tolerant aster species, and along with 'Clara Curtis' chrysanthemum and 'Vera Jameson' sedum, these three quietly pretty perennials belie their tough constitutions.

Some of the myriad hybrid mums have retained their hardiness and dependability. If there is a particular one that strikes one's eye, there's no harm in trying and hoping. In a friend's garden, an unknown variety with pearl-like, white flower buttons comes back like clockwork, with no pinching or dividing, year after year.

The largest chrysanthemum is the Hungarian daisy, *Chrysanthemum uliginosum* (aka *C. serotinum*), a stately spray of white flowers that greets the gardener at eye level. A need for staking plagues this otherwise garden worthy plant, and pinching is to no avail, for it blooms quite late and if pinched, may not have enough time to bloom at all. Placed in the background and closely packed in with larger grasses and other big perennials, it is highly effective. The smaller, more brilliant white daisies of four-foot *Boltonia asteroides* var. *latisquama* 'Snowbank' have captured the hearts of more gardeners, but for alkaline soils on the lighter side, the Hungarian daisy is much better suited. I have watched my stunted, chlorotic boltonia struggle along for two years, and have come to the conclusion that it is better off elsewhere. In a moister garden, the last giant crimson and rose flowers of *Hibiscus moscheutos* would make a perfect foil for the froth of white boltonia daisies. Hungarian daisy, on the other hand, looks great paired with the mauve panicles of the hardiest of the maiden grasses, *Miscanthus sinensis* 'Gracillimus', or with the burgundy-toned fall foliage and silver plumes of ravenna grass, *Erianthus ravennae*. The tallest of the asters, *Aster tataricus*, needs these as a backdrop, for its form is a bit anorexic. Sprays of its powder blue daisies grow skyward and last well over a month, much longer than most of its kin.

▶ *Autumn-flowering crocus pokes through ripening* Nigella *pods, blue sheep's fescue and the last flowers of* Alchemilla alpina.

Of all the asters, I will always consider the deep purple forms of New England aster the most representative of autumn. When paired with goldenrods, as they are throughout the fields of the eastern half of the States, the two combine in a way that still outranks even the most original and lovely autumn garden contrivances I have seen. The jaunty buff vertical spikes of three-foot feather reed grass, *Calamagrostis* x *acutiflora* 'Stricta', and the more open tawny and rust panicles of four-foot Indian grass, *Sorghastrum nutans*, make ideal companions. 'Hella Lacy', a more compact three- to four-foot form of *Aster novae-angliae*, combined with *Solidago sempervirens*, replay in my garden the autumnal meadows of my memory.

The Foliage of Fall

Color in the autumn garden is more than blossoms, however. While many perennials and annuals continue bravely late into the season, it is the combination of these flowers with the complex tapestry of changing foliage color, both in woody plants and in the herbaceous, that gives autumn its richness. Fresh green becomes the exception rather than the norm; evergreen plants suddenly leap forth with emerald intensity after a spring and summer of blending shyly into the background. Somber black-green firs and pines pair beautifully with gold and russet ash and plum trees planted among them. Icy blue Colorado spruces and junipers vie for attention with crimson burning bush and orange-red sumacs.

On a smaller scale, many perennials are also touched by autumn's colorful kiss: The leaves of bergenia and the carmine-flowered forms of *Dianthus deltoides*, the maiden pinks, both take on garnet tones still framed by a froth of white alyssum. Hints of plum appear in the tips of aggressive blue *Sedum reflexum*, fighting it out with the equally ambitious hardy iceplant, *Delosperma nubigenum*. The latter's succulent chartreuse mats are showing touches of the ripe raspberry color they become in the depths of winter. Blues and silvers shimmer all

▲ Hosta tardiflora *blooms in mid-autumn.*

▲ *Silver and gray foliages frame 'Waterlily' colchicum in Rob Proctor's garden.*

▼ *Hardy* Cyclamen hederifolium *graces the base of ferns in Mary Ellen Tonsing's shaded garden.*

the more intensely with the interjection of straw yellow, amber and red. A steely fountain of blue avena grass becomes a principal player as balloon flower goes gold next to it; a blue juniper shimmers with orange-red *Zauschneria* flowers as a partner. Small naked autumn crocus flowers, a cool lavender hue, poke up in front of a sculptural mass of maroon sempervivums. Some peonies join the foliage party, while others are more modest, preferring to remain a dull green to the last. A shocking pink anemone-flowered one I have no name for is the finest—it seems to have the need for attention, both in its brilliant spring display and now, as it glows apricot near the huge, sprawling blue leaves of sea kale, *Crambe maritima*. A tuft of tawny Siberian iris foliage completes this scene. Magenta colchicums raise their leafless blossoms through a cloak of scarlet leadwort foliage; the last few of leadwort's brilliant flowers stud the picture like blue sequins.

Many shrubs also turn fiery come autumn. Every year at this time I marvel at the surreal scarlet of burning bush, *Euonymus alata*, and think perhaps I should break down and plant one. But the bush is just too nondescript the other fifty weeks of the year for me to give it precious garden space, so I continue to enjoy the plants vicariously elsewhere. The shrubs in my private infrared landscape must also hold their own at other times of the season. Crimson pygmy barberry changes from its summer color of muted maroon to flaming russet, enhancing the tawny daisies of hardy mum 'Mary Stoker'. Short days and cooler nights transform the glossy, narrow green leaves of low-growing, drought-tolerant sand cherry, *Prunus besseyi*, to burgundy. A must with these rich red foliage tones is some ice blue foliage—perhaps a few tufts of blue sheep's fescue or blue avena grass, a petite 'Blue Star' juniper or a squat, four-foot dwarf blue spruce variety like 'Globosa' or 'R. H. Montgomery'. Both the purple-leaved forms and plain blue-green species of drought-tolerant smoke bush, *Cotinus coggygria*, have fabulous foliage throughout the growing season. Plumes of flower panicles, turning from peach in midsummer to buff to almost white in autumn, give the shrub its common name. In the autumn, the "smoke" is joined by fire as the foliage turns a smoldering orange.

The most beautiful fall planting I have ever seen included no annuals, perennials, trees or shrubs. It was a gathering of rambunctious vines on a ten-foot cyclone fence. The fire-engine red, palmate foliage of Virginia creeper (*Parthenocissus quinquefolia*) formed the backdrop, like royal tapestry. *Clematis paniculata* was still in bloom, wafting its sweet scent from cascading creamy flowers. Lace vine (*Polygonum aubertii*) contributed a froth of just barely over-the-hill, translucently white flowers. Entwined throughout were the seedheads of three clematis vines—those of yellow-flowered lemon-peel clematis, *Clematis tangutica*, and *C. orientalis*, a silky silver, and native *C. ligusticifolia*, a parade of cottony puffballs. The colors and textures of this casual vertical garden, which I doubt was planted with much thought aside from wanting to cover the ugly fence with some tough, fast vines, can match the most well-orchestrated herbaceous border in early summer. The image, in all its loose, ripe abundance, speaks more eloquently than any prose for the garden in autumn.

PLANTS FOR FALL FIREWORKS

KEY
D: insists on dry conditions.
S: prefers some shade.
M: blooms from summer.
PP: featured in plant portrait section.

PERENNIALS AND BULBS BLOOMING IN AUTUMN
Aconitum carmichaelii monkshood **S**
Agastache giant hyssop **M**
Anaphalis pearly everlasting **M, S**
Anemone x *hybrida, A. hupehensis* Japanese anemone **S**
Aster **PP**
Asteromoea mongolica
Boltonia asteroides
Callirhoe buffalo rose **D, M, PP**
Ceratostigma plumbaginoides **M, S**
Chrysanthemum uliginosum
Chrysanthemum weyrichii
Chrysopsis golden aster
Chrysothamnus rabbitbrush **D**
Cimicifuga simplex bugbane **S**
Colchicum naked boys
Coreopsis x 'Moonbeam' **M**
Crocus autumn crocus **PP**
Cyclamen hederifolium **S**
Delosperma cooperi purple iceplant **D, M**
Dianthus pinks **D, M**
Eriogonum buckwheat **D,M**
Eupatorium coelestinum hardy ageratum **S**
Eupatorium maculatum Joe Pye weed
Eupatorium rugosum white snakeroot **S**
Gaillardia x *grandiflora* Indian blanket **D, M**
Gaura lindheimeri apple blossom grass **M**
Gentiana asclepiadea willow gentian **S**
Gentiana septemfida **M**
Geranium sanguineum var. *striatum* **M**
Gutierrezia sarothrae broomweed **D, M**
Helenium autumnale Helen's flower **M**
Helianthus maximiliani Maximilian's sunflower
Hemerocallis daylily late selections
Hibiscus moscheutos swamp mallow **M**
Hosta plantaginea **M, S**

Hosta 'Royal Standard' **M, S**
Hosta tardiflora **S**
Lespedeza thunbergii bush clover
Lobelia cardinalis cardinal flower **M, S**
Malva mallow **M, PP**
Melampodium leucanthum blackfoot daisy **D, M**
Oenothera speciosa Mexican evening primrose **M**
Patrinia **M, S**
Perovskia Russian sage **M**
Physostegia virginiana obedient plant **M**
Psilostrophe paperflower **D, M**
Ratibida columnifera prairie coneflower **D, M**
Rudbeckia black-eyed Susan **M, PP**
Salvia azurea azure sage
Sedum 'Autumn Joy'
Sedum 'Ruby Glow'
Sedum spectabile
Senecio longilobus silver groundsel **D, M**
Solidago goldenrod **M**
Stachys coccinea red betony **M**
Sternbergia autumn daffodil
Tricyrtis toad lily **S**
Vernonia noveboracensis cast-iron plant **M**
Viguiera multiflora showy goldeneye **M**
Zauschneria California fuchsia **D, PP**
Zinnia grandiflora Rocky Mountain zinnia **D, M**
(See list of frost-tolerant annuals in chapter 6.)

FALL FOLIAGE COLOR PERENNIALS
Amsonia tabernaemontana blue stars
Bergenia cordifolia pigsqueak
Boltonia asteroides
Ceratostigma plumbaginoides leadwort
Euphorbia epithymoides cushion spurge
Geranium cranesbill
Lysimachia vulgaris circle flower
Paeonia peony
Persicaria (Polygonum) affinis border jewel
Platycodon grandiflorus balloon flower
Schizachyrium scoparium little bluestem
Sedum
Veronica longifolia

SHRUBS
Aronia chokeberry

Berberis barberry
Cotinus smokebush
Cotoneaster acutifolius Peking cotoneaster
Cotoneaster apiculatus
Cotoneaster divaricatus
Euonymus alata burning bush
Forestiera neomexicana New Mexico privet
Jamesia americana wax flower
Peraphyllum ramosissimum squaw apple
Physocarpus monogynus nonebark
Prunus plum, cherry
Rhus sumac
Rosa nitida
Rosa rugosa
Rosa virginiana
Spiraea
Syringa oblata
Vaccinium blueberry, huckleberry
Viburnum opulus European cranberry bush
Viburnum trilobum cranberry bush

TREES
Acer maple except *A. negundo* box elder
Amelanchier serviceberry
Celtis occidentalis hackberry
Cercis canadensis redbud
Cladrastis lutea yellowwood
Cornus mas
Crataegus hawthorn, most species
Fraxinus ash
Gleditsia triacanthos honey locust
Larix larch
Malus crabapple, some species
Populus tremuloides aspen
Prunus plum, cherry, most species
Pyrus calleryana 'Autumn Blaze' callery pear
Pyrus ussuriensis Ussurian pear
Sorbus mountain ash, many species
Viburnum prunifolium black haw viburnum

VINES
Parthenocissus quinquefolia Virginia creeper
Vitis vinifera 'Purpurea' purple-leaf grape

IX

The Winter Garden: Myth or Reality

Over the years, I've read several articles and books on the English winter garden. Unusually hued conifers and broad-leaved evergreens filled the sumptuous pages. I realized, after some delightful delusions, that I was really reading a continental gardener's version of *Alice in Wonderland*. While Colorado winters are replete with teasing interludes of sunny, sixty-degree days in January and February, often cajoling crocus, snowdrop and iris out of their slumber a good month or so before they appear in milder maritime climates, the inevitable minus-thirty-degrees-Fahrenheit night significantly alters one's choice of evergreen plants.

Broad-leaved evergreens, especially, resent the marked changes in temperature and the desiccating sun and wind of western winters. The most sheltered, shaded north side or a swaddling of burlap are necessary for success with even the most hardy of this group of plants. A protective wrap, as far as I'm concerned, totally negates the whole purpose of evergreen plants—just when their foliage is most needed and appreciated, it must be wrapped up like a mummy, only to reappear come spring, when all the deciduous plants are beginning to dominate the garden once again. Suffice it to say that while I miss the rhododendrons and azaleas of my childhood, I have no intention of coddling them in this manner, and the high alkalinity of my soil would demand yet more intervention. I grow a few semievergreen hardy daphnes—*Daphne* x *burkwoodii* 'Somerset' and the variegated 'Carol Mackie' and sprawling *D. cneorum*, but were it not for their wonderfully fragrant flowers, I would pass them by. The choice of needled evergreens, the conifers, is much greater, but several otherwise quite winter-hardy genera like *Chamaecyparis*, *Taxus* and *Thuja* need special siting to avoid that same winter sun and wind that wreaks havoc with the broadleaves. Golden and variegated forms also are susceptible to burn and browning.

Remarkably, while the choice of woody plants is much more limited compared to Washington, D.C., Seattle or Dublin, evergreen perennials thrive. Several are not well known or well grown in those milder, moister climates, preferring the drier winter air and soil of the continental West. Others are common old regulars on both sides of the Atlantic, that suddenly show evergreen tendencies given dependable, intense sunlight. Many perennials I remember turning to amorphous blobs of half-rotted leaves

(preceding pages) The stems and fruit of Ephedra americana var. andina *brighten the cold, dreary face of a rock.*

184

in Philadelphia maintain handsome form until early spring. Then the old leaves finally succumb, not so much to winter as to priority given the young growth now beginning to emerge. So, while the traditional choices for winter garden interest are not of much use in our climactic extremes, with a smattering of fine conifers, a selection of deciduous trees and shrubs that have beautiful bark, the addition of interesting dried seedheads and brightly colored berries and a generous helping of the vast number of evergreen perennials, the winter garden can be a wonderful tapestry of color, form and texture.

I'm very fond of winter, and although my tolerance for cold gets worse each year and I'm beginning to understand the exodus of the aged to Florida and Arizona, I still can't imagine a gardening year without a few months of soft slumber, both for the plants and the gardener. Winter feeds the spirit, fills one with the energy and desire to start out fresh, to face the renewal of spring with delirious optimism. A friend from the San Francisco area once protested that they, too, have seasons and cycles. While I don't doubt that, I can't imagine December without the rituals of coiling hoses, oiling tools, washing and stacking pots. There is a sense of quiet accomplishment, of reflection, of preparing for the next cycle in all that busy work. How I would miss the silver veil of a November hoarfrost, the peach-lit evening sky before a January snowstorm or the silence that awakens me the next white morning. Most of all, spring's first crocuses and damp, humusy smell wouldn't be half as welcomed.

And yet, looking at photographs of the bright, colorful blur that was the summer garden, one can't help but grow wistful. The varied shapes and brilliant colors of flowers are one of the strongest attractions of gardening. Now that the quieter, more reflective months are here, there's time to ponder the hows and whys of plants. Flowers are bright and showy for a reason—to attract pollinators, not just enraptured gardeners. Something quite similar is at play with what are now the brightest spots in the garden—berries and fruits. These orange, yellow, red and blue orbs are beckoning to be eaten. Then they can be digested and the enclosed seeds expelled elsewhere, to start the cycle anew. I'm not one to make jellies and jams of even the more acceptable, run-of-the-mill subjects like grapes and strawberries, so my interest in berries and fruits is purely aesthetic. But the prospect of a visual feast is a strong motivator.

 I've been partial to shrub and species roses over the modern hybrids for *Roses for Hips* many years now, mainly due to having spent three years of my life pruning, mulching, feeding, watering and spraying four hundred prima-donna hybrid teas and floribundas where I was employed. Come fall, my prejudice is amply rewarded. While the majority of species and shrub roses only offer one long burst of bloom in early summer, in the autumn many are given to the wonderful habit of making fruits, called hips. I planted only two roses in hot west part of the garden because they needed to be larger—six feet or more—and more drought-tolerant than those in the east-facing rose garden. The red-leaf rose, *Rosa glauca* (aka *R. rubrifolia*), with its plum-silver-copper foliage

185

▲ Hoarfrost touches evergreen sunrose leaves with silver.

▲ Rosa rugosa.

▲ Rosa x alba 'Semiplena'.

and canes, and gray-green, fuller *R. x alba* 'Semiplena', both bloom only once, in late spring. The reward for their short flowering season is the ample production of lovely oval orange hips, pendulous in the case of the pink-flowered red-leaf rose, and more upright on white-flowered *R. x alba*. The apple-scented sweetbriar rose (*R. eglanteria*) joins in with a bounty of small reddish, round hips.

Two other roses that tolerate drier conditions and need no coddling in the form of pruning, feeding, spraying or winter protection, which I grow out back where the dogs greatly limit the plant palette, are *Rosa woodsii* and *R. rugosa*. Both have superb foliage and fruit, not usually the first things that come to mind when one considers a rose. *R. woodsii* is a western native with spreading habits, especially if overwatered. Its glaucous blue-green foliage shows hints of pink in the newer growth, and the canes are burgundy. Small, sweetly scented, single pink flowers bloom profusely for several weeks in early summer. By late summer, on through the fall and into winter, hundreds of tiny, round cherry red, hips punctuate the dense bush. The queen of the hip-making roses is *R. rugosa*. While the newer rugosa hybrids tempt me with their showier flowers in a wider color range, I delight in the old-fashioned species and single forms come autumn and winter, for they truly make one of the most spectacular fruit displays imaginable. One-inch, shiny tomato-like hips bedeck the ends of the branches, seeming all the showier when contrasted with the dark green leaves. They are said to make a fine, tart jelly rich in vitamin C. I opt for enjoying the hips on the bush for as long as possible. If the birds don't eat them, they remain attractive, if somewhat darker and wrinkled, well into winter.

More Fruits and Berries

Many other members of the rose family make beautiful fruits—the haw-thorns, cotoneasters, firethorns and crabapples to name a few of the more familiar. Unfortunately, this group of plants is also susceptible to an often fatal disease called fire blight, where at first a few twigs appear scorched, then whole branches; and soon thereafter the whole plant succumbs. No dependably successful treatment has been found; the key is to select varieties of these plants that have been bred for resistance to this disease, and to site them and grow them according to their needs, minimizing stress.

Many people in the "higher ranks" of horticulture have started to sneer at crabapples, as they do at junipers, in deference to the stupid unwritten rule that anything very popular is somehow inferior. I selected two crabapples for my garden—they were the first trees I planted. Nothing can match them for small size, spring flowers, soil and climate adaptability and fall fruit display. The varieties I planted are known for fire blight resistance and dependable fruiting: 'Ormiston Roy', which has been slightly af-flicted in a bad year, with pink buds opening to single white flowers in early spring and small, abundant orange fruit as well as a burnished bronze bark; and 'Adams', com-pletely unscathed thus far, with single, old-rose flowers and larger crimson fruit.

The question of fruit persistence into winter has more to do with the local birds' palate than with climate or the tree's physiological state. Some crabapples are stripped in a matter of days, while others are totally ignored. Just as we have MacIntosh, Granny Smith and Golden Delicious adherents, local bird populations have their definite tastes. My nine cats keep a large and diverse avian population at bay, forcing the birds to covet all the seeds and fruits and insects in my garden from the safety of my neighbor's large trees and fence. Similar frustration is imposed on those less desirable animals of the garden—bushy-tailed suburban rats, known in polite circles as squirrels, and mice and voles, known collectively as "vice." So, whether it be due to discriminating local tastes or my feline troops, fruit persists well in this garden, brightening the snowy winter landscape.

Less common rose family members are the *Aronia* species, also known forbiddingly as chokeberries. Whether birds or small mammals actually choke on them, or whether some unfortunate curious early settler had such an experience upon tasting the berries, I'm not sure. The showy red or black fruits do persist well into winter, unmolested by the animal kingdom even in gardens filled with hungry wildlife. Chokeberries make large shrubs, with modest white flowers in the spring, and outrageous red and purple fall foliage, which gives way to the clusters of handsome fruit. The aronias need a somewhat moist soil, but otherwise are quite adaptable and bone hardy.

Many large, treelike junipers bear showy blueberries. Some individuals bear more heavily and are more productive some years than others. Hiking in the Rocky Moun-tain foothills and coming across a tree laden with the aquamarine fruit is a delight on a bleak November day. I add a few to the fir holiday wreath for natural sparkle. The less they are handled, the better; the waxy, white bloom that gives the berries their frosted look is easily worn off.

My favorite plant for fruit is the bayberry, which grows wild along the Eastern seaboard, yet thrives in the coldest inland climates provided they aren't too arid. It is a large, nondescript shrub, tolerant of clay or sandy soils, but definitely not a candidate for the showier, more manicured parts of the garden. When rubbed or crushed, the leaves and berries release the wonderful bayberry fragrance used to scent candles. The tiny fruit, found only on female plants, forms dense clusters all along the branches and remains throughout the winter. The little bayberries have a most unusual color—soft, pearly gray with a white cast. They mirror the colors that evoke their native habitat—the gray and white of lonely gulls, creaking clapboard houses, rocking boats and a wintry, white-capped ocean that are all part of an off-season visit to an Atlantic beach resort.

Viburnums are a group of shrubs and small trees that make beautiful fruit, usually red but sometimes purple or yellow. Unfortunately, few keep their fruit for more than a month, and even fewer are tolerant of harsh winters, strong winds, dry summers or alkalinity. The majority of the diverse genus thrive on the coasts. However, both the European and American cranberry-bush viburnums (*Viburnum opulus* and *V. trilobum*) are tough enough, given adequate moisture, for most continental climates. Their opulent red fruit clusters last well into winter. The handsome, three-lobed foliage of the American cranberry bush contributes its share of fall foliage color, turning tones of flame.

New Mexico privet, *Forestiera neomexicana*, is a large, dense shrub ideal for hedging and screening. Its yellow flowers, appearing on naked branches before the leaves, are reminiscent of a toned-down forsythia. This tough, drought-tolerant shrub also has good yellow fall color, but my main reason for liking it are the enormous amounts of small blue fruits it bears, which last well into winter.

 Beyond berries and fruits, the richly hued and textured bark of various woody *Bark* plants takes on a newly important role once the leaves have dropped. A well-known group of shrubs grown for their bark are the red- and yellow-stem dogwoods. They need harsh annual pruning in the early spring; only the youngest growth has the brilliant bark color, so the plant must be rejuvenated by being cut almost to the ground each year to promote next fall and winter's crop of bright stems. Often I find pruning them coincides with Easter and this gives me a good use for the twigs—I put them in a large vase and hang eggs from them. I've also seen them combined beautifully with forced, blooming stems of cherry, almond and forsythia in an early spring arrangement. But the greatest pleasure is to see the red twigs peeking out of a thick bank of snow, or the golden ones set off by a background of dark evergreens.

► Juniperus squamata 'Blue Star' is a slow-growing evergreen for light shade.

▼ Crabapple fruit.

▲ In winter, dwarf Colorado spruce 'R.H. Montgomery' is a focal point in Denver Botanic Gardens' Rock Alpine Garden.

I am counting on my amur cherry, *Prunus maackii*, planted towards the setting sun, to develop its characteristic peeling cinnamon bark. Its many small, lacy white flowers in spring are appealing, but the bark is what I went for. So far, it is a shiny copper but has not begun to exfoliate. The leaves fall quite early, turning a warm yellow before they drop, and the gleaming naked silhouette graces the garden for the next six months.

For those gardens with more moisture-retentive soils, an extra vigorous variety of the American river birch, *Betula nigra* 'Heritage', is a welcome candidate to replace all those disease- and pest-ridden weeping and paper birches. The bark of 'Heritage', while not white, is fabulous. Patterns of cream, bronze and peach peel off in thin layers that catch the rays of the low fall and winter sun and glow bronze. This birch is resistant to the birch borer, tolerant of shade, grows quickly and can take heavy clay soils.

The last tree I planted on the west side of the house is a favorite of mine from childhood: serviceberry or shadblow, *Amelanchier alnifolia*. Species and subspecies of this genus grow wild throughout North America. All bloom very early, before the leaves appear. Apparently this tree flowered at the time those who died in the winter were finally buried in the thawing ground, hence the folk name serviceberry. The flowers themselves are white, small, diaphanous and

▲ *Woolly veronica and sempervivum weave a muted evergreen tapestry.*

▶ Sedum spathulifolium *'Cape Blanco'.*

◀ Delosperma nubigenum, *a hardy iceplant, carpets the winter garden in raspberry red.*

▼ Sedum spurium *'Red Carpet'.*

would hardly be noticed were there leaves or other flowers with which to compete. I planted my serviceberry with the neighbor's dark spruce as a backdrop to accentuate the white flowers against its somber needles. In autumn, serviceberry's leaves turn all shades of orange and red, lasting several weeks before leaving the smooth, dove gray bark to carry on through the winter.

Evergreens Winter in the mountainous West conjures up images of high country pines, spruces and firs wearing a sparkling dusting of snow, thanks to the indelible imprint of countless postcards and posters. In my small garden on the plains, I find it hard to feel that same sense of beauty when the hulking blue spruce belonging to my next-door neighbor drapes its snow-laden branches all over my plants. I fight its thirsty roots with inordinate amounts of compost, manure and water for the struggling plants that attempt to grow nearby. I battle its mighty, impenetrable year-round shadow, scouring my books, catalogs and memory for planting ideas for its inhospitable dry shade. My neighbor, with all good intentions and sympathy for the plight of my spruce-scourged plants, recently decided to limb up the behemoth. I now have more light and a pathetically humiliated tree to look at.

The message behind all this bellyaching is that one can experience that same magical, snow-sprinkled winter view without sacrificing the rest of the garden, simply by choosing smaller evergreens. Many cone-bearing, needle-leaved evergreens, also called conifers, are tolerant of heat and drought; some can take highly alkaline soils, and many tolerate strong, drying winter winds. In short, they are well prepared to take the daunting conditions handed them.

Rock gardeners have long known the value of the so-called "dwarf conifers." I hate that name for it forever will remind me of a remark a friend once made in a poorly designed garden where specimens of the lovely plants were plunked around haphazardly, without any thought to integrating them with the other plants. He said they looked like gnomes. I like to think that in all but the most horrid gardens, these graceful plants act as living statuary, giving structure and permanence to the landscape. Rock gardening, with stones and evergreen mat- and cushion-forming plants, offers beauty year-round, and to this, small conifers add indispensable height, form, texture and color.

Slow-growing, modestly sized conifers can enhance other garden styles just as well. In my wild cottage garden, the havoc of herbaceous plants can easily turn to mush in winter and appear unkempt in the summer and fall. Small conifers provide the visual anchors the garden needs. They are truly my statuary, for they change less than any other plants in the garden, looking the same year-round except for a few weeks in late spring when the new flush of growth gives them a brighter, more luminescent demeanor. While I appreciate fine statuary in other gardens, it has never suited my temperament or wallet. I'll take the dark green tussocks of a bird's nest spruce over some stone cherub or, heaven forbid, concrete snail or rabbit. Sundials, on the other hand, have always fascinated me. At the risk of sounding pathetically practical, perhaps I'm attracted to the fact they have a function beyond the merely decorative. And yet, since I haven't a clue how to set or read them, I feel that acquiring one would be a highly pretentious addition to my garden. While I show little humility or restraint in color combinations or choice of unusual plants, I'm quite a prude about statuary. So it is to the smaller conifers that I have turned.

For the sunny, hot, drier part of the garden, several pines are ideally suited. The dwarf form of Austrian pine, *Pinus nigra* 'Hornibrookiana', is a tough, elegant, mounded bush growing to only five or so feet in height and girth. It is densely cloaked in long, somber, dark green needles, which offset the silver-gray pointed buds at the tips of each branchlet. Alkaline soils, winter cold, sun and wind, as well as fierce summer heat have little effect on this pine. In more humid climates, it succumbs to diplodia blight, but in the arid West, given a bit of additional watering, it is as healthy as a horse.

Super-hardy Scots pine also has several small forms. *Pinus sylvestris* 'Watereri' tops out at fifteen feet and has a nice blue cast to its short, twisted needles, while 'Beauvronensis' stays more green, compact and bushlike at four feet. 'Glauca Nana' combines blueness with small stature—I have two fine specimens, both of which barely blinked after being planted right before a heat wave, only to be pelted by hail two months later. They were the most hail-tolerant conifers in the garden.

For a truly tree-shaped pine that is small in stature, Japanese white pine (*Pinus parviflora*), with its abundant cones and gracefully irregular growth habit, is ideal. There is a bluer form, 'Glauca', a bit more short and stout. I recommend two other tough, beautiful pines, if one has the patience to deal with growth of less than two inches a year. Swiss stone pine (*P. cembra*) and native bristlecone pine (*P. aristata*) both have dense green needles. The bristlecone pine's sport whitish resin spots on the needles, prompting many uninitiated gardeners to worry about an imaginary infestation of insects. Once the panic of ignorance is overcome, the resin actually can be considered an aesthetic asset. It probably has some relationship to this pine's remarkable drought tolerance. In fact, most bristlecone pine deaths in cultivation can be directly attributed to overzealous watering.

For a cooler garden with moister, more acidic soil, stunning Tanyosho pine, *Pinus densiflora* 'Umbraculifera', is the perfect specimen plant. Its flat-topped, multistemmed habit and orange-red bark have made it a much sought-after focal point in the garden. Mature specimens are generally ten to fifteen feet tall. My favorite pine back East for its fine, flexible needles is the lovely Eastern white pine, *P. strobus*. Its smaller varieties, such as 'Nana' and 'Blue Shag', retain that irresistible softness. Yet all forms of Eastern white pine need conditions I cannot give them. I have killed two of these beauties via drought and alkalinity.

▶ Arctostaphylos nevadensis, an early spring bloomer, is one of few broadleaf evergreens to thrive in bitter cold, sunny, dry winters.

(facing page) Red-stem dogwood adds a vibrant note of color to somber evergreens at Denver Botanic Gardens.

▲ Hardy evergreen heath, Erica carnea 'Springwood White', blooms in late winter.

Both of these more moisture-loving pines are very hardy, and in the coolness of more northerly gardens or those at higher elevations, they succeed given good soil. I am sorely jealous when I see them.

The same can be said for another Eastern native, not a pine, but the familiar small-needled drooping denizen of many an Eastern stream hollow and spring gulch, the Canadian hemlock. This is a tree out of the mists of fairy tales. I remember the mushroomy smell and the darkness of a hemlock grove in central Pennsylvania, the needle-littered forest floor giving rise to hundreds of ghostly white Indian pipes. The hemlock's various dwarf, weeping forms—five foot 'Bennett', 'Cole', larger 'Sargentii', 'Pendula', among others—are a vision of grace in the garden. I only wish I could give them what they need: a cool root run, a good amount of shade, some extra water and a slightly acidic soil. Many regional gardens could easily support a flourishing miniature hemlock or two; it's a shame one doesn't see more of them.

The conifers most forgiving of my garden's daunting conditions are the prickly, resilient spruces. That overbearing Colorado spruce next door actually has several well-behaved cousins. *Picea pungens* 'Fat Albert' stays a respectably small (though wide—up to fifteen feet across), brilliantly blue tree, and plump little 'R. H. Montgomery' rarely exceeds four feet. Rounded, shrublike 'Globosa' is even smaller, lacking a leader, and 'Blue Mist' grows prostrately like a turquoise drape.

The blue spruces are not actually drought tolerant; they are strong competitors for available water—in other words, they rob all surrounding plants of their fair share. All the more reason to stick with the smaller forms, encircling them with dryland plants. I grow cerise and white sunroses at their feet in one part of the garden, and fiery red prairie-fire penstemon where the hotter colors abound. What they lack in water hospitality, they make up in resilience to heavy snow loads (many conifers are prone to breakage), fierce sunlight and dry air. In the heat of the summer, I spray mine with the hose every day or so to keep spider mites at bay. They are healthy, beautiful garden statues.

Another overused hulk in the suburban landscape is the Norway spruce, unmistakable for its somber, dark, drooping silhouette, like some giant, morose monk. It also has several small relatives. *Picea abies* 'Pumila Nigra' is a dense, flat-topped bush, just as tough as its gargantuan progenitor. The dark needles set off a planting of yellow broom flowers beautifully in the spring and make a striking snow-capped picture in winter. 'Nidiformis' is another; its name appropriately means "shaped like a nest." It remains low and rounded, achieving four feet at maturity. I have found the Norway spruce varieties a bit touchy the first year after transplanting in the garden. Their new growth is particularly frost- and drought tender, and they take a while to get established. It is not a plant for the very hottest, driest gardens; mine do best on the north and east sides of the house where they get at least a half day of sun, yet not the heat of the day. The same conditions are appreciated by my miniature Serbian spruce, *P. omorika* 'Nana', with short dark green needles softly touched with blue.

The sun-baked areas of the garden should be reserved for the toughest of that much-maligned group, the junipers. Poor junipers; they have become the pariahs of the status-conscious gardening world. With their varied sizes, shapes, colors and growth habits, and with the adaptability and resilience of several of the species, it is no wonder they have been overused by the landscape industry for well over three decades now. Still, at the risk of being sneered at by my snobbier gardening friends, I am happy to include several great junipers in my garden. For a narrow exclamation point in the garden, a well-placed 'Skyrocket' juniper is without peer. The petite, sparkling blue shrublet *Juniperus squamata* 'Blue Star' grows best in light, dry shade for me, turning lightly plum-colored in winter. The finest winter color transformation is among the spreading *J. horizontalis* tribe; blue 'Plumosa', also known as the Andorra juniper, and 'Prince of Wales' lead the pack into purpledom. They spread several feet, ideal for larger bank plantings, yet I prize their winter color so much that I have made them room. Smaller 'Holden Arboretum' juniper remains blue year-round.

Winter exaggerates different microclimates in the garden. The northern side of the house enters a Rip Van Winkle-esque period each year about November, staying buried for the next four months in successive layers of snow, defrosting only once the gloomy shadow of winter has been lifted with the spring equinox and higher arc of the sun. Many of the more traditional garden plants thrive in this enforced slumber. The snow protects them from severe temperature fluctuations, making this an ideal site for some of the marginally hardy things as well as the tougher plants harking from the northern temperate regions of the world. Many of the more well known perennials appreciate the predictability of such a site. In the sunniest parts of the garden, far from the shadow of the house, day temperatures can vary sixty degrees from night and the soil rarely freezes much below a few inches. This kamikaze climate often spells death for those plants that awaken and break their dormancy at the slightest warming trend. These areas are best left to plants with origins in climactically similar regions—either natives of the continental West or plants from the harsh, sunny steppe regions of eastern Europe and central Asia. Basking in the deceptively warm winter sun of Tadjikistan or Colorado, evergreen foliage abounds, in all shades of green, purple, gray, silver, russet and blue. Winter gardening now becomes more than a wishful vision fueled by too many fancy gardening books from the traditional gardening mentor, Great Britain. These plants, with their muted colors and rich textures, have all the beauty of a fine, softly sun-faded Persian carpet.

In my sunny winter garden, silvers, grays and blues predominate, lending a shimmer to the garden that blends well with the peach-mauve of the flagstone paths. Between the stones, gray woolly thyme (*Thymus pseudolanuginosus*), greener, tinier *T. serpyllum* 'Minus', lichen-like pewter *Raoulia australis* and the tiny silver pussytoes, *Antennaria parvifolia*, meander. While I intended for these plants to be tough and take a bit of foot, wheelbarrow and cat traffic, they are so beautiful that I can't help but pamper them, playing hopscotch over them rather than walking normally, much to the amusement of my neighbors.

Flanking and softening the edges of the paths, several old favorites grown in maritime gardens show new tendencies toward good evergreen foliage with the dry air and strong sunlight of Colorado. Furry lamb's ears, the gray rosettes of basket-of-gold and the fine-textured platinum of lavender cotton and some of the sunroses spill over the hard, cold stone. Icy mats of *Veronica incana*, while only blooming for a few weeks in early summer, earn their many places in my garden by virtue of their wonderful, almost-white winter foliage. Several rarer, more refined counterparts to these commoners are encroaching on their garden space. While the rarer, finer-textured, equally silver *V. cinerea* will never replace *V. incana*, several other plants may need to start worrying about their status. The longer flower period and the finer texture of both blossoms and foliage of *Alyssum montanum*, has convinced me to replace its coarser, rangier lookalike basket-of-gold except for the

Perennials for Winter Beauty

197

pale yellow and apricot varieties. Lamb's ear is also losing ground—it gets ugly and woody in only a couple of years and tends to hold on to half-dead foliage, while the narrower, equally silver and furry foliage of pale yellow-flowered *Sideritis scardica* stays fresh-looking and neat year after year.

Huge, flat, scalloped rosettes of the biennial horned poppy, *Glaucium flavum*, and its smaller, more curled and convoluted relative *G. corniculatum*, dominate the blues. A more unusual biennial poppy, *Papaver triniifolium*, has the laciest blue foliage of all. While I've never liked the horned poppy's flaccid flowers and really only tolerate the plant for its foliage, it too may soon become history, since the newcomer poppy matches it in the foliage department and beats it hands down regarding flowers. A three-month succession of soft apricot-orange, well-formed blossoms covers the blue foliage, making the horned poppy's insignificant, dirty gold flowers look like used Kleenex in comparison.

Tufts and tussocks of blue fescue, blue avena grass and several species and varieties of dwarf pinks add softness to the foliage picture. *Euphorbia myrsinites*, a prostrate, snakelike tangle of waxy gray-blue stems and leaves, lolls on the ground. Large, wavy-edged blue clumps of *Penstemon palmeri* foliage grab one's attention; the cross-shaped blue-gray rosettes of *P. grandiflorus* are smaller yet highly architectural.

Blue spruce sedum, *Sedum reflexum*, takes on dusky plum tints as winter settles in. More plum and purple hues are contributed by a variety of common garden thyme called 'Porlock', and the winter color of native prairie-fire penstemon, *Penstemon pinifolius*. Candytuft and the crimson-flowered form of *Dianthus deltoides* are more maroon than purple, while the leathery mats of native sulphur flower, *Eriogonum umbellatum*, border on a plummy brown, almost liver-like color. Being of the generation that loved Jimi Hendrix, psychedelia and the color purple, I can't have enough of this hue and am always on the lookout for more plants with purple winter foliage. *Sedum album* 'Murale', with little sausagelike leaves, is next on the want list.

For brighter reds, various hens and chicks, especially the appropriately named variety 'Borscht', dot the landscape with ruby rosettes. Hardy iceplant (*Delosperma nubigenum*) unfortunately is now confined to only a few peripheral areas where its enthusiastically spreading ways aren't a problem. I would like to have more of its brilliant rose-red mats threading through the garden but am resigned to watching it drip out over the far curb, which it does with great flamboyance, like a melting raspberry sherbet. A thug of similar proportions is the ever-popular silver-leaved snow-in-summer, *Cerastium tomentosum*, which I also love but have banished to a narrow strip between the lilac hedge and the sidewalk. Its small silver leaves remain attractive for most of the winter, especially if the plant has been mercilessly sheered once or twice during the growing season, resulting in denser, more compact foliage.

Green winter foliage frames the more exotic silvers, blues, purples and reds, enhancing them through contrast. Bright *Santolina virens*, the green species of lavender cotton, and the more muted green tangle of dwarf mormon tea (*Ephedra minima*) and various brooms set off the flashier foliage plants. Aggressive woolly veronica (*Veronica pectinata*) softens the

▲ *Hardy cacti and other drought-loving evergreens give the hell strips winter interest.*

▶ *Rose hips in snow.*

▼ *Snow-capped rabbitbrush,* Chrysothamnus nauseosus, *and George the cat soak up some winter sun, waiting for spring.*

▼ Acantholimon *mounds are the porcupine statuary of the winter garden.*

straight lines where the garden meets the sidewalk by spilling a good foot out on the cement. Sea thrift's small fluorescent green tufts evoke the lush grass of spring. The dark, almost black-green whorls of the early flowering yellow crucifer *Alyssoides graeca* contrast starkly with the perfect silver pinwheels of several *Physaria* species. Old spring-blooming regulars moss phlox (*Phlox subulata* and *P. bifida*) contribute dense, needlelike mats of a more olive green. Tiny *Yucca harrimaniae* and its larger cousins the narrow-leaved *Y. angustissima* and broader, agave-like *Y. baccata* add green architecture to the soft mats and mounds.

Even the dormant, shaded north side of the house is graced with a few evergreen perennials. I've steered clear of the tough and ubiquitous vinca, ivy, creeping grape holly and carpet bugle since they prefer to be the sole inhabitants of an area. I did tuck a few pieces of glossy, deep purple *Ajuga reptans* 'Atropurpurea' in the cracks between the stone path and the steps up to the house, where I'm fairly confident its adventurous ways will be contained. Less invasive perennials with pretty winter foliage greet me as I step outside the front door: the softly mottled rosettes of native coralbells, the finger-like foliage of *Helleborus foetidus*, and the large, cabbagy leaves of *Bergenia cordifolia*, which would turn a lovely deep red in more sun but remain dark green in the shade. If I had a bit moister, more acidic soil, I would plant European ginger (*Asarum europaeum*), its glossy, kidney-shaped leaves unmatched in polish and finesse. They can transform a brown, bleak winter scene and then play perfect host to the pristine white flowers of the earliest snowdrops as spring returns.

The winter garden combines the beauty of the season gone by with the promise of seasons yet to come. Last year's silvery maiden grass plumes, button-like chocolate *Rudbeckia* seedheads, rusty red rose hips mingle with evergreen foliages of all shapes and hues to keep the gardener's hopes alive, just as they continue to nourish and strengthen the plants themselves. And soon enough, on a warm day in late January or February, one looks deep into the heart of a seemingly lifeless rosette and finds the faint hint of a bud, a shoot, an unfurling leaf. Winter always keeps its promise of spring.

PLANTS FOR WINTER BEAUTY
Most of these prefer full sun and a well-drained soil on the dry side.

KEY

S: prefers some shade.

PP: featured in plant portrait section.

PERENNIALS WITH ATTRACTIVE PERSISTENT FOLIAGE
Achillea yarrow
Aethionema stone cress

Agave parryi century plant
Agave utahensis century plant
Ajuga reptans carpet bugle **S**
Alyssoides graeca
Alyssum montanum mountain
   basket-of-gold **PP**
Anacyclus depressus Mt. Atlas daisy
Antennaria pussytoes **S, PP**
Arabis rock cress **S**
Arenaria montana sandwort
Armeria sea thrift

Arum lords and ladies **S**
Asarum (not *A. canadense*) ginger **S**
Aubrieta purple rock cress **S**
Aurinia saxatilis basket-of-gold
Bergenia cordifolia pigsqueak **S**
Campanula persicifolia peach-leaf bellflower **S**
Centaurea stricta
Cerastium snow-in-summer
Coryphantha vivipara
Delosperma nubigenum hardy iceplant
Dianthus pinks

200

Dracocephalum botryoides
Echinocereus hedgehog cactus
Epimedium barrenwort **S**
Erica carnea heath **S**
Erigeron compositus cutleaf daisy
Eriogonum buckwheat **PP**
Euphorbia myrsinites donkeytail spurge
Euphorbia rigida spurge
Festuca ovina var. *glauca* blue sheep's
    fescue
Galax fairy wand **S**
Geranium macrorrhizum creeping cranesbill **S**
Geranium x *cantabrigiense* **S**
Globularia
Goniolimon statice
Hedera helix ivy **S**
Helianthemum sunrose
Helichrysum everlasting—some
Helictotrichon sempervirens blue avena
    grass
Helleborus **S**
Hepatica liverleaf **S**
Hesperis matronalis sweet rocket **S**
Heuchera sanguinea coralbells **S**
Heucherella tiarelloides **S**
Iberis candytuft **S**
Kniphofia red hot poker
Lavandula lavender
Limonium sea lavender
Lychnis coronaria rose campion **S**
Mahonia repens creeping mahonia **S**
Marrubium horehound **PP**
Neobesseya missouriensis
Onopordum Scots thistle
Onosma alboroseum **S**
Onosma sericeum **S**
Opuntia
Papaver triniifolium Armenian poppy **PP**
Pediocactus snowball cactus
Penstemon beardtongue **PP**
Persicaria (Polygonum) affinis border jewel **S**
Phlomis russeliana **PP**
Phlox bifida sand phlox
Phlox subulata moss phlox

Physaria bladder pod
Poa baldensis
Raoulia vegetable sheep **S**
Salvia cyanescens
Salvia lavandulifolia
Santolina lavender cotton
Saxifraga **S**
Schivereckia podolica
Sedum
Sempervivum hens and chicks
Sideritis **PP**
Silene vulgaris ssp. *maritima* sea campion
Stachys byzantina lamb's ear
Synthyris missurica **S, PP**
Tanacetum densum var. *amani* partridge
    feather
Tellima grandiflora fringecups **S**
Teucrium germander
Thymus mastichinus thyme
Thymus pseudolanuginosus woolly thyme
Thymus serphyllum mother of thyme
Tiarella foamflower **S**
Townsendia Easter daisy
Verbascum mullein
Veronica **PP**
Vinca minor **S**
Viola labradorica **S**
Waldsteinia barren strawberry **S**
Yucca

EVERGREEN WOODY PLANTS
Abies fir
Arctostaphylos bearberry, kinnikinnick,
    manzanita
Cercocarpus ledifolius curl-leaf mountain
    mahogany
Daphne cneorum garland daphne
Daphne x *burkwoodii*
Ephedra joint fir
Genista broom
Juniperus
Microbiota decussata
Picea spruce
Pinus pine

Tsuga hemlock

BARK PLANTS
Betula nigra 'Heritage' birch
Cornus sericea redstem dogwood, 'Flaviramea'
    yellowstem
Physocarpus ninebark
Pinus bungeana lacebark pine
Populus tremuloides aspen
Prunus maackii Amur cherry
Ulmus parvifolia lacebark elm

FRUITS AND BERRIES
Aronia chokeberry
Arum lords and ladies **S**
Belamcanda chinensis blackberry lily
Berberis koreana Korean barberry
Berberis thunbergii barberry
Cotoneaster
Crataegus hawthorn
Ephedra joint fir
Forestiera neomexicana New Mexico privet
Hippophae rhamnoides buckthorn
Ilex holly **S**
Juniperus
Ligustrum privet
Mahonia—some **S**
Malus crabapple
Myrica pensylvanica bayberry
Neobesseya missouriensis berry cactus
Opuntia humifusa prickly pear cactus
Opuntia phaeacantha prickly pear cactus
Pyracantha coccinea firethorn
Rhus typhina staghorn sumac
Rosa eglanteria sweetbriar rose
Rosa gallica
Rosa glauca red-leaf rose **PP**
Rosa moyesii
Rosa rugosa
Rosa woodsii Woods rose
Rosa x *alba* **PP**
Viburnum trilobum cranberry-bush
       viburnum (others don't last)

X

*Portraits of
Indispensably
Undaunted Plants*

(preceding pages) Passing over lamb's ear and Salvia x superba *'East Friesland', a swallowtail flutters to Rocky Mountain penstemon for nectar.*

The following plants are all hardy in northern Colorado to at least minus thirty-five degrees Fahrenheit. They have proven themselves to me in the flesh, not just from enticing pictures in books and catalogs full of wishes. These plants possess superior ornamental qualities along with their adaptability to harsh climates, and in many cases are not yet well known. I've included some combinations I particularly like, for it seems more people ask me this sort of aesthetic advice than the nuts and bolts information. The latter, of course, is also included. The pronunciation guide is not meant to be a rigid put-off—it is a guide, nothing more. There is no wrong way to pronounce a botanical name unless the syllables are out of order or a person's name is mangled in the process. Common names are included when known; in some cases, the plant is still too uncommon to have one.

Alcea rugosa (al-SEE-a roo-GOH-sa)

This kissing cousin to the old-fashioned hollyhock is one of the finest recent garden introductions for harsh climates. While hollyhocks have thrived here for years, even neglected and without water in abandoned gardens and homesteads, they go through an annual denuding when rust sets in and ruins the lower half of their foliage just as they go into flower. *Alcea rugosa* is mercifully resistant to rust and a bit more long-lived in the garden too, perhaps because it doesn't experience the stress of disease. It looks very much like a single yellow form of *A. rosea*, but closer scrutiny reveals darker green, more wrinkled and deeply lobed foliage and a stronger lemon yellow color to the flower. The flower is also a bit larger and frillier along the petal margins than single hollyhocks. All in all, this is an imposing five- to seven-foot plant but with a sweet, old-fashioned look about it. *A. rugosa* blooms in midsummer for over a month; if the central flower stalk is removed once spent, side shoots will continue blooming into autumn. It makes a good companion to the steely blue spheres of globe thistles (*Echinops* spp.) and does best in full sun and average garden soil. The plant grows easily and quickly from seed, but unfortunately much is mislabeled and really only a pale yellow single-flowered variant of *Alcea rosea*.

205

Allium christophii (AH-lee-um kris-TAW-fee-eye)
STAR ONION

This bulb opens its spherical galaxies of silver-lavender stars in early summer. If one is to grow but one of the myriad ornamental onions, this is it. Star onion needs full sun and a well-drained soil, and can take it quite dry. Contrary to most other bulbs as large and showy, it puts out relatively scant foliage, a real blessing once the flowers have gone over and the leaves begin to decline. The flower heads are truly spectacular, between eight and twelve inches in diameter yet still graceful. The individual flowers have an almost metallic sheen, giving the plant added sparkle. Star onion usually grows about fifteen to eighteen inches tall; sometimes it reaches two feet. It cuts and dries beautifully, so it might also be a good choice for the kitchen garden if one wants to preserve its beauty in situ elsewhere. Star onion looks fabulous with soft colors—white, cream, pale yellow, pink and silver, and also with deep purples and magentas. It is a great companion for show-stopping Armenian cranesbill, *Geranium psilostemon*, with black-eyed, shocking pink flowers. A bit of silver partridge feather foliage adds the finishing touch to the combination. Star onion, like most of the *Allium* genus, can be grown easily from seed but takes several years to bloom this way, and good bulbs can be bought for a reasonable price through the mail from several specialty bulb brokers, so it seems a waste of time to bother with seed.

Alyssum montanum (ah-LISS-um mon-TAH-num)
MOUNTAIN BASKET-OF-GOLD

Once one meets this plant, its coarser common cousin *Aurinia saxatilis*, the old-fashioned basket-of-gold, will most certainly end up in the compost heap. While the latter boasts some fine cultivars, including a pale apricot ('Sunny Border Apricot') and lemon yellow ('Citrina'), a variegated one called 'Dudley Neville' and a double form, the plain old basket of gold pales next to the longer bloom time, prettier growth habit and superior foliage of *Alyssum montanum*. Mountain basket-of-gold offers a profusion of bright yellow flowers similar in form to the annual sweet alyssum's. They begin to bloom very early in the spring, continuing for a good six weeks. If cut back hard, the plant will rebloom sporadically later in the season. *A. montanum* forms a six-to-eight inch-tall, foot-wide mound when in full flower. The gray-green foliage is small yet profuse along the semiprostrate stems. Mountain basket-of-gold is short-lived yet self-sows with abandon. If the spent flowers are removed promptly before seed formation, plants will live longer. The seedheads are quite pretty, however, giving the plant the appearance of a pale greenish yellow bloom until completely dry and tawny. Mountain alyssum needs strong colors for companions. The dark indigo blue spikes of biennial *Dracocephalum nutans* look good at the end of *Alyssum montanum*'s bloom; early on, orange and red tulips and chartreuse donkey-tail spurge, *Euphorbia myrsinites*, hold their own against its vibrant spring display on my hell strips. Full sun and a lean soil produce the best plants, but mountain basket-of-gold is quite adaptable to most garden conditions except shade.

Antennaria parvifolia (an-teh-NA-ri-a par-vi-FOH-li-a)
PUSSYTOES

Pussytoes owe their endearing name to their tiny flower heads—several fuzzy balls arranged in tight clusters. *Antennaria parvifolia* is the most drought tolerant of the genus and also has the most ornamental evergreen foliage. It is native to the plains, often seen growing in picturesque silver-gray patches with small hardy ball cacti amid vast stretches of buffalo grass. In mid-spring, the flowers rise up on two- to six-inch stems above the prostrate mat of leaves. Usually they are creamy white, turning buff as the involucre dries and expands to a small fluffy dandelion-like head, but they vary a great deal in nature. Some flower selections have a rose tint in bud, some come in a purer white. Just west of Cheyenne, Wyoming, I found one colony

almost chartreuse in flower that glowed at me beneath menacing, charcoal gray afternoon thunderclouds. The foliage of this charming little spreading ground cover is a lovely gray-silver, made up of many tight little rosettes. It is ideal between flagstones in light, dry shade or as a ground cover for small bulbs. Deep purple *Iris reticulata* 'Pauline', golden *Crocus ancyrensis* or hot lipstick pink *Tulipa humilis* look wonderful backed by pussytoes' silver mat. An extra minute form, 'McClintock', with rosettes smaller than a pencil eraser, needs the confines of a rock garden or trough to show off its intricacy. In cool, cloudy climates, pussytoes likes full sun, but closer to its harsh native haunts it prefers a bit of shade; the grasses of the prairie provide this in nature. Pussytoes grows most easily from division, but seed sown generously will germinate well, too.

Aster ericoides (AS-ter eh-ri-KOY-dees)
HEATH ASTER

This is my favorite aster; I consider it the baby's breath of the fall garden. Masses of tiny white, pink or pale lavender flowers hover in stiff, heathlike sprays two to three feet above a small, humble clump of leaves. Heath aster grows wild in sunny dry spots in the eastern half of North America and has proven to be one of the more drought-tolerant asters in the garden although it would not survive completely without supplemental water in drier climates. In rich, moist soil it can be a bit invasive. Heath aster grows easily from root or stem cuttings, or division. In the warm, low sunlight of an autumn afternoon, the thousand tiny daisies attract the last of the season's honeybees. With lavender fall-blooming *Crocus speciosus* at its feet, both the bees and the gardener can enjoy an end-of-the-season delight.

Atriplex hortensis **'Rubra'** (AH-tri-plex hor-TEN-sis 'ROO-bra')
RED ORACH

This annual was originally grown as a vegetable, for its young foliage and stems have a salty, spinach-like taste. The red-leaved form, however, has entranced many and is now more of an ornamental than anything else. Once seen backlit by the sun, the color of bruised raspberries, red orach becomes an absolute necessity in the spring and early summer garden. If allowed to grow on rich, moist soil, it can reach five to six feet. Full sun is best. The flowers are not showy, but the seeds are red and plant themselves helter-skelter for early, cool-weather germination next spring. I usually only allow a few plants to flower and go to seed; the foliage display declines rapidly with the onset of hot weather. Red orach mingles well with hot colors—brilliant orange-red Oriental poppies, crimson fernleaf peonies, scarlet Maltese cross—and with pale colors and white. It frames the shimmering pale yellow blossoms of the old-fashioned bearded iris 'Flavescens'. A friend and I salvaged a small start of this iris from a group of luminescent clumps that grew out in the middle of nowhere, miles from civilization, on the rolling high plains at the Wyoming-Nebraska border, survivors of a vanished homestead. Bearded iris snobs disdain its dog-ear shape and small flowers, but I am honored to have it grace my garden. Red orach is just the right companion.

Callirhoe involucrata (ka-lih-ROW-ee in-voh-loo-KRAH-ta)
PRAIRIE WINE-CUP, POPPY MALLOW, BUFFALO ROSE

This evocative plains wildflower is a sturdy, dependable perennial in the sunny, dry garden. It blooms tirelessly from late spring through early autumn, sending up a parade of showy, open-faced, one-to two-inch mallow cups of the richest wine red with a contrasting white eye. Pink and white forms are sometimes seen in nature but so far have not been selected for in the trade. Buffalo rose is a sprawling, ground-hugging plant; a mature, happy specimen can cover an area three to four feet in diameter each season, yet is completely noninvasive underground. In winter the long stems wither and a deep emerald evergreen rosette of fresh leaves forms in the heart of the plant, at the top of its long, probing taproot. The deep green foliage remains attractive until late in the growing season, a welcome effect among the typical dusty sage greens and pervasive silvers of the dry garden. Because of its lanky nature, this plant looks best draped over a berm or raised bed, spilling over a wall or scrambling through more solid plants. It festoons silver lamb's ear at the edge of my garden, lapping onto the hot pavement. The vibrant magenta blossoms look best with silver-leaved and white, blue or lavender-flowered companions—blue flax, perovskia and many of the hardy salvia clan including big-leaved biennials *Salvia sclarea*, *S. argentea* and *S. aethiopsis* (the first two have dependably perennial forms,) the long-flowering pale lavender-blue spikes of silver-leaved *S. cyanescens*, and more well known, cooking sage and its purple-leaved form *Salvia officinalis* 'Purpurea' and narrow-leaved variant *S. lavandulifolia*. Buffalo rose is temperamental and sporadic to germinate; a pot of seed stratified all winter will germinate a seedling here and there throughout the spring and summer, and again the following year. Self-sown seedlings in the garden are common, however.

Catalpa speciosa (ka-TAL-pa spee-see-OH-sa)
WESTERN CATALPA

I am totally confused about this tree's reputation. One of horticulture's finest authorities on woody plants, Michael Dirr, claims western catalpa is of limited use in the landscape. Nonhorticultural neighbors complain it is messy because it drops long, pencil-like beans and large, tropical-looking foliage in the fall. Now what deciduous tree doesn't drop its leaves? The fruit and foliage are large and coarse, making cleanup easier than for most trees. Western catalpa is adaptable to almost any soil, considerably drought tolerant for a tree of its size, hardy to at least minus forty degrees Fahrenheit, fast-growing yet not nearly as prone to breakage as other instant-gratification trees like Siberian elms, poplars or silver maples, and has fabulous leaves and flowers to boot. In the case of this wrongly maligned tree, I say ignore both the authority and the ignorant neat-freak. When western catalpa has expanded its heart-shaped, ten-inch leaves and bursts into a mass of frilly white early summer bloom, the exotic lushness of the tropics pays a welcome visit. Western catalpa's narrow crown makes it a good street tree. Easy from seed or cuttings, this great native American tree will grow two to three feet a year, reaching fifty to sixty feet on average at maturity, sometimes more.

Clematis integrifolia (KLEH-mah-tis in-teh-gri-FOH-li-a)
BUSH CLEMATIS

I feel almost sacrilegious refuting one of the world's finest plantsmen, Graham Stuart Thomas, but since this is a matter of taste, not knowledge, perhaps I can get away with it. Besides, plants come first and this plant needs a fan club. In his classic book *Perennial Garden Plants*, Thomas snubs bush clematis, calling it a dull plant. Hogwash. *Clematis integrifolia* is one of the most charming midsummer-blooming perennials, easy to grow in sun or light shade, best in good garden soil. The nodding two-inch flowers are a soft mid-blue, pretty with any color. Bush clematis does for the July border what nepetas do earlier on—they are ideal go-betweens, setting off showier flower colors and shapes yet having a quiet beauty all their own. For the many daylily-crazed gardeners out there, I suggest a hearty dose of *C. integrifolia*—it will transform the most boring monoculture of those popular plants. Bush clematis tends to clamber and sprawl a bit, typically to three feet in height and width, and is not shy about clutching and leaning on its neighbors. This breaks the formal tension between the daylily clumps, softens their stiff outlines and harmonizes with all their colors. The plant is also lovely with the deep magenta forms of *Rosa rugosa*. Bush clematis grows well from semihard cuttings. It takes several years to grow into a vigorous plant, like its climbing cousins, but is carefree and extremely long-lived thereafter. It tends to show signs of life frighteningly late in the spring, but will return dependably. There is a compact selection, 'Hendersonii', that is said to reach only eighteen inches and be extra floriferous.

209

Crambe maritima (KRAM-bee ma-RIH-ti-ma)
SEA KALE

Sea kale was originally grown as a vegetable; when blanched, its leaves have a mild, sweet cabbagy taste. That same foliage convinced gardeners to grow it as an ornamental. In early spring, a ruffle of young, smoky purple foliage breaks through the ground, gorgeous with early red tulips. By mid-spring it has expanded considerably and turned a waxy aquamarine. The rest of the season, the wavy-edged glaucous leaves loll about, covering a good two feet of ground. Fragrant creamy white flowers in loose broccoli heads bloom in late spring; some gardeners go so far as to remove them so the plant will spend its energy on making the more desirable foliage. *Crambe maritima* reaches about eighteen feet in height, so is useful toward the

front of the sunny border as a heavily textured blue exclamation point, especially effective with vivid colors. It needs a well-drained, good garden soil for the best foliage, one that never dries out completely. Sea kale grows easily from seed without stratification. I have two large clumps, one for an early summer accent with a linear fountain of similarly turquoise blue avena grass and screaming orange biennial Siberian wallflowers. The other combination takes the limelight late in summer; sea kale anchors the purple haze of sea lavender flowers and a large stand of the bright rose daisies of purple coneflower 'Bright Star', an especially prolific selection with showier flowers than the straight species.

Crocus speciosus (KROW-kus spee-see-OH-sus)
AUTUMN CROCUS

Crocus speciosus is one of the easiest bulblike plants to grow, tolerating most soils, full sun to light shade and a good bit of drought. I can't have enough of it and I tuck its little corms all along the paths. The four- to six-inch-tall flowers appear quite late in the fall, looking just like their spring brethren—lavender chalices open to the sun, enticing the last bees to visit their brilliant orange stigmas and anthers. Like the larger rose-pink naked boys of late summer and early autumn, the colchicums, *C. speciosus* flowers without its foliage. Colchicums have large, ungainly foliage in the spring which dies down during the summer; autumn crocus sends up thin, unobtrusive foliage right after it flowers, which continues to elongate until winter finally snuffs it. Because the flowers are naked, all the more reason to plant them with attractive foliages of companion plants. Rock cresses—*Arabis* spp.—work well, as do the many mat- and mound-forming thymes, veronicas and sedums. *Sedum kamtschaticum* often turns a brilliant orange-red in the fall, a wild and wonderful contrast with the crocus flowers. *Crocus speciosus* reproduces heartily by seed and cormlets; the colonies will increase exponentially over the years. Larger flowered and deeper purple selections are sometimes available for the autumn crocus connoisseur, as are other rarer and more demanding species.

Cynoglossum amabile (sih-noh-GLAW-sum ah-MAH-bee-lay)
CHINESE FORGET-ME-NOT

For those smitten by pure sky blue, a flower color so rare and delightful, this plant is just the thing. Chinese forget-me-not is technically a biennial, though it blooms the first year from seed. One- to two-foot-tall sprays of airy blue flowers grace the garden for two months in the summer. The plant grows easily from seed started indoors or sown directly in the garden; young transplants tolerate light frost so they can be put out early in the spring. Once well situated and blooming, Chinese forget-me-not can be counted on to self-sow quite a bit. It does best in morning sun or light shade, in average garden soil that never goes totally dry. I grow it with the peach-buff David Austin rose 'Bredon'. It is also lovely with all colors of daylilies. Pink and white forms exist, but I couldn't be less interested—that wonderful blue is the plant's raison d'être and can't be outdone.

Cynoglossum nervosum
(sih-noh-GLAW-sum ner-VOH-sum)
HOUND'S TONGUE

    Hound's tongue has a deeper true blue color than its annual cousin—that blue found in some gentians and delphiniums that sends many gardeners into rapture. It is an easy plant for morning sun or dryish light shade, reaching two feet in height and spread. The foliage is dull green and narrowly oval. In late spring, clusters of forget-me-not flowers, similar to alkanet, bloom for three weeks. *Cynoglossum nervosum* grows easily from stratified seed. It is lovely with early orange, gold or yellow daylilies. I grow it in light, dry shade with golden feverfew and the silver-netted foliage and yellow flowers of *Lamiastrum galeobdolon* 'Herman's Pride'.

211

Dracocephalum nutans (dra-koh-SEH-fa-lum NOO-tans)
    This biennial member of the mint family has become an indispensable self-sowing presence in my hot, dry hell strips. A long-bloomer, as so many biennials are, *Dracocephalum nutans* sends up a stiff, vase-shaped twelve- to eighteen-inch clump of rich indigo flower spikes for six to eight weeks. The calyces surrounding the blue flowers are a dark burgundy, adding to the color display. The flowers are longer lasting and the plant more drought tolerant than lookalike *Salvia* x *superba*, which resides in less harsh conditions elsewhere in the garden. An added feature is that its stems and calyces turn a bronze-maroon color as the flowers fade, so the plant remains attractive over a month after bloom has actually ceased. This also allows the seed to fall for next year's crop. The foliage is unremarkable but takes up very little space the first year; typical yearlings are four inches tall and wide. The next spring, at the tail-end of

golden *Alyssum montanum*'s bloom, the spikes begin to open. They are equally at home with pink and rose dianthus and the fragrant, sugar pink foam of stone cress (*Aethionema grandiflorum*) as they are with hot colors. I especially like them as a dark anchor to the bright red spires of *Penstemon eatonii* and *P. barbatus*, with deep gold *Linum flavum*, and as a dark backdrop to each morning's fleeting parade of orange poppy flowers, courtesy of *Papaver pilosum*. *Dracocephalum nutans* needs full sun. It can grow in more pampered garden conditions but the flowers lose much of their rich coloration.

Epilobium angustifolium 'Album'
(eh-pi-LOW-bee-um an-goos-ti-FOH-li-um)
WHITE FIREWEED, WHITE WILLOW HERB

This beautiful plant is the white form of the equally beautiful rose-purple thug, fireweed, known for colonizing vast expanses of fire-ravaged areas including London after the Blitz and the post-eruption Mount St. Helens area. White fireweed is not as invasive. Supposedly there is an entirely well behaved white form that remains a polite clump. Mine runs about quite a bit, but only at about half the rate of the aggressive colored form. Fireweed grows three to five feet tall, with medium green whorled leaves that arise from the ground in the spring like parasols. In early summer, elegant spires of white flowers begin to open. The white form I managed from seed may not be the well-behaved form but it blooms at least a month longer than the straight pink species—for two months, well into August. Fireweed does well in sun or light shade and needs moist soil to flourish. I grow it with lilies and shrub and old garden roses in a well-watered and manured east-facing area. Fireweed grows from pieces of the obnoxious underground runners and from stratified seed.

212

Eranthis hyemalis (eh-RAN-this hee-eh-MAH-lis)
WINTER ACONITE

Winter aconite bears irresistible yellow buttercup-like flowers in late winter. Each plant sends up one flower, held aloft over a clown-collar of green leaves. It is one of the earliest bulblike plants to bloom, often preceding snowdrops, which make good companions in the moist, humusy, lightly shaded sites both plants prefer. Winter aconite is actually a tuber, not a bulb, and is very prone to drying out in storage, which is the main reason so many people fail with it. One should soak the pealike tubers in water for a day before planting or, preferably, transplant clumps of the plant soon after flowering. Once happy and settled in, *Eranthis hyemalis* will self-sow, forming great colonies of yellow, ideal for carpeting beneath casual shrub plantings or under shade trees. *E. cilicica* is very similar but slightly finer textured, blooming a week or so later.

Eriogonum umbellatum
(eh-ree-AW-goh-num um-beh-LAH-tum)
SULPHUR FLOWER

So many breathtaking North American wild-flowers are all too fleeting in flower and not much for year-round interest in the garden. Sulphur flower bucks that trend; this widespread western mountain buckwheat is truly a four-season perennial. Many subspecies and named selections exist, from large three-foot shrubby types to almost prostrate alpine mat-formers. All have evergreen, leathery foliage, usually dark green but sometimes grayish on the top and white-felted beneath. All bloom heavily in early summer, with sulphur yellow compound umbels of long-lasting flowers, sometimes paler, an almost cream color. These flower heads in turn remain showy as they dry and go to seed; the seedheads are a warm rusty red color. The entire plant then goes on to turn a maroon or purple-brown fall color. Some actually turn a good red by early winter. Sulphur flower is also quite adaptable, tolerating sun to light shade, completely dry, unamended soil to good garden soil with occasional irrigation. Consistently moist soil, however, will do in the plant. Sulphur flower is easily grown from seed or basal cuttings. It is especially effective with blue flax or the showy indigo spikes of *Penstemon strictus*, a tractable, long-lived beardtongue.

Eryngium giganteum 'Miss Willmott's Ghost' (eh-RIN-jih-um jih-GAN-tee-um)
SILVER SEA HOLLY

The hardier members of the sea holly genus are unusual perennials grown for their thistly flower heads, generally a prickly combination of a collar-like bract and a central inflorescence in shades of steely blue or silver. *Eryngium giganteum* is more biennial than perennial, but self-sows with a vengeance. It has the most silvery flower heads of the group, shimmering on stiff, branched stems in the heat of midsummer and lasting for a good month. The plant grows two to three feet tall and needs full sun and a well-drained but not dry-as-dust soil. To get the plant started, one needs to find fresh seed and winter-stratify it. Once a few plants are thriving and blooming, progeny are bound to follow. Ellen Willmott, a talented and opinionated Edwardian gardener, is said to have sprinkled seed of this plant in gardens she visited where they later arose, ethereally silver, hence 'Miss Willmott's Ghost'. Apparently, she was also quite a prickly, stiff character, so I imagine it is just as likely that one of her legion of hired gardeners named the plant after a nasty run-in with her—a bit of wishful thinking, no doubt. *E. giganteum* is lovely with the pink or white spires of gas plant, *Dictamnus albus*.

Fallugia paradoxa (fa-LOO-ji-a pa-ra-DOH-xa)
APACHE PLUME

This fine-textured shrub from the Southwest is dependably hardy to at least minus forty degrees Fahrenheit, especially if the individual plant harks from stock from the colder ranges of its natural habitat. Apache plume is so named for its showy fruits, fluffy long-lasting achenes reminiscent of pasque-flower seedheads but of a russet-mauve color. This shrub grows four to six feet tall and at least that wide, a casual but impressive twiggy mound. The small, cut foliage is semievergreen, gray-green on top and downy-white below. The stems and twigs are also covered with white felt. In early summer, many single, white, one-inch flowers open, resembling roses. Bloom continues sporadically into the autumn, when the shrub is at its best, covered in a ruddy smoke of seed while still studded with the occasional pristine white flower. *Fallugia paradoxa* needs full sun and a lean, dry soil or it becomes misshapen, scraggly and limp. The most effective siting of Apache plume is where the beautiful seedheads can be appreciated backlit by the low morning or afternoon sun.

Foeniculum vulgare var. *purpureum* (fuh-NEE-kew-lum vul-GAH-ray pur-POO-ri-um)
BRONZE FENNEL

This fast-growing, self-sowing herb is grown mainly for its luxuriant plum-bronze foliage—soft, ferny and perfect as a foil for bold flower shapes and colors. Whether framing a hot red daylily or a cool white rose, this plant is an indispensable mixer. Bronze fennel is not reliably perennial when winter temperatures dip below minus twenty-five degrees Fahrenheit. Winter mulching with dried leaves helps. It grows so quickly from seed that its billowing three- to four-foot-tall presence can be counted on even if grown as an annual. Full sun and a well-drained soil on the dry side produce the best coloration and stiffer stems less likely to sprawl. Removing flower stalks as they develop helps keep the foliage attractive longer. By late summer, the plant will stubbornly insist on blooming at the expense of the leaves; the unremarkable flat-topped clusters, reminiscent of a muddy yellow version of Queen Anne's lace, will produce seed to ensure fennel's presence the following year should a cold winter kill the parent plant. The seeds, foliage and stems all can be used for cooking and baking; their delightful anise scent is a treat for non-chefs like myself whenever I happen to rub against the plant in the garden. When sited by a gate, bronze fennel will release its aroma every time the gate is opened and brushes upon it. Occasionally, a few brightly striped caterpillars come to dine; with a large clump of the plant or several specimens, their damage will go unnoticed and when they visit at a later date, transformed into elegant swallowtail butterflies, the sacrificed stem or two of the fennel will be well worth it.

One of the best uses of this lovely plant is as a backdrop to the smoky colored arilbred irises, suffused with maroon, bronze and brown casts and often with deep velvety purple-brown signals, dark spots at the base of the falls that look like inky thumb prints. With bronze fennel's soft, smoky foliage at its freshest in the spring, it works as the perfect foil for these exotic, dramatic flowers. Some especially nice iris cultivars are maroon-netted 'Oyez', dusky lavender and tan 'Onlooker' with dark signals and similar but more compact 'Jewel of Omar'.

Humulus lupulus 'Aureus' (HOO-mew-lus LOO-pew-lus 'AW-reh-us')
GOLDEN HOPS VINE

This vigorous vine dies down to the ground each year, yet manages to put on ten to fifteen feet of growth year after year. In the most severe winter climates, it is grown as an annual. Golden hops vine is perfect for morning sun or light shade and will tolerate some drought, although it performs best in good garden soil with regular moisture. It has attractive, large-lobed leaves of a soft yellow, more gold in the sun, more chartreuse in the shade. It is one of the few golden-leaved plants that comes true from seed rather than reverting back to all green. In late summer and fall, unusual bracted flowers appear, also chartreuse, looking like a cross between a shrimp and a pinecone. All in all, the foliage color and vigorous carefree nature is what make this vine a worthy garden plant. It lights up a dark tree trunk or rough-hewn wood arbor. Allowed to twist and twine its golden arms around clematis' profusion of summer flowers, whether white as shown here or Jackman's purple, this good vine becomes sublime.

Hydrangea arborescens 'Annabelle' (hy-DRAN-ja ar-bo-REH-senz)

Few shrubs thrive and flower in the shade; 'Annabelle' hydrangea does. This plant has become widely available and its popularity is well deserved. The hardiest hydrangea, it offers a lush effect, dependability and fabulously showy flowers for the shaded garden or one that gets morning sun. From midsummer well into fall, its lovely foot-wide balls of flowers add much to the landscape. Annabelle hydrangea is a medium-sized, casual-looking shrub in leaf, typically three to four feet tall and wide. In harsh winters when the mercury dips to below minus ten or so, as it usually does in my garden, the plant dies down to the ground each year. This is no problem at all since the winter interest of its coarse, sparsely branched twigs is virtually nil. The foliage of this shrub is large and a good dark green, perfect for setting off the creamy white flower trusses. 'Annabelle' is by far the best form—the species has insipid flowers and other selections tend to flop to the ground. Annabelle hydrangea is not a plant for dry shade or poor soil—an annual topdressing of compost will help plump up the plant. Where happy, it suckers a bit. I grow mine with white and green variegated redstem dogwood and white-flowered musk mallow (*Malva moschata* 'Alba'). As the giant flower trusses start to fade, they turn a pretty pale green, remaining effective well into fall. They are great in dried arrangements, wired onto a wreath form or as naturalistic Christmas tree ornaments. To complete my pale, quiet shady composition, I add a smattering of annuals each year—the old-fashioned, fragrant, white flowering tobacco, *Nicotiana alata*, the pale green nodding bells of *N. langsdorfii* and the cool-colored flowers of *N.* 'Lime Green'.

Iris aucheri (EYE-ris AW-ker-eye)

This bulbous iris blooms early each spring, a breathtaking vision of ethereal blue after a long, hard winter. Its flowers, though large, seem almost surreally delicate, yet this iris is one sturdy little customer, accustomed to the rocky, sunbaked hillsides of Asia Minor. *Iris aucheri* is a member of the juno irises, a group of tough, hardy, often drought-tolerant plants with appealing glossy apple-green foliage arranged in opposite sheaths along the stem. *I. aucheri* grows six to nine inches tall, in full sun and dry soil. The pale flowers are sweetly fragrant, pretty when paired with the white candytuft-like early flowers of *Schivereckia podolica*, a refined version of *Iberis sempervirens* for drier spots.

216

Knautia macedonica (NOW-tee-a ma-seh-DOH-ni-ca)
RED PINCUSHION FLOWER

This short-lived perennial blooms ceaselessly from late spring until after frost and then self-sows prodigiously. It is another of those plants whose relative scarcity I can't fathom, for its floriferous ways, adaptability, hardiness and stunning one- to two-inch

crimson-burgundy flowers make it a must for the sunny garden. In lean soil it grows about a foot tall and wide; with more moisture and greater fertility, it doubles these dimensions and starts to sprawl a bit. *Knautia macedonica* looks especially good with all sort of silver foliage, with the chartreuse sprays of alchemilla in the moister garden, and with cream-colored flowers such as the double-flowered dropwort, *Filipendula vulgaris* 'Flore Pleno', some peony cultivars and the whorled flower spikes of *Phlomis russeliana*. It also makes a nice companion to old garden roses.

Lathyrus latifolius (LAH-thih-rus la-ti-FOH-li-us)
PERENNIAL PEA

Perennial pea is a tried-and-true cottage garden plant—a vine found in many older gardens throughout Europe and North America. Long-lived, inclined to self-sowing and hardy to drought, heat and cold, it's no wonder the plant is so widespread. Ironically, one is hard-pressed to find it in the trade. I had to grow my perennial peas from seed. The large seed germinates quickly and easily when soaked in scalding hot water for a few hours until it imbibes. Discard the seeds still floating after half a day in water—they are probably not viable. Perennial pea typically reaches six or more feet in a season, then dies back to the ground in harsh climates like Colorado's. The large flowers bloom in clusters all along the vine and are bright rose-pink, unfortunately not fragrant. They make nice cut flowers. Deadheading greatly improves this plant's performance: bloom season continues from early summer into fall if spent flower clusters are cut off before they form seed. A lovely white form known as 'Albus' or 'White Pearl', depicted here, is available from some seed sources. Perennial pea vine climbs by tendrils. It will not cling to wood or masonry surfaces. I stapled some inconspicuous black netting, the kind sold for protecting fruit from birds, to our cedar picket fence to help the pea climb. Perennial pea does best in full or half-day sun. It will tolerate quite a bit of drought but the best growth and bloom results if it is not grown bone dry. This vine—both rose and white forms—looks great fighting it out with the floriferous, summer-blooming clematis group that includes velvety purple Jackmanii and the wonderful, smaller-flowered viticella hybrids.

217

Lavatera thuringiaca (la-vah-TEH-ra thoo-rin-jee-AH-ka)
SHRUB MALLOW

Shrub mallow is a five-foot-tall and four-foot-wide semiwoody plant that nevertheless dies down to the ground each year. It is grown all over Europe, yet scarce in the States. I've found it to be completely hardy in northern Colorado. Attractive, sage green, lobed foliage, somewhat maple-like, clothes the coarse, upright branches, giving shrub mallow a valuable shrublike role at the back of the border. In the sagging days of mid- and late summer, the gardener is treated to a four-week-long succession of clear, two-inch pink mallow flowers, especially effective with the wispy lavender-blue wands of Russian sage. Adaptable shrub mallow can take quite dry or more mesic conditions, as shown by its command performance in both England and Colorado, but needs full sun for good flowering. It grows easily from both seed and stem or root cuttings. 'Barnsley' is a pretty white selection with a contrasting rose eye, named for Rosemary Verey's famed garden in England where it was found.

Lilium regale (LEE-lih-um ray-GAH-leh)
REGAL LILY

This is one of the easiest lilies to grow and one of the most beautiful. If I were to grow but one lily, it would be the regal. Hardy, disease-resistant, vigorous and long-lived, adaptable to almost any soil as long as it is well drained and not allowed to dry out completely, the regal lily is every bit worthy of its name. In mid-summer, sturdy six-foot-tall stems are crowned with a whorl of large, long-lasting flowers. The white blossoms are trumpet-shaped, flaring up to six inches wide, tinged purple or burgundy on the outside. They are heavily perfumed. Though adaptable, the plants will perform best in full sun in a sandy loam enriched with lots of compost. Each year the planting grows stronger, sending up more stems and flowers. Regal lilies have been popular ever since they were introduced early this century, and are widely available. They are much less likely to have viral problems than most other lilies, but buying them from a reputable source is still a good precaution. I grow mine in front of purple-leaved cistena plum to show off the flowers. The lilies are close to the path, temptingly near the nose. Silver lamb's ear fronts their lanky stems; annual red orach pops up in between, adding more burgundy to the scene.

218

Linum flavum (LEE-num FLAH-vum)
GOLDEN FLAX

Golden flax is an easy sun-loving, drought-tolerant perennial. Its clusters of warm yellow flowers open on foot-high stems in late spring and early summer for several weeks. Prompt deadheading encourages sporadic flower stalks throughout the rest of the summer. The ground-hugging foliage rosettes persist well into winter and are deep green, a w   ful foil for the bright flowers. They also add a lush green note to the predominant gray   ed foliage colors

of a water-wise landscape. In early spring, I cut the straggly rosettes back hard, forcing new, vigorous, less woody growth from the crowns. *Linum bulgaricum* and *L. dolomiticum* are supposedly separate species; I can't tell them from *L. flavum*. Apparently *L. bulgaricum* is the best for intense heat and drought tolerance. For the life of me, I don't know which one I grow, but my golden flax thrives in the unwatered "hell strips" with a gravel mulch, paired with the imposing four-foot-tall red flower spikes of *Penstemon barbatus* and shorter indigo purple *Dracocephalum nutans*. The pale sage green velvet of *Marrubium rotundifolium* foliage cools the scene. In the occasionally irrigated west-facing part of the garden, golden flax keeps company with the foot-tall deep blue spikes and silver foliage of *Veronica incana* 'Saraband'. Golden flax grows easily from seed.

Malva moschata (MAL-va moh-SHAH-ta)
MUSK MALLOW

Musk mallow is a tough yet sweet-looking hollyhock relative for light shade or morning sun. It sports a mass of glossy, deep emerald green foliage, growing from a central rosette, ultimately reaching two feet in height and spread. Over a period of six to eight weeks from midsummer until early autumn, the plant produces many pink or white one- to two-inch mallow flowers. The white variety, *Malva moschata alba*, is especially effective in light shade for it is one of the purest whites of any flower, and the contrasting foliage is so dark and handsome. Musk mallow grows easily from stratified seed and self-sows quite a bit in the garden. In a moister, lightly shaded site, it makes a good companion to 'Annabelle' hydrangea, the blue-purple spikes of midsummer-blooming monkshoods such as *Aconitum henryi* or *A. napellus*. In my drier shade, it grows with the tall, airy lavender flower sprays of *Thalictrum delavayi* and the tropical-looking pink flowers of naked ladies, a great old-fashioned bulb for late summer.

Marrubium spp. (ma-ROO-bi-um)
HOREHOUND

Horehounds are semiwoody perennial shrublets grown for their tough constitutions and wonderful felted foliage, usually rounded and crinkled or wavy along the edge, like small pieces of gray or chartreuse velvet. The common horehound from which throat lozenges were once made, *Marrubium vulgare*, is the dullest of the bunch, a nondescript small gray-green shrub, coarse and lanky in growth habit. *M. incanum* is a dense eighteen-inch mound of silver-gray leaves, the perfect color foil in smaller gardens where large artemisias take up too much space. *M. cylleneum* boasts chartreusy sage foliage and a more prostrate habit a foot or so tall and a bit wider. Its flowers, unlike the inconspicuous white blooms of the other species, are pale lavender and a bit more ornamental but the foliage is still the reason for this plant's place in the sunny dry garden. It looks superb with the strong lavender-rose of long-blooming sprawler *Verbena bipinna...r* with equally floriferous magenta *Callirhoe involucrata*. *Marrubium rotundifolium*, pictured at right, ...ompletely prostrate, even cascading, with noncrinkled, spoon-shaped leaves of the finest pale green velvet, with a lighter cream rim around them. It is a refined treasure of the finest order, whether playing the star of the planting or the ideal foil for small, brilliantly-colored plants such as the orange-scarlet prairie-fire penstemon, *Penstemon pinifolius*, or coppery and burnt orange selections of sunrose such as *Helianthemum nummularium* 'Seattle', 'Pumpkin' or 'Henfield Brilliant'. All the horehounds grow easily from stratified seed or semihard stem cuttings.

Nepeta sibirica (neh-PEE-ta sih-BEE-ri-ka)

This long-flowering perennial is, as its botanical name would suggest, hardy to viciously cold winters. It is easy to grow from seed or cuttings and tends to sucker from the roots, so I can't imagine why it is so scarce among generous gardeners or in the trade. It is one of the finest border plants in the mint family, sending up three- to four-foot tall spikes of large periwinkle blue flowers that blend with any and all companions. The misty blue color and spike form as well as this nepeta's large size and somewhat rambunctious ways make it an ideal companion to old garden roses, whose rounded flowers and rose, pink, mauve and white hues are perfectly complemented. For smaller gardens, the cultivar 'Souvenir d' André Chaudron', also known as 'Blue Beauty', only reaches eighteen inches. Full sun to light shade is best, as is a soil average in fertility and moisture. If treated too well, the plant becomes floppy and extremely invasive. *Nepeta sibirica* blooms from peony season on until well into the doldrums of midsummer, for an impressive total of six to eight weeks. I especially like it with the cool, lemon yellow of the large-flowered daylily 'Irish Limerick' and the Ozark sundrop, *Oenothera macrocarpa*, sprawling in front.

Oenothera brachycarpa (ee-NAW-theh-ra brah-kee-KAR-pa)
ROCKY MOUNTAIN SUNDROP

I first saw this plant's luminous three- to four-inch lemon yellow flowers glowing like beacons from road cuts in northern Colorado. It was a cloudy day, so they hadn't closed yet, as they do on sunny afternoons. I thought they were the well-known Ozark sundrop, *Oenothera macrocarpa* (formerly *O. missouriensis*), but once I got up close, I realized that while the flowers were indistinguishable, the foliage and growth habit were totally different. This sundrop's flowers emanated from a neat six-inch rosette of narrow, somewhat shiny dark green leaves, not the untidy flopping olive-green mass that supports the Ozark sundrop. This evening primrose had all the best qualities of the well-known one and none of the bad. Now that I've grown it for several years, I can also attest to its greater drought tolerance. It grows from stratified seed and takes a couple of years to reach the size necessary to support a large number of flowers. My four-year-olds bloom every evening and morning for three months from late spring through late summer with the help of my deadheading. If allowed to form seedpods, the plant stops blooming much sooner. On early summer mornings, before the heat of the day has set in, I enjoy the radiant flowers along with that day's crop of blue flax and pink, peach, cream and white sunrose flowers, fresh and pristine before the heat knocks down their fragile petals.

Omphalodes verna (om-fah-LOW-dees VER-nah)
NAVELWORT, BLUE-EYED MARY

I first saw this plant in great gentian-blue forget-me-not masses under exotic pale yellow and peach rhododendrons in Ireland and was smitten. I never thought this shade- and moisture-loving plant could grow here in Colorado, let alone make it through the winter, but it was worth a gamble. Blue-eyed Mary has been spreading slowly on the north side of my house for four years now, a well-behaved sweetheart of a ground cover framing the small yellow and white daffodil 'Jack Snipe'. Blue-eyed Mary grows to only six inches or so in height; the intense blue flower sprays start to bloom before the foliage has unfurled and finish about three weeks later. A lovely white-flowered form exists, but I have not been able to find it in the trade. *Omphalodes verna* can be grown from fresh seed or easily divided. It deserves much more use in shaded gardens on this side of the Atlantic.

Origanum spp. (oh-RIH-ga-num)
SHOWY OREGANO

221

Several unusual species and hybrids of this genus have large bracts from which the lavender, white or rose-purple flowers protrude. The bracts, often tiered and chartreuse, call to mind those of the tender shrimp plant grown indoors. They are the showiest aspect of the inflorescence and are appealing for six weeks or more before disintegrating in late summer. When I worked on the British Isles, oreganos were heavily in vogue much like hellebores are right now. In the harsher climate of the continental United States, several oreganos are making themselves a happy home. A few can't take the cold winter temperatures, but the following have proven hardy in northern Colorado over several years. *Origanum acutidens* has large chartreuse bracts and white, inconspicuous flowers. It thrives on my hell strips, and in the more pampered part of the sunny garden it likes to be cut to the ground once the bracts are no longer showy and makes a semicascading eight- to twelve-inch mound. It is lovely with hot pink flower clusters of annual catchfly, *Silene armeria*. *Origanum amanum* is smaller and more fine-textured in flower and leaf, growing only about six inches tall and not quite a foot wide. Its bracts are pink and the flowers long and protruding, a good rose-purple, making the inflorescence the showiest of the genus. I give it afternoon shade. *O. libanoticum*, pictured here, has narrow chartreuse bracts with lavender flowers in long shrimplike drooping heads. It grows a foot or so tall and wide and is wiry and fine-textured. *O. laevigatum* 'Hopley's' is the latest to bloom, in August. An airy, foot-tall plant with blue-green foliage, its wiry dark maroon stems hold up a profusion of rose-pink flowers in plum colored bracts. It is pretty with silver and chartreuse foliages such as lamb's ear or *Marrubium cylleneum*, and as a fine-textured foil to the exotic-looking pink flowers of the late-summer-flowering bulb naked ladies, *Lycoris squamigera*. *Origanum laevigatum* does best in full sun with average garden soil and moisture. All the above oreganos grow well from stratified seed or semihard cuttings.

Paeonia mlokosewitschii
(pay-OH-ni-a mlo-ko-seh-VI-chi-eye)
MOLLIE THE WITCH PEONY

Here is another fabulous garden plant—bone hardy, beautiful and easy to grow—yet just about impossible to come by. I had to grow mine from seeds ordered from overseas, a long-winded process that involved several years of nursing and coddling. Peonies are slow to produce commercially and not particularly happy in the confines of plastic one-gallon pots, but that doesn't seem to deter the nurseries from carrying a good number of the common lactiflora hybrids. A fine selection of bare-root plants can also be had through mail-order sources for fall planting. So where is poor Mollie the witch? *Paeonia mlokosewitschii* is a wonderful perennial for east-facing or lightly shaded gardens. Its lush, lobed gray-green foliage, often edged burgundy, makes a shrublike two-foot mound. The sumptuous pale yellow flowers are single and cupped, up to six inches across, especially effective in softly lit areas. It is one of the earliest peonies to bloom, along with the crimson flowers of its cousin the fern-leaf peony, *P. tenuifolia*. Beautiful Mollie combines especially well with pale foliage such as golden feverfew. A touch of blue—the forget-me-not flowers of *Brunnera macrophylla* or the airy powder-blue clusters of *Phlox divaricata*—completes a perfect spring picture in good moist garden soil.

Papaver somniferum (pah-PAH-ver som-NIH-feh-rum)
OPIUM POPPY

This annual poppy grows in the gardens of innocents, self-sowing and blooming with beautiful abandon—even though the seedpod's milky sap is the chief source of opium. As a teenager, I remember seeing opium poppies on a visit to relatives in Austria. I fell in love with the two- to four-feet high, pale gray-green plants and their large, diaphanous single, semidouble and double blooms. The semidoubles look like peony flowers; the doubles are the least graceful of the lot, a bit like crumpled clods of used tissues. I could not find a source for the plants back in the States, so I grew my first batch from seed scraped off the top of a bagel. My first crop of opium poppies were pale salmon singles. White, lavender, maroon, red, pink and deep purple versions can be had if one hunts in old cottage gardens or pilfers some seed from abroad. Most European plant society seed lists include several selections, as do English seed catalogs. Opium poppy flowers range from two to five inches across, blooming in early to midsummer for about a month. They then dry quickly, the foliage politely shriveling to nothing. The plant leaves no unattractive dead remnant behind, only a humble tawny stem and saltshaker-like seedpod to rattle in the wind and spread about next year's progeny. Opium poppies need full sun and a soil on the dry side. They should be sown where they are to grow for they hate being transplanted. Fall sowing results in better germination the next spring. I'm feeling a bit puffed up and proud that a temptingly lickable grape purple single form that cropped up in my garden a few years ago has been named and is being spread through gardeners' networks as 'Lauren's Grape'.

Papaver triniifolium (pa-PAH-ver tri-ni-ee-FOH-li-um)
ARMENIAN POPPY

Most poppies thrive in harsh continental climates, with the help of long taproots, moisture-conserving hairy or waxy foliage and a massive production of easily germinated seed to ensure progeny. Armenian poppy is a promiscuous biennial, self-sowing dependably. It is as beautiful in the first year of growth with its lacy blue doily of a foliage rosette as it is in the second when a stiff one to two foot candelabra of buds opens diaphanous pale orange flowers on a daily basis for well over a month in late spring and early summer. The finely cut, hairy blue foliage compliments the unusual flower color beautifully. Full sun and dry, hot conditions are best, but Armenian poppy is quite adaptable, growing in muggy East Coast gardens as well as in cool, moist Irish ones. It is pretty with rue, blue flax and the furry silver lamb's ear lookalike *Sideritis scardica*.

Penstemon digitalis **'Husker Red'** (PEN-steh-mon dih-ji-TAH-lis)

Of the large and varied penstemon genus, this plant is probably the most adaptable and easy to grow. 'Husker Red' penstemon is one of the more dependably long-lived of this notoriously short-lived group of plants, and likes the same conditions that most traditional border perennials do—morning or full sun and an evenly moist yet well-drained soil of moderate fertility. Thus it fits in the well-prepared part of the garden where the peonies, columbines and asters might go. Aesthetically, it also has more in common with these plants than the wild dryland penstemons or exacting alpine ones. 'Husker Red' makes a dense, lush eighteen-inch mound, a definite presence rather than the insubstantial foliage so many other penstemons leave behind when out of bloom. The plant is named for its fabulous leaves, dark burgundy in color, and for the football team of the University of Nebraska. It is at the extensive penstemon breeding program of that institution that the plant originated. The straight species, *Penstemon digitalis*, is an undistinguished white- or lavender-flowered plant with green leaves. 'Husker Red' combines white flowers with that fascinating, mysterious dark foliage and, presto, a classic garden plant is born. The best way to grow the plant is to obtain divisions of the finest deep purple forms rather than from seed. Much of what is floating around in the trade under the name is inferior, with foliage more green suffused with purple rather than the pure wine color of the original selection. When in flower in early summer, the plant rises to two to three feet. The seedpods and stems are also strongly purple, so I don't hurry to remove them once the flowers have dropped. Design ideas for integrating this plant are limitless. I grow several large clumps with peach and cream Asiatic lilies in front of the flesh pink shrub rose 'Sparrieshoop'. Elsewhere, its dark foliage provides a good foil for white flowers in the spring: first moss phlox 'Colvin's White', then candytuft, next the nodding drops of pewter-leaved *Onosma alboroseum* and finally shrubby potentilla 'Abbotswood' and sandwort (*Arenaria montana*). Blush pink Lancaster geranium keeps the penstemon company throughout the summer and into fall.

Penstemon procerus (PEN-steh-mon proh-SEH-rus)

When I moved to Colorado from Pennsylvania, the wide world of penstemons opened its doors, when before I had struggled with a few persnickety, half-hardy hybrids and a handful of underwhelming southeastern species. A great many species of this large genus like it hot and dry. *Penstemon procerus* is a bit less exacting, adaptable to full sun or light shade and to moist or quite dry soils. It also forms a good, rich green, glossy prostrate mat of linear foliage, making a decent ground cover, path-edger or front-of-the-border plant. Most penstemons suffer in the foliage department and even those that have attractive leaves rarely create a form of much substance save some of the shrubbier, less tough northwestern natives. Easy-to-please *P. procerus* has delicate flower-heads of a vibrant lavender-blue, rising a little less than a foot above the foliage. In my garden it blooms for about a month in mid- to late spring, along with paler powder blue *Phlox divaricata*. Then the green foliage dukes it out with golden moneywort (*Lysimachia nummularia* 'Aurea') the rest of the summer and fall, making a refined yellow and green swirl at the front of the east-facing border where it is never allowed to dry out completely. In light, dry shade, it blooms a bit less profusely but is still a good performer. Like so many in its genus, *Penstemon procerus* grows quickly and easily from stratified seed, blooming the second year.

224

Phlomis russeliana (FLOH-mis ru-seh-li-AH-na)

This superb perennial lends unmatched architectural flower form and great textural foliage to the garden. It forms a heavy mound of large, velvety mid-green leaves, a good foot and a half tall and wide. In late spring and early summer, showy two-foot stalks tiered with whorls of tawny buff flowers rise up from the foliage. *Phlomis russeliana* looks good among shrub roses. I like it best with the warmer tones, such as peach-pink 'The Fairy' and 'Sparrieshoop', creamy 'Windrush' and butter yellow 'Goldbusch' and 'Golden Wings'. Maroon and copper foliage also looks wonderful with the plant, such as *Heuchera micrantha* 'Palace Purple' or a shrubby backdrop of crimson barberry or cistena plum. It grows in front of the latter in my garden, with the tall, grassy foliage of the old-fashioned spuria iris, white and yellow *Iris orientalis*, as a companion. I salvaged this elegant, tough iris from behind a dilapidated old shed in our backyard when we moved in; everyone I know who grows it has a similar tale to tell when asked for its source. Both plants grow best in full sun or a half day of sun with an average soil and water regime. *Phlomis russeliana* grows easily from stratified seed or division.

Primula elatior (PRIH-mew-la eh-LAH-tee-or)
OXSLIP

Most primroses sulk in hot summers and dry air. The charming oxslip, long on grace and toughness, does fine in the north-facing shade of my house. In Ireland, where I first met this plant, I was instantly taken by its dainty yet generous flower display of sweetly fragrant sulphur yellow flowers clustered on foot-tall stems. Later on in the season I came to respect the plant for its unscathed foliage. While other primroses were either yellowed and withering or made into mincemeat by an ever-expanding crew of slugs and snails, the oxslip foliage remained deep green and healthy. Here in hot Colorado summers, I've found the main primrose pest to be spider mites, but again, the oxslip remains untouched. *Primula elatior* is easily grown from fresh seed, stratified over the winter. I have since learned my particular plants are of the subspecies *carpathica*, with hairy gray undersides to the foliage. Perhaps this leaf adaptation has helped them tolerate the harsher extremes of Colorado's climate so well. In early spring, right by the front door, I am greeted by their fragrant display, along with the ice blue flowers of my favorite lungwort, *Pulmonaria saccharata* 'Roy Davidson', and the somber, nodding plum flowers of Lenten rose, *Helleborus orientalis*.

Rosa foetida bicolor (RO-sa FEE-ti-da by-CO-lor)
AUSTRIAN COPPER ROSE

This most vibrant of shrub roses is also one of the toughest, tolerant of drought, cold, lean soil and wind. In fact, it is the one of the few roses that actually does better in harsh, semiarid conditions; in milder, moister climates, it is plagued by black spot. Scruffy, gnarled specimens survive in neglected gardens and old farmsteads, full of viciously thorned, dead gray wood. Come mid-spring, however, even the most forlorn specimen comes alive for two to three weeks with the most beautifully hued single blossoms cascading down its tired old canes. Burnt orange never looked so good. Given just a modicum of care—pruning out the oldest canes every few years and watering the shrub a handful of times during the driest part of the summer—Austrian copper rose becomes a vase-shaped shrub when out of bloom, not a showstopper but nothing to hide either. The shrub grows four to five feet tall and not quite as wide. Since the base is usually a bit bare on more mature individuals, companion plants especially enhance the plant—perhaps the bronzy maroon foliage of crimson pygmy barberry, or the gentian blue of alkanet, *Anchusa azurea*. Occasionally branches of Austrian copper rose will revert to its parent, a golden yellow rose, all on the same bush, which can be pruned out or left for its interesting effect.

Rosa glauca (RO-sa GLAW-ka)
RED-LEAF ROSE (SOMETIMES SEEN AS *ROSA RUBRIFOLIA*)

The red-leaf rose is grown more for its foliage than anything else. The leaves have an indescribable metallic pewter color suffused with bronze, mauve and burgundy. The young canes are reddish maroon. Red-leaf rose is one of the most drought-tolerant shrub roses, equally at home in full sun and light, dry shade, where it becomes more silver with less reddish overtones. A large, rather sparse, upright, arching shrub growing up to ten feet tall and four to six feet wide, this rose looks best with its marvelous foliage used as a foil to enhance flowers in front. It would be the perfect backdrop to a water-wise pink, purple, silver and white scheme of artemisias, purple verbenas, pink sidalceas, cottage pinks, lavender, the purple-eyed white flower spikes of *Verbascum chaixii* 'Album', baby's breath and the white and rose spikes of *Dictamnus albus*. The reason *Rosa glauca's* dusky foliage isn't as useful with the fiery end of the color spectrum is that its small single flowers, born in late spring, are a soft rose color. In the fall, drooping cherry-like hips extend red-leaf rose's long season of good looks. Minimal care is needed—an occasional pruning out of old, scraggly canes helps invigorate the bush and keep it neat.

226

Rosa x alba 'Semiplena' (RO-sa AL-ba seh-mee-PLAY-na)

This shrub rose belongs to the tough alba race of roses, known for their hardiness, adaptability and beautiful, disease-free, gray-green foliage. While cultivars such as 'Königin von Dänemark', 'Maiden's Blush' and 'Madame Plantier' offer larger, fully double blooms, the flowers of 'Semiplena' are more liberally produced and the plant has a nicer shrub form. An added bonus comes in the fall when the leaves turn a warm straw yellow strewn with a myriad of oval orange hips. 'Semiplena' does well in sun or light shade and is quite drought tolerant for

a rose. It reaches six to eight feet quickly, in three years, becoming an arching, graceful shrub, dense with gray-green leaves. The cool color of the foliage sets off the cascades of shimmering pure white semidouble flowers perfectly. The flowers' simple innocence is matched by their fragrance, a clean, sweet rose scent. In the back of my west-facing border, this rose joins the huge white blossom cloud of perennial *Crambe cordifolia* and the giant silver rosette of self-sowing biennial Scots thistle for an imposing silver and white triumvirate in late spring.

Rubus deliciosus (ROO-bus de-li-see-OH-sus)
BOULDER RASPBERRY

This graceful deciduous shrub is native to the Rocky Mountains. Its long, sparsely branched, arching stems reach six to eight feet. Lobed fresh-green leaves cloak the copper-brown stems; the ruddy bark is shreddy on older wood. In mid-spring, last year's canes are covered in large, two-inch white flowers reminiscent of single roses. A hybrid between *Rubus deliciosus* and its southern counterpart from Mexico, *R. trilobus*, is even showier. Called 'Benenden', it has flowers three inches across and grows more quickly than boulder raspberry, putting out many new canes each year. I grow 'Benenden' in the shade of a limbed-up old Colorado spruce. It has appreciated an annual fix of compost and manure, but basically it is thriving in quite dry shade. Full sun is best in cool, cloudy climates and light understory shade where summers are hot and sunny. 'Benenden' has been hardy here in northern Colorado for four years, but with its southern lineage, it may be questionable in the harshest northern regions. Boulder raspberry is bone hardy. Mine blooms with tall sweet rocket (*Hesperis matronalis*) in shades of purple, lavender and white; *Anemone canadensis*, the snowdrop anemone, an invasive but disarmingly pretty ground cover for dry shade; and the white haze of hearty little sweet woodruff, even more rampant and carefree, ideal beneath large shrubs. To encourage young canes and to make the bush more appealing, prune out the oldest canes every few years. Incidentally, I've never known either raspberry to make a decent berry; they are hard and dry.

227

Rudbeckia triloba (rud-BEH-ki-a try-LOW-ba)

This is my favorite black-eyed Susan, yet it is one of the most difficult to find in the trade. Like too many good plants, it carries on in old gardens, unknown to most. A short-lived perennial, *Rudbeckia triloba* self-sows its legacy. Stratified seed comes quickly and easily, blooming the second year. The foliage forms a rosette of rough, dark green lobed leaves about a foot tall and wide. Well into autumn, four- to six-foot stalks arise, stiff and not in need of staking if grown lean, in full sun and on the dry side. These burst into great masses of small golden daisies with chocolate eyes, like a baby's breath of black-eyed Susans. The eyes remain attractive dark buttons in the winter landscape. *R. triloba* does quite well in light shade, too, but tends to flop a bit. It tolerates all but the wettest or driest soils. I enjoy mine with the stiff, compact New England aster selection 'Hella Lacy' for a combination that evokes memories of purple and gold autumnal Pennsylvania roadsides.

Salvia jurisicii (SAL-vi-a joo-ri-SIH-si-eye)
UPSIDE-DOWN SAGE

Upside-down sage has become my favorite substitute for catmint as a filler in the drier parts of the sunny garden. Both are a foot or a little taller; both have gray-green foliage and softly spiked lavender-blue flowers. While I still grow and love catmint, I'm getting tired of finding it half-chewed and then rolled upon by one of my pleasure-seeking feline addicts. *Salvia jurisicii* does not attract them in the least. While the plant doesn't flower for quite as long a period as catmint—it starts a week or two later, and is finished in three—the entire aspect of the plant is much more refined, and the finely cut, featherlike hairy foliage is far superior. As with catmint, any color consorts well with upside-down sage. I've mixed it extensively in the pastel hell strip, with mounds of dianthus, frothy sugar pink stone cress and white Serbian yarrow softening the spikes of various penstemons. *S. jurisicii* grows easily and quickly from stratified seed. It will also grow with a bit more water, if the soil is well drained, but must have full sun.

228

Salvia sclarea (SAL-vi-a SCLA-ree-a)
CLARY SAGE

This coarse-textured, beautiful medicinal herb has a controversial aroma—pungent yet clean, with a slightly bitter edge. It is generally grown as a biennial, but variety *turkestanica*

tends to be perennial. The species typically grows three feet tall, but a recent introduction, nicknamed "superclary," reaches heights of five to six feet, wonderful with tall yellow verbascums at the back of the sunny, dry garden. Clary sage forms a hairy, gray-green, foot-wide rosette of foliage the first year. The following year, in early summer, it sends up stiff candelabra-shaped spikes of flowers. Showy bracts and calyces are responsible for the overall iridescent, opal-like effect, blending white, chartreuse, lavender and pink. These also help extend the ornamental season of the plant long after the flowers have come and gone, to a total of six weeks or more. Some forms have a distinct rose-purple hue in the stems and bracts. These can be selected for in a batch of seedlings, for the young foliage also shows hints of red. Clary sage self-sows with abandon. It does best in full sun but can tolerate light shade. It is a superb plant to bridge the gap from the late-spring floral flush into the doldrums of midsummer, lovely with magenta and silver *Lychnis coronaria*, pale daylilies, mulleins or the moonlight yellow daisies of *Anthemis tinctoria* 'E. C. Buxton'.

Scabiosa ochroleuca (sca-bee-OH-sa ok-ro-LEW-ka)
YELLOW PINCUSHION FLOWER

This pretty, fine-textured perennial blooms from midsummer well into autumn so profusely and for such a prolonged time that I think this accounts for its relatively short lifespan—it literally blooms itself to death. Fortunately the plant is easy to grow from seed and tends to self-sow a bit. In full sun and a lean soil, a profusion of one-inch, pale yellow flower heads rise on wiry stems above a mound of deeply cut gray-green leaves. In full bloom, the plant is a good two feet tall and wide. In a sunny garden on the dry side, this lovely scabious looks especially good fronting the taller pow-

der blue haze of Russian sage and the shrubby mass of *Lavatera thuringiaca*, that great pink late-summer mallow. The color, while cool and enticing on a sunny day, emanates a special glow at dusk, that same magical light so many of the evening primroses possess. There is a choice form with silver-felted leaves called *Scabiosa ochroleuca* var. *webbiana*, but I have not found a source.

Scutellaria supina (skoo-teh-LA-ri-a soo-PEE-na)

A well-composed garden strikes a balance between showstoppers and a good support-ing cast. *Scutellaria supina* is the perfect filler plant—a dense, fine-textured, long-flowering plant that grows in semiprostrate foot-wide mounds. Its foliage is a healthy mid-green, unusual for such a heat- and drought-tolerant plant. In late spring, pale yellow, hooded flowers open in short spikes in great numbers. They continue on for a good six weeks and when cut back will send up another smaller batch in late summer, much like another great filler in the mint family, misty blue catmint. *S. supina*'s flowers have a quiet color perfect with pink, purple, lavender and blue. Around dusk, however, like so many pale yellow flowers, it comes alive and the shimmering mounds become fea-tures in the evening garden, along with the large, lumi-nescent evening primrose flowers. *S. supina* does best on my hot strips, but grows adequately in amended soil with a bit more moisture as well. Full sun is a must. It grows quickly from stratified seed and self-sows a bit in the garden. I grow it at the stark bases of a mass of lavender *Penstemon grandiflorus*.

Semiaquilegia ecalcarata (seh-mi-ah-kwi-LEE-ji-a ee-kal-kah-RAH-ta)

This dainty little spring-bloomer looks like a miniature columbine. Its dusty rose blossoms dangle from wiry, dark, almost black stems. A good common name might be wine-drops, for they have the exact color of wine stains on a white damask table cloth. *Semiaquilegia ecalcarata* does best in an eastern exposure or light, dappled shade. Where I grow it in full sun, it is helped by the sanctuary of a cool root run under the flagstone path. The plant's airy flowers and beautiful scalloped foliage rosettes—also very similar to a small columbine and a dusky plum as they unfurl in early spring—are ideal at the edge of paths. Only coralbells can give a similar effect—a refined foliage rosette at the edge and dainty flower stems to wave above. Soft pink-and-white-striped moss phlox *Phlox subulata* 'Tamanonagalei' harmonizes well with the little wine-drops. They are somewhat short-lived, like most columbines, but self-sow a bit and are simple to grow from stratified seed, fresh or old.

Sideritis scardica (sy-der-EYE-tis SCAR-dih-ka)

This genus is packed with perennials and small shrubs with lovely, felted silver foliage, but many are not hardy in cold temperatures. *Sideritis scardica* is. In leaf, it resembles a refined lamb's ear, forming low four- to six-inch mounds about double in girth. It thrives in hotter, drier sites than does lamb's ear, and doesn't tend to die out in the center as often. In late spring, woolly flower stalks rise, again similar but much more refined than those of lamb's ear. The small flowers, instead of a washy lilac, are a soft yellow, perfect with silver. Once bloom is over, the foliage is not as ragged-looking as that of a post-flowering *Stachys byzantina*. *Sideritis scardica* grows easily and quickly from stratified seed. It forms an indispensable softening mat at the edge of my hell strips, where unamended soil and less than fourteen inches of moisture allow only the toughest to flourish. Whether fronting the lavender and orchid spikes of *Penstemon grandiflorus* and *P. secundiflorus*, or the delicate apricot flowers of Armenian poppy, it is a cornerstone of my hot, dry plantings.

Symphytum x *uplandicum* 'Variegatum'
(sim-FY-tum up-LAN-dih-cum va-ri-eh-GAH-tum)
VARIEGATED COMFREY

Here is a plant that should be in all shady gardens, provided they aren't too dry. Variegated comfrey grows large—three to four feet tall and almost as wide—with impressive, rough-textured, oval, sage green leaves edged in creamy yellow. One plant can light up a boring green scene. The flowers, blooming in late spring and early summer, are small drooping lavender bells, not much to write home about but not unattractive either. Variegated comfrey should not get direct sunlight or else it will scorch; besides, bright light bleaches out the contrasts of the variegation, making it visually ineffective. It is lovely in the shade with the lavender flower puffs of *Thalictrum aquilegifolium*, and with the shade-loving, graceful powder blue campanula cousins of the *Adenophora* tribe. The only way to grow variegated comfrey is to get a division.

251

Synthyris missurica (SIN-thi-ris mi-SOO-ri-kah)
This lovely evergreen perennial is native to the Great Basin and has proven itself completely hardy in the severe continental climate of Colorado. It is a small, refined plant for a shady spot that doesn't dry out completely. Its shiny, rounded, leathery leaves are similar to those of East-Coaster *Galax urceolata*, the fairy wand. In early spring, *Synthyris missurica* sends up many dense, foot-tall grape-hyacinth-like spikes of ageratum blue flowers, especially pretty with the pristine white water-lily-like flowers of double bloodroot, *Sanguinaria canadensis* 'Multiplex', or with small early daffodils. The seed germinated well for me after stratification, but it was four years before my plants were large enough to flower. The plant, a true native treasure, is well worth the wait.

Syringa reticulata (si-RIN-ga re-TIH-kew-lah-ta)
JAPANESE TREE LILAC

This lovely tree, like the similarly coarse-textured, luxuriantly summer-blooming catalpa, has a lush, almost tropical effect and yet is hardy well below minus thirty-five degrees Fahrenheit. Once mature, Japanese tree lilac has a beautiful shiny, lenticel-covered bark. The showy flower panicles are creamy white; their fragrance is not the best, but were it not for the obvious comparison with this tree's sweet-scented shrubby cousin, the common mildew- and borer-plagued lilac, no one would complain about the smell. The tree blooms in early summer, after the majority of woody plants' flowering flush is over. A mature tree lilac is said to reach thirty feet tall and half as wide. I beg to differ after seeing the beautiful specimen at the Nebraska Agricultural Experiment Station in North Platte, which is at least twice this size and easily as broad as tall. From a distance, this impressive individual has the lush foliage, dense crown and showy flowers reminiscent of a horse chestnut. For the small garden, variety *mandshurica* remains a multistemmed, eight to twelve foot form. Japanese tree lilac does well in moderately fertile, well-drained but slightly moist soil, and blooms best in full sun. It is an easy, disease- and pest-free flowering tree given a decent garden soil, and deserves much more popularity.

252

Tanacetum niveum (ta-na-SEE-tum ni-VAY-um)
SNOW DAISY

When I first saw this froth of tiny pristine white daisies shimmering in the Rock Alpine Garden at Denver Botanic Gardens, where I've met countless other unusual and superb plants, it was love at first sight. Beautiful silver foliage, reminiscent in form of its more shade- and moisture-loving cousin feverfew, forms a foot tall and wide mound. Then in late spring the plant doubles in size when its ethereal white cloud of flowers begins to open. The show continues for well over a month. Self-sown seedlings pop up generously. Why is this plant so scarce?

Though not particularly long-lived, it grows easily and quickly from seed, blooming the second year, and transplants well at a young age so one needn't be worried about losing it. It is also quite adaptable, growing in the moist, well-fed soil at the foot of a white 'Iceberg' rose and a clump of bronze fennel as well as in the sunbaked, unamended and unwatered stuff on my hell strips. There it softens the brilliant cacophony of ruby red Greek valerian, *Centranthus ruber*, and a host of large blue, pink and cerise desert penstemon species.

Tanacetum parthenium 'Aureum'
(formerly *Chrysanthemum*)
(ta-na-SEE-tum par-THEH-ni-um AW-reh-um)
GOLDEN FEVERFEW

Feverfew is an old-fashioned, short-lived perennial once used medicinally. Its foliage is highly aromatic and said to repel many insects; the plant is sometimes grown with roses for that reason, aside from the fact that the dainty, white, miniature mumlike flower sprays are a visual complement. The golden form of feverfew is especially nice—its chartreuse-yellow foliage lights up a shaded area. Feverfew is one of the best plants for light shade somewhat on the dry side, though it also does well in morning sun. Full sun all day is fine in cool, cloudy climates, but in most parts of this continent the flowers go over too quickly and the foliage burns out. Feverfew grows quickly and easily from unstratified seed; the golden form comes true. It self-sows so thickly that it can become a bit weedy. I combine it with the gentian blue flowers of *Cynoglossum nervosum* in dryish shade, and with Siberian forget-me-not (also tolerant of dry shade) and the large lemon yellow flower globes of *Trollius europaeus* 'Superbus' in a moister spot. Feverfew has single, semidouble and double-flowered forms and makes a superb cut flower. Misguided breeding has given rise to cauliflower-like dwarf forms—no thank you.

Thermopsis fabacea (ther-MOP-sis fa-BAY-see-a)
GOLDEN BANNER

While several different golden banners grace much of North America, most of these are either too invasive or not drought tolerant enough to compete with this splendid Asian species for space in the undaunted garden. This perennial forms a leafy, vase-shaped, medium green clump of large cloverlike leaves, about two feet in height and girth. In late spring, *Thermopsis fabacea* sends up foot-long lupinelike flower spikes of a luminescent sulphur yellow, much cooler yet more radiant than the brassier yellows of most of our native species. It is stunning with blue flax and blue avena grass in the sunny garden. A soil average in moisture and fertility is best. The plant will also tolerate light shade. *T. fabacea* grows slowly, usually taking at least three to four years from seed before blooming, but is long-lived and carefree once established with its clumps improving year after year. Germination is very good if the seeds are soaked in a scalding hot water bath first and then stratified.

Tulipa batalinii (too-LEE-pa bah-tah-LIH-nee-eye)

Species tulips are not grown enough; they are the perfect bulbs for harsh, continental climates. If one grows a handful or more species, their gemlike, brilliant flowers will brighten the garden from late winter well into mid-spring. Once gone over, these petite plants leave behind little of the ugly ripening foliage that their larger hybrid relatives do. One of the finest and longest-blooming species tulips is tiny *Tulipa batalinii*, a creamy yellow sweetheart only four to six inches tall. It has a rounder, plumper, more recognizably tuliplike flower than most of the species, and carries on for a month in mid-spring, nearly twice as long as other tulips. As with the majority of species tulips, a sunny spot with well-drained soil that dries out in the summer is ideal. 'Bright Gem' is a stronger yellow; 'Bronze Charm' is a warm coppery color. Species tulips are very forgiving of the procrastinating, disorganized gardener. They don't dry out quickly in storage and can be planted very late in the fall—I've been known to poke several hundred in with frozen hands while being snowed upon in November. I grow *T. batalinii* throughout much of the garden—in the buffalo grass lawn with many other tiny, drought-tolerant bulbs; through the ground cover *Sedum reflexum*, with striped bearded iris in the sunny, lightly watered part of the garden; and with early robin's egg blue *Penstemon nitidus* in the hell strips. 'Bronze Charm' is especially lovely with a cascade of purple rock cress.

234

Verbascum undulatum (ver-BAS-cum un-dew-LAH-tum),
WAVY-LEAF MULLEIN

This biennial is grown for its sumptuous foliage, a wavy-edged, two-foot wide rosette covered in pale yellow felt as if dusted by sulphur. The measly flowers rise up the second year in anorexic spikes, but one needs to look past them and let them form seed in order to enjoy the offspring's foliage the following year. The fact that the flowers are thin and not too tall, reaching only about two feet in height, is actually a blessing, for it makes for easier placement of this mullein in the landscape. So many mulleins have wonderful, broad yet low foliage rosettes the first year, inviting the gardener to place them in the foreground for close scrutiny. The second year, they often become five- to ten-feet-high behemoths. *Verbascum undulatum* can be placed safely at the front. Full sun and a dry soil makes the best foliage—tighter, wavier and more sulphur yellow. Mulleins are grown easily from unstratified or stratified seed. They are highly promiscuous so garden-collected seed may not come true to species. Wavy-leaved mullein doesn't develop the undulate edges until a good-size seedling. I almost threw my whole first batch out, thinking I'd been cheated. The foliage is smashing in early summer with the deep green leaves and rich yellow flowers of golden flax and the iridescent purple flower globes of star onion, *Allium christophii*, and for some serious drama later on, with the magenta spikes of the compact prairie gayfeather *Liatris spicata* 'Kobold'.

Verbena rigida (ver-BEE-na RIH-ji-da)

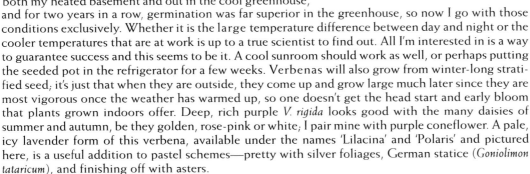

This attractive summer-and fall-blooming plant fortunately is annual in cold climates, for its aggressive spreading underground roots have made it a noxious weed in warmer southern regions. *Verbena rigida* begins to bloom in July, carrying on until after the first light frosts. Full sun and a hot but not too dry site are preferred. Its showy purple flower clusters are held stiffly erect on one to two foot, sparsely leaved stems. Butterflies find them irresistible. Verbenas can be temperamental to grow from seed. Some authorities say they need complete darkness to germinate; others insist they need light. Neither situation proved helpful for me. In my experience, it seems that verbenas like a cool but not freezing period of several weeks before germination. I had attempted several species of verbenas in both my heated basement and out in the cool greenhouse, and for two years in a row, germination was far superior in the greenhouse, so now I go with those conditions exclusively. Whether it is the large temperature difference between day and night or the cooler temperatures that are at work is up to a true scientist to find out. All I'm interested in is a way to guarantee success and this seems to be it. A cool sunroom should work as well, or perhaps putting the seeded pot in the refrigerator for a few weeks. Verbenas will also grow from winter-long stratified seed; it's just that when they are outside, they come up and grow large much later since they are most vigorous once the weather has warmed up, so one doesn't get the head start and early bloom that plants grown indoors offer. Deep, rich purple *V. rigida* looks good with the many daisies of summer and autumn, be they golden, rose-pink or white; I pair mine with purple coneflower. A pale, icy lavender form of this verbena, available under the names 'Lilacina' and 'Polaris' and pictured here, is a useful addition to pastel schemes—pretty with silver foliages, German statice (*Goniolimon tataricum*), and finishing off with asters.

Veronica pectinata (ve-RAH-ni-kah pek-ti-NAH-ta), WOOLLY VERONICA

Woolly veronica is a fabulous evergreen ground cover for full sun and dry conditions. It forms a dense mat of gray-green leaves that are strongly toothed, giving the whole mass a refined texture. During the dormant season, the foliage takes on a slightly plum cast. The plant grows about four inches tall and spreads slowly but indefinitely if allowed. In mid-spring, flowers of classic veronica blue open in great sheets, lasting for about a month. Sporadic flowers dot the plant all summer long. I grow woolly veronica at the edge where my garden meets the town sidewalk. It grows out onto the hot concrete with abandon, softening the harsh lines. In bloom, it resembles blue water lapping out from the garden. Cultivars 'Alba' and 'Rosea' have a lower-growing, more scraggly pewter gray foliage which doesn't make nearly as dense a ground cover as the straight species, nor do they bloom with the same abandon. Besides, who can forego that wonderful blue for

a washy rose or white? Woolly veronica grows from seed, cuttings and most easily, from division. I started the many square feet that edge the garden from a handful of small shreds begged off a friend. Woolly veronica is a good companion to vigorous selections of standard dwarf bearded irises, complementing their bold vertical form and showy flowers with a fine-textured fuzzy mass of color. An unknown cool lemon yellow dwarf iris I was given by a friend makes a memorable April combination with my blue ocean of *Veronica pectinata*. Woolly veronica does best in full sun but will tolerate light shade. It likes to be grown on the dry side, but is more vigorous if not completely left to Colorado's sparse rainfall. I grow a patch of it near the vibrant orange-red *Tulipa vvedenskyii*, one of the more vigorous and later-blooming of the botanical tulips. Woolly veronica is ill-suited as an actual ground cover over bulbs, for its dense, aggressive and quite deeply probing root system outcompetes the bulbs.

Viola corsica (vy-OH-la COR-sih-ka)
CORSICAN PANSY

This sweet little plant is the most adaptable, long-flowering garden plant I can think of. It is in bloom twelve months out of the year when not covered in snow. It self-sows in the most appropriate nooks and crannies, brightening any new neighbor with its velvety purple flowers. Corsican pansy is a short-lived perennial, not nearly as leafy and overbred-looking as its cousin the common pansy. The flower is much more charming—smaller, with the upper petals distinctly shaped from the bottom, giving it a jaunty Mickey Mouse look rather than the broad, flat, expressionless faces of pansies. It enjoys cool or hot weather, sun or light shade, a moist or very dry soil. Corsican pansy grows easily and quickly from stratified seed and will make itself at home in the garden in no time, relieving the gardener of any further seeding. Aside from the earliest bulbs, this plant is one of the most welcome harbingers of spring, its purple flowers dotting the grays and tans of a still-dormant landscape. Later it mingles effortlessly with sea thrift, candytuft and various moss phloxes and dwarf bearded irises. Through summer and into fall, a steady parade of bloom is to be expected. What more could one ask of a plant?

Zauschneria spp. (zow-SHNEH-ri-a)
CALIFORNIA FUCHSIA

I immediately think of this plant when asked about the usefulness of hardiness zones for herbaceous perennials. I remember what a fuss was made over these beautiful orange-red autumn-flowering plants in public gardens overseas and on the East Coast. They seemed completely undependable, flowering like crazy some falls, barely blooming in others and dying completely more winters than not. Zone seven, after all, is what they had been designated. I was convinced they were temperamental half-hardies from California that should be relegated to seasonal container display. An autumn visit to the Rock Alpine Garden at Denver Botanic Gardens changed that. There, in great fiery masses, were over a dozen different selections of *Zauschneria* that had been thriving there for several years. This genus is a taxonomic nightmare. It has been stuck in with *Epilobium* recently. After growing a number of supposedly different species from seed and finding the seedlings often more distinct and variable within a single species, I feel justified beyond my botanical ineptitude to avoid any attempts at classifying them here. I've grown three distinct forms in my garden for four years. So-called *Z. arizonica* is a robust, hairy light green beast that spreads by underground runners, reaching two to three feet by autumn, wonderful with blue foliages such as rue, Colorado spruce or blue avena grass, or with golden rabbitbrush. So-called *Z. garrettii* grows wild in mountainous parts of Wyoming and Idaho, and is said to be the hardiest. It is much smaller and less invasive, with narrower foliage, staying below a foot in height. A few of my seedlings actually lie prostrate to the ground like red pancakes. The prettiest form I have is metallic silver in leaf, and the foliage is slimmer and smaller than the others'. The flowers are a deeper red but not quite as profuse. It looks like descriptions of *Z. cana*, but I never knowingly grew that species. 'Glasnevin' is a fine-textured cultivar not hardy for me. Hardier color selections of California fuchsia include 'Solidarity Pink', a washy peach pink, and 'Album'. I am much in favor of the reds. They are the floral fireworks, the grand finale of the autumn garden. For best flowering, keep them on the dry side in lean soil, but not completely without water, and site them where they get the most heat from the sun—a south- or west-facing slope is ideal. This ensures that they get the long season of heat they need for good flowering. California fuchsia grows easily from spring cuttings or stratified seed.

GROWING FROM SEED

Many of the plants mentioned in this book aren't readily available, either locally or through the mail. This is where seed comes in: Were it not for these small, dry, humble things, adventurous gardening pioneers and those of us with limited budgets would never be able to grow the number or variety of plants we do.

Until sown, seed is best stored dry and cool but not frozen. Most of my hardy perennials and annuals are kept in the refrigerator in sealed, alphabetized tupperware containers, crowding out my husband's beer collection. Seeds of tropical annuals and questionably hardy perennials from Mexico, Australia, California and the like are stored at room temperature. In humid regions, seed stored at room-temperature benefits from placement in airtight containers with silica gel added as a desiccant.

I get my seed from various sources. Some is collected in the wild. Much comes via seed exchanges offered through membership to plant societies—the North American Rock Garden Society, Alpine Garden Society, Scottish Rock Garden Club, Hardy Plant Society, Species Iris Group of North America and American Pensemon Society all have excellent seed exchanges. Some seed comes from generous fellow horticulturists, and a bit from the ever-changing roster of mail-order seed companies.

PERENNIALS

I have two distinct seed rituals. The first involves perennials. The majority of hardy perennial seed benefits or even requires a cold, moist period to ready it for germination. Unless I know otherwise, I give all such seed the same treatment. I sow the seed during the January and February doldrums when little else is impinging on my time. I make a fifty-fifty mix of sterile, soil-less seed-starting media carried by most nurseries and garden centers and coarse washed sand, available from gravel pits, cement plants and many building supply stores.

Certain seeds have hard coats and/or chemicals within that inhibit germination—notably many plants in the pea, morning glory and iris families. These I first soak in hot water for a day, changing the water frequently. Plants in the buttercup family—clematis, pulsatilla, columbine, peony, hellebore, among others—are best sown as fresh as possible. These go in the refrigerator in zip-lock bags with slightly moist, sterile medium as soon as I can harvest them. I plant them in pots, medium and all, come midwinter. If the seed arrives late in the year, I soak it in successive water baths for several days before sowing it.

I reuse washed four-inch plastic pots (stable and easy to pack into a small space) year after year. For a week in the depths of winter, the kitchen becomes a potting shed. I fill trays of pots with soil, assembly-line fashion, label them with pencil—durable against the elements—and sow the seeds thinly on top of the soil. Then I sprinkle one-eighth inch of fine gravel (one or two grades coarser than the sand) on top—this protects the seed from being splashed out and helps keep the temperature and moisture more uniform.

Then the pots are plunked in the bathtub with an inch or so of water in it, to soak up from the bottom. The gravel on the top darkens once the pot is saturated. I let the pots drain, and then nature performs the cold-and-moist magic to ready the seeds for spring germination. I put them outside on the north side of my shed, which stays shaded throughout the winter. This prevents the seed from experiencing the wide temperature fluctuations of warm, sunny winter days. If one lives in a climate with much winter rain, a cover over the pots is a great help. The ideal cover, however, is a blanket of snow.

As the seedlings come up in the spring, they are moved to sun or shade, depending on their needs. I fertilize them with a weak solution of soluble general purpose plant food every other week or so. By late spring, some are large enough for transplanting—dibbling—into their own container. I use two-and-one-quarter-wide, three-inch-deep standard plastic pots for this, and plant them in the same media mix used for sowing unless it is a rare moisture-loving plant, which receives no sand in its mix.

Dibbling carries on well over the Fourth of July; most of the plants, with regular fertilizing, are ready to be planted in the garden by late summer and fall. A few slower, weaker growers are overwintered in cold-frames and planted out the following year.

ANNUALS

Annuals have an entirely different routine. These I sow from March through April, depending on how quickly they are known to germinate and grow. On their first attempts at seed-raising, many overzealous gardeners, myself included, sow too early and are then stuck with a jungle of huge seedlings competing for light, food and water. By the time it is warm enough to plant them into the garden, the plants are spindly and obscenely bare at the bottom from crowding, hardly ready for the wilds of the great outdoors. I now err on the late rather than early side of sowing dates.

While window-sill growing is certainly a viable option, I've found that plants grown under fluorescent lights are much better. Any heated room with electricity and a floor that can stand getting a little dirty and moist will do. I started a large vegetable and cut flower garden in a dormitory closet in college. The eery glow of the lights and the earthy smell emanating from beneath the door prompted many a suspicious (or envious) glance from those certain I was growing monstrous marijuana plants in there.

These days I have expanded my facilities to our heated basement. Under eight four-foot shoplights, I start about one hundred different types of annuals and vegetables each spring. I use the cheaper cool-white fluorescent bulbs rather than any fancy grow-light, for the wider range of wavelengths the more expensive bulbs offer are not necessary to germinate and grow seedlings. Forty-watt cool-white fluorescent bulbs need very little electricity and can be used for two to three years' crops.

A cheap light timer—the kind used during vacations to fool burglars—helps free me from a fixed schedule. I set the timer to turn on the shop lights for eighteen hours, then six hours off.

With annuals and a warm indoor situation, cleanliness is next to godliness. While the pots for sowing perennials are merely washed in warm water before reuse, the six-inch flats I use for starting annuals are scrubbed each year in hot water and bleach. I use no other containers: My seedlings go direct from germinating flat to garden. I don't have the time or patience of more exacting growers to transplant the annual seedlings to their own individual container or cell once they have developed their first set of true leaves.

The annual "soil" is a fifty-fifty mix of the same soilless medium I use for perennials, and coarse-grade vermiculite. This provides a balance of aeration and water-retention suitable for most annuals. I sow annual seed in one-eighth-inch-deep furrows I make in the mix by pressing a pencil. Those few plants that require darkness to germinate are covered by potting mix. The others are lightly pressed into the furrow with the pencil. I then water the flats from the bottom in the tub, as with the perennials.

After the flats drain, I encase each in a clear plastic grocery produce bag. This keeps the mix moist and the environment ideally humid for germination, a miniature greenhouse of sorts. I blow into the bag to make room for the young plants to raise their heads above the soil mix, then close it tightly with a twist-tie and place it a foot or so under the lights. I check the flats daily for germination. If left too long in the bag once they come up, the seedlings become leggy and prone to disease. As soon as some seedlings are up, I remove the flat from the bag and put it a couple of inches under the light bulbs.

As the seedlings grow, I raise the lights on chains with S-hooks. I continue to water from the bottom, placing the flats in a barely blue plant-food solution in old kitty-litter pans. As spring progresses, the annuals are then hardened off by being shuffled outside for the day, inside for the night for about a week before they are planted in the garden. The cold-hardy annuals go out a good month and a half before the tender, heat-loving ones such as the peppers and tomatoes. I've never grown tired of growing annuals from seed—brimming summer vases, jars of homemade salsa and dried flower wreaths in winter make it more than worth my while.

 **REFERENCES**

The American Rock Garden Society and Denver Botanic Gardens. *Rocky Mountain Alpines*. Portland, Oreg. Timber Press, 1986.

Bailey, Liberty Hyde and staff of Liberty Hyde Bailey Hortorium. *Hortus Third*. New York: Macmillan, 1976.

Barr, Claude A. *Jewels of the Plains*. Minneapolis: University of Minnesota Press, 1983.

Beales, Peter. *Classic Roses*. New York: Holt, Rinehart and Winston, 1985.

Bryan, John E. *Bulbs* vols. I and II. Portland, OR: Timber Press, 1989.

Deno, Norman C. *Seed Germination Theory and Practice*, 2nd edition. State College, PA. 1993.

Dirr, Michael A. *Manual of Woody Landscape Plants*, 3rd edition. Champaign, Ill. Stripes Publishing Company, 1983.

Mathew, Brian. *The Smaller Bulbs*. London: Batsford Ltd., 1987.

Rehder, Alfred. *Manual of Cultivated Trees and Shrubs Hardy in North America*, 2nd edition. New York: Macmillan, 1974.

Sabuco, John J. *The Best of the Hardiest*. Flossmoor, Ill. Good Earth Publishing Ltd., 1985.

Schenk, George. *The Complete Shade Gardener*. Boston: Houghton Mifflin, 1984.

Woods, Christopher. *Encyclopedia of Perennials*. New York: Facts on File, 1992.

PLANTS FOR FRAGRANCE

KEY:

F: foliage fragrant.

E: fragrant in the evening and at night.

Arctostaphylos manzanita (some)
Artemisia sage **F**
Buddleya butterfly bush
Calycanthus floridus sweet shrub
Caragana pea shrub (some)
Caryopteris blue mist spirea **F**
Catalpa
Chamaebatiaria millefolium fern bush **F**
Cladrastis lutea yellowwood
Clematis (some)
Comptonia peregrina sweet fern **F**
conifers many **F**
Cornus mas Cornelian cherry
Cowania mexicana cliffrose
Cytisus broom (some)
Daphne
Elaeagnus angustifolia Russian olive
Genista broom (some)
Gleditsia triacanthos honey locust
Holodiscus rock spirea
Kerria japonica
Lonicera honeysuckle (some)
Maackia amurensis amur maackia
Mahonia grapeholly

FRAGRANT TREES, SHRUBS AND VINES

Magnolia
Malus crabapple (some)

Myrica pensylvanica bayberry **F**
Philadelphus mock orange
Prinsepia sinensis
Prunus cherry, plum (some)
Purshia tridentata antelope brush
Rhododendron periclymenoides pinxterbloom azalea
Rhododendron prinophyllum roseshell azalea
Rhus aromatica fragrant sumac **F**
Ribes aureum clove currant
Robinia locust
Rosa (many)
Rosa eglanteria sweetbriar rose **F**
Syringa lilac (some)
Tilia linden (some)
Viburnum carlesii spice viburnum
Viburnum x carlcephalum
Vitex agnus-castus chaste tree **F**
Wisteria

FRAGRANT PERENNIALS AND GROUND COVERS

Adenophora lilifolia ladybells
Aethionema stone cress
Agastache giant hyssop **F**
Alyssum montanum mountain basket-of-gold
Androsace rock jasmine (some)
Aquilegia caerulea Rocky Mountain columbine
Aquilegia chrysantha golden columbine
Arabis rock cress
Artemisia sage **F**
Astrantia Hattie's pincushion
Bergenia pigsqueak
Berlandiera lyrata chocolate flower
Calamintha calamint **F**

Chamaemelum nobile Roman chamomile **F**
Chimaphila pipsissewa
Convallaria majalis lily-of-the-valley
Coronilla varia crown vetch
Corydalis fumitory (some)
Crambe sea kale
Dianthus pinks (some)
Dictamnus gas plant **F**
Dodecatheon shooting star
Dracocephalum dragon's head (some) **F**
Epigaea repens May flower
Erodium storksbill (some) **F**
Erysimum wallflower
Filipendula queen of the meadow, dropwort
Galium odoratum sweet woodruff **F**
Gaura coccinea bee blossom
Geranium macrorrhizum creeping cranesbill **F**
Glechoma hederacea ground ivy **F**
Helichrysum (some) **F**
Hemerocallis daylily (some)
Hesperis matronalis sweet rocket **E**
Hosta (some)
Hyssopus hyssop **F**
Inula hookeri
Iris bearded group (some)
Jurinea
Lavandula lavender **F**
Lupinus lupine (some)
Melissa officinalis lemon balm **F**
Mentha mint **F**
Mertensia chiming bluebells
Monarda bee balm, horsemint **F**
Nepeta catmint **F**
Oenothera evening primrose (some) **E**
Onosma (some)

Paeonia peony (some)
Pardanthopsis dichotoma vesper iris E
Penstemon palmeri
Perovskia Russian sage F
Phlox (some)
Primula primrose (some)
Ptilotrichum spinosum spiny alyssum
Pyrola wintergreen
Ruta rue F
Salvia (many)F
Santolina lavender cotton F
Saponaria officinalis bouncing Bet E
Satureja savory F
Schrankia sensitive briar
Sedum spectabile showy stonecrop
Tanacetum (some) F
Teucrium germander (some) F
Thymus thyme F
Valeriana valerian
Viola odorata sweet violet
Xerophyllum beargrass
Yucca (some)

FRAGRANT ANNUALS, BIENNIALS AND TENDER PLANTS

Abronia sand verbena E
Agastache giant hyssop F
Ageratum houstonianum
Anethum graveolens dill F
Angelica archangelica
Artemisia annua sweet Annie F

Asperula orientalis blue woodruff
Brachycome Swan River daisy
Calandrinia rock purslane
Calendula officinalis pot marigold F
Centaurea imperialis sweet sultan
Cheiranthus wallflower
Coriandrum sativum coriander
Cosmos atrosanguineus chocolate cosmos
Datura angel's trumpet E
Dianthus barbatus sweet William
Eschscholzia California poppy
Foeniculum vulgare fennel F
Hedysarum coronarium French honeysuckle
Helichrysum licorice, curry plant (some) F
Heliotropium arborescens cherry pie
Iberis annual candytuft
Ipomoea alba moon vine E
Lantana
Lathyrus odoratus sweet pea
Layia tidy tips
Limnanthes douglasii poached egg flower
Lobularia maritima sweet alyssum
Lunaria annua money plant, honesty
Malcomia virginica Virginia stock
Matricaria recutita German chamomile F
Matthiola stock E
Mentzelia blazing star E
Mirabilis four o'clock E
Monarda citriodora lemon mint F
Nemophila baby blue-eyes
Nicotiana flowering tobacco (some) E
Ocimum basilicum basil F

Oenothera evening primrose (some) E
Pelargonium geranium (some) F
Petroselinum crispum parsley F
Petunia x hybrida (some)
Phlox drummondii annual phlox (some)
Reseda odorata mignonette
Salvia sage (some) F
Scabiosa atropurpurea pincushion flower
Silene armeria none-so-pretty, annual catchfly
Tagetes marigold F
Tanacetum parthenium feverfew F
Trachymene caerulea blue lace flower
Tropaeolum majus nasturtium F
Verbena (some)

FRAGRANT BULBS

Asphodeline Jacob's rod
Crocus (some)
Cyclamen
Eremurus foxtail lily (some)
Galanthus snowdrop
Hyacinthus orientalis hyacinth
Iris (many bulbous)
Leucocrinum montanum sand lily
Leucojum aestivum summer snowflake
Lilium lily (many)
Lycoris squamigera naked ladies
Muscari grape hyacinth
Narcissus daffodil (some)
Puschkinia scilloides Russian squill
Trillium wake robin (some)
Tulipa (some)

PLANTS THAT ATTRACT BUTTERFLIES AND HUMMINGBIRDS

KEY:

B: butterflies and/or moths.

H: hummingbirds.

TREES, SHRUBS AND VINES THAT ATTRACT BUTTERFLIES AND HUMMINGBIRDS

Amorpha leadplant B
Arctostaphylos manzanita H
Berberis barberry B
Buddleya butterfly bush B, H
Campsis radicans trumpet creeper H
Caragana pea shrub H
Caryopteris blue mist spirea B
Catalpa H
Ceanothus fendleri B, H
Ceanothus integerrimus deer brush B, H
Cercis canadensis eastern redbud B, H
Chaenomeles speciosa flowering quince H
Chrysothamnus rabbit brush, chamisa B
Clematis (some) B, H
Crataegus hawthorn B, H
Fallugia paradoxa Apache plume B

Hibiscus syriacus rose-of-Sharon B, H
Holodiscus rock spirea H
Hypericum St. John's wort B
Kolkwitzia amabilis beauty bush B, H
Lathyrus latifolius perennial pea vine B
Ligustrum privet B
Lonicera honeysuckle B, H
Malus crabapple H
Philadelphus mock orange B
Physocarpus monogynus ninebark B
Potentilla fruticosa shrubby potentilla B
Prunus cherry, plum H
Rhododendron periclymenoides pinxterbloom azalea B, H
Rhododendron prinophyllum roseshell azalea B, H
Rhus sumac B
Ribes currant, gooseberry B, H
Robinia locust H
Rubus raspberry B
Spiraea spirea B, H
Symphoricarpos snowberry, coralberry B, H
Syringa lilac B, H
Tilia linden, basswood B, H
Vaccinium blueberry, huckleberry B
Viburnum B

Vitex agnus-castus chaste tree B, H
Wisteria H

PERENNIALS, GROUND COVERS AND BULBS FOR BUTTERFLIES AND HUMMINGBIRDS

Achillea yarrow B
Aconitum monkshood B
Agastache giant hyssop B, H
Ajuga carpet bugle H
Alcea rosea hollyhock H
Allium ornamental onion B
Anaphalis pearly everlasting B
Antennaria pussytoes B
Anthemis tinctoria golden marguerite B
Aquilegia columbine B
Arabis rock cress B
Armeria sea thrift B
Asclepias tuberosa butterfly weed B, H
Aster B
Astilbe B
Astragalus vetch B
Aubrieta stone cress B
Aurinia saxatilis basket-of-gold B
Calamintha calamint B

Campanula bellflower **B, H**
Castilleja Indian paintbrush **H**
Centaurea knapweed **B**
Centranthus ruber Greek valerian **B**
Cephalaria yellow pincushion flower **B**
Ceratostigma plumbaginoides leadwort **B**
Chelone turtlehead **H**
Chrysanthemum daisy **B**
Chrysopsis golden aster **H**
Cirsium thistle **B, H**
Colchicum naked boys **B**
Coreopsis tickseed **B**
Coronilla varia crown vetch **B**
Crocosmia **H**
Crocus speciosus autumn crocus **B**
Dalea prairie clover **B**
Delphinium **B, H**
Dianthus pinks **B, H**
Dicentra bleeding heart **B**
Digitalis foxglove **H**
Echinacea purple coneflower **B**
Echinocereus triglochidiatus claret cup cactus **H**
Echinops globe thistle **B, H**
Epilobium fireweed **B, H**
Erigeron fleabane **B**
Eriogonum buckwheat **B**
Eryngium sea holly **B**
Erysimum wallflower **B, H**
Eupatorium Joe Pye weed, snakeroot **B**
Filipendula queen of the meadow, dropwort **B**
Gaillardia Indian blanket **B**
Geranium cranesbill **B**
Gladiolus byzantinus hardy gladiolus **H**
Glechoma hederacea ground ivy **B, H**
Haplopappus golden ray **B**
Helenium autumnale sneezeweed **B**
Helianthemum sun rose **B**
Heliopsis sunray **B**
Hemerocallis daylily **B, H**
Hesperis matronalis sweet rocket **B**
Heuchera coralbells **H**
Hibiscus rose mallow **H**
Hieracium hawkweed **B**
Hosta **H**
Hymenoxys perky Sue **B**
Hyssopus hyssop **B**
Iberis candytuft **B**
Iris **B, H**
Knautia macedonica **B**
Kniphofia red hot poker **B, H**
Lavandula lavender **B, H**
Liatris gayfeather **B, H**
Lilium lily **B, H**
Limonium sea lavender **B**
Linaria toadflax **B**
Lithospermum canescens, L. carolinense puccoon **B**
Lobelia **B, H**
Lupinus lupine **B, H**
Lychnis chalcedonica Maltese cross **H**
Lychnis coronaria rose campion **H**

Lythrum purple loosestrife **B**
Malva mallow **B**
Marrubium horehound **B**
Melissa officinalis lemon balm **B**
Mentha mint **B, H**
Mertensia chiming bluebells **H**
Mimulus monkey flower **H**
Mirabilis four o'clock **B, H**
Monarda bee balm, horsemint **B, H**
Nepeta catmint **B, H**
Oenothera evening primrose **B, H**
Opuntia prickly pear cactus **B, H**
Origanum oregano **B**
Penstemon **B, H**
Perovskia Russian sage **B**
Phlox **B, H**
Physostegia virginiana obedient plant **H**
Platycodon grandiflorus balloon flower **H**
Polemonium Jacob's ladder **B**
Primula primrose **B, H**
Prunella selfheal **B**
Pulmonaria lungwort **H**
Ratibida Mexican hat, prairie coneflower **B**
Rudbeckia black-eyed Susan **B**
Ruellia wild petunia **B**
Salvia sage **B, H**
Saponaria officinalis bouncing Bet **B, H**
Scabiosa pincushion flower **B, H**
Scrophularia red figwort **H**
Sedum spectabile showy stonecrop **B**
Senecio groundsel **B**
Silene laciniata fire pink **H**
Solidago goldenrod **B**
Sphaeralcea cowboy's delight **H**
Stachys coccinea red betony **H**
Stanleya prince's plume **H**
Symphytum comfrey **B**
Thelesperma greenthread **B**
Thymus thyme **B**
Tulipa **H**
Valeriana valerian **B**
Verbena bipinnatifida **B, H**
Vernonia noveboracensis ironweed **B**
Yucca **H**
Zauschneria California fuchsia **H**

ANNUALS, BIENNIALS AND TENDER PLANTS FOR BUTTER-FLIES AND HUMMINGBIRDS

Ageratum houstonianum **B**
Ammi majus annual Queen Anne's lace **B**
Antirrhium majus snapdragon **B, H**
Begonia **H**
Browallia speciosa **H**
Calendula officinalis pot marigold **B**
Canna **H**
Centaurea cyanus bachelor's button **B**
Cheiranthus wallflower **B, H**
Cleome spider flower **B, H**
Consolida ambigua larkspur **B, H**

Coreopsis tinctoria calliopsis **B**
Cosmos **B**
Dahlia **B, H**
Daucus carota Queen Anne's lace **B**
Digitalis purpurea giant foxglove **H**
Echium viper's bugloss **B**
Fuchsia **B, H**
Gazania rigens treasure flower **B**
Gilia/Ipomopsis skyrocket **H**
Gomphrena globosa globe amaranth **b**
Helianthus annuus sunflower **B**
Heliotropium arborescens cherry pie **B**
Impatiens **B, H**
Ipomoea morning glory, cypress vine **H**
Isatis tinctoria woad **B**
Kallstroemia grandiflora desert poppy **B**
Lantana **B, H**
Lavatera trimestris annual mallow **B**
Layia tidy tips **B**
Limonium sinuatum statice **B**
Linaria maroccana toadflax **B, H**
Lobelia erinus **B, H**
Lobularia maritima sweet alyssum **B**
Lunaria annua honesty, money plant **B**
Machaeranthera Tahoka daisy **B**
Matthiola stock **B**
Maurandya snapdragon vine **H**
Mimulus monkey flower **H**
Mirabilis **B, H**
Monarda citriodora lemon mint **B**
Nicotiana flowering tobacco **B, H**
Onopordum Scot's thistle **B**
Pelargonium geranium **B, H**
Petunia x hybrida **B, H**
Phacelia campanularia desert bluebells **H**
Phaseolus coccineus scarlet runner bean **H**
Phlox drummondii annual phlox **B, H**
Reseda odorata mignonette **B**
Rudbeckia hirta annual black-eyed Susan **B**
Salvia sage **B, H**
Scabiosa atropurpurea pincushion flower **B, H**
Silene armeria none-so-pretty **B**
Silybum marianum milk thistle **B**
Tagetes marigold **B**
Thelesperma greenthread **B**
Torenia fournieri wishbone flower **H**
Tropaeolum majus nasturtium **B, H**
Verbena **B, H**
Verbesina encelioides butter daisy **B**
Vinca major periwinkle vine **H**
Viola pansy **B**
Zinnia **B, H**

Notes:
Boldface indicates photograph.
PP: plant portrait.